AGAINST THE FLOW

'In loving memory of my father, Peter Caffari.
The man who inspired, encouraged
and supported me.'

AGAINST
THE
FLOW

THE INSPIRING STORY OF A TEACHER
TURNED RECORD-MAKING YACHTSWOMAN

DEE
CAFFARI

WITH ELAINE BUNTING

LONDON

Published by A & C Black Publishers Ltd
38 Soho Square, London, W1D 3HB
www.acblack.com

ISBN 978-07136-8441-4

A CIP catalogue record for this book is available from the British Library.

This book is produced using paper that is made from wood grown
in managed, sustainable forests. It is natural, renewable and recyclable.
The logging and manufacturing processes conform to the environmental
regulations of the country of origin.

Typeset in Haarlemmer MT 10.5/13.5pt by
Palimpsest Book Production Limited, Grangemouth, Stirlingshire
Printed and bound in Great Britain by MPG Books Ltd, Bodmin, Cornwall

CONTENTS

FOREWORD

Patrick Snowball
Aviva Executive Director; March 2001–June 2007

When I first met Dee she was a rookie skipper, inexperienced on the corporate circuit, but was already planning her first circumnavigation of the globe against the prevailing winds and currents in the 2004–2005 Global Challenge Race. Instinctively, I trusted her. Maybe my military training enables me to spot an inner strength in someone that sits at the very core of them: a fortitude and resourcefulness that fires the spirit and frees it to do something extraordinary. Dee is one such person.

During the Global Challenge Race, Dee was tested to the limit. A crew member with a life-threatening medical condition needed immediate treatment. Dee's calm, decisive leadership ensured that this man's life was saved. Undaunted by this and other adventures, Dee chose to test herself by following in the footsteps of Sir Chay Blyth to become the first woman to sail single-handed around the world the 'wrong way'. I would have expected nothing less from her. Her 'impossible voyage', as it was called in Sir Chay's day, was not without its risks but, at Aviva, our decision to support her attempt was straightforward. She had the knowledge, a boat – not surprisingly called *Aviva* – that could do the job, and the will to succeed. With Dee at the helm, it was always going to be a winning combination.

It's easy to believe in Dee – simply because she is so believable. She is unpretentious, charming and, perhaps because of her days as a teacher, a natural communicator. She lives close to the edge and that is when she is at her best. Her passion for challenge gives her life purpose and, by example, helps to shape the lives of people around her.

Dee personifies a can-do, forward thinking attitude and at Aviva we are proud of what she has done – and what she may yet do.

PREFACE

James Cracknell

If nobody can hear you, are you really screaming? This flashed through my mind as I was 100 feet up *Aviva*'s mast. Although I wasn't the most relaxed I'd ever been I didn't feel like screaming, reassured by the sight of Dee below me guiding her 'soulmate' across a glassy Solent on a beautiful July day.

What would have made me scream? Being stuck up here with broken climbing gear, struggling to replace a computer chipboard, whilst at the bottom of the world in the Southern Ocean during the worst storms for fifty years, looking down at the deck knowing there was nobody on board to help you out and the nearest human was busy orbiting the Earth. But screaming in that situation probably wouldn't suffice.

Maybe a salty sea-dog, born in wellies and a sowester, could have coped in a situation like that. But not someone from landlocked Hertfordshire, who only started sailing six years earlier and the first time she'd sailed *Aviva* on her own was to the start line.

That is what makes Dee remarkable; not that she was the first woman to go 'the wrong way round' but the way that she did it, on a small budget with hardly any preparation time and with a smile on her face. Knowing her you'd think she was too sociable and gregarious to spend 178 days alone at sea, but this is what makes her so special. She has found a way to unlock the inner strength that is within every one of us, and for that as much as the circumnavigation she is an inspiration.

In a world where we want everything right here, right now without having to make any effort or sacrifice, Dee is testament to the fact that the greatest rewards do not come easily – and if they did they wouldn't be any fun, would they?

PREFACE

Sir Chay Blyth

Being first to climb something, sail somewhere or explore some hidden corner of the earth used to be what it was all about. Think Columbus, Magellan, Joshua Slocum, pioneers all. Their voyages were firsts; those who followed in their wake had to seek out and overcome other challenges.

But in these critical times people find it easy to sneer at the accomplishments of others. They point to satnav, electronic autopilots, satphones and the magic equipment that streams weather data almost endlessly from the on-board computer. It all seems too easy today, and if it goes wrong air-sea rescue will pluck you from the ocean and have you home in time for tea.

Maybe they are right. Maybe technology has taken something away from modern day adventure, but some things do not change. Let those critics who carp and sneer sweat for months (years maybe) to raise the necessary money, to win backers, to build the yacht, and, yes, to put in all the high-tech kit and let's see them embark on a voyage of their own.

Let us see them drive a 72 foot yacht which would normally be crewed by 18, sail across the Southern Oceans of the world against the wind and currents, against the whole terrestrial spin of the globe. To stand at the helm and steer for hours at a time with the winds and waves crashing against you almost ceaselessly. To stand and fight in that desolate place where the seas come as big as houses that roll and break over and over again on top of you and your yacht, where day turns to night and the seas do not discriminate either between you or the time of day. Damage has to be repaired and the yacht has to be kept driving forward. No satnav phone helped anyone go through that.

The Impossible Voyage may no longer be impossible. But it remains hard – very, very hard. In all recorded history only five people have circumnavigated the globe from East to West against the prevailing winds and currents. Dee Caffari is one of these five Impossible Voyagers.

I feel proud that in coming safely home along a track I pioneered more than 30 years ago Dee Caffari has written herself into history and we can now all bask in her reflected glory. This is her story.

ONE

A Voyage of Extremes

Something was wrong. I climbed up the companionway ladder and shone my torch into the cockpit. *Aviva* reared up on each wave and slammed into the trough beyond with a terrible crash. The boat juddered and flexed before starting the ascent up the face of the next wave. Water crashed over the deck and cascaded in deafening torrents across the cockpit. For the first time since I had left Portsmouth in November I was afraid.

The beam of the torch lit up a mass of tangled ropes in the cockpit, some streaming out astern of us. I clipped my lifeline on and crawled out on my knees. As I moved away from the shelter of the tiny cuddy a wall of freezing water swept me off the cockpit floor and washed me aft until my lifeline snatched taut. My face was pressed up against the cold, hard surface of a winch. I struggled to get upright again and when I did I was stunned by the fury of the storm. In the darkness I could see the foaming white of breaking waves all around us, their tops ripped off by the wind and whipped away in spume. The air was choking with salt and I fought for breath. Reefed down to a tiny amount of sail and at times submerged beneath tons of solid water, *Aviva* crashed on to windward.

I fought to retrieve the trailing lines with my frozen hands and crept forwards again, unclipped myself and clambered back down into the cabin. Below deck the din was less deafening but more worrying. I wedged myself in behind the chart table and watched the numbers on the wind instruments rise and rise. It had been 60 knots not long ago. Now every flicker of the numbers was higher, and I saw 70 for the first time. I had been through the Southern Ocean before in this boat and I had absolute confidence in her. *Aviva* could handle it. But could I? Dealing with a breakage or a crisis now would be close to impossible.

I turned up some music in the hope of drowning out the noise but it was no use. The jarring thud of the boat crash landing in the troughs, the high-pitched wail of the wind through the rigging, the sound of water coursing over the decks, even the creaking of the mast structure as it reverberated into the bilge could not be masked. I turned the music off again. However much it put me on edge I needed to listen to the commotion. The smallest change to the pattern would probably be my first clue that something was not right.

The low pressure system I was in was small, only about 400 miles across, but it was moving fast and tearing southeast at about 45 knots. This was an asymmetric system and the winds on the south were not quite as ferocious as those to the north, so my aim was to sail south as fast as I could. If I didn't manage this, there was worse to come: an intense and far more vicious secondary low was being generated behind this weather system.

For the next three days the wind did not subside. I went through these two storms back to back. There were winds of more than 60 knots at times and there was no opportunity to recover in between. The noise, the motion and the worry made sleep impossible. I had not eaten or rested, and after three days of this attrition I was exhausted. My thoughts were disturbed and disconnected. Every time I shut my eyes I had visions of breaking waves. If I nodded off I would waken seconds later with a jolt, scared that *Aviva* was breaking up or taking in water.

That same week, after the storms had finally passed over us, I saw icebergs for the first time. They were all around us, beautiful and deadly. When the icebergs were close they showed up on radar but if they were at a distance at all they were lost in the swell. I shut the watertight doors, got a supply of emergency gear ready and prayed. In my diary I wrote:

'In the night there is very little I can do but keep my fingers crossed, pray the radar alarm picks any icebergs up and continue to head north. This will be another night with very little sleep but plenty of worry.'

The fear and despair I felt as *Aviva* and I were surrounded by ice were new to me. This was the lowest point in my mission to become the first woman to sail alone non-stop round the world against the prevailing winds and currents. I could see no way out. Yet 24 hours later my whole outlook had changed. Tears and despair weren't going to change anything; I just had to buck up and get on with it.

The extremes of emotions that I went through on this voyage amazed me. When it felt as if I couldn't go on, somehow I turned things round and came out the other side with even more determination. Even when I had gone for days and sometimes a week with only a few hours' sleep and very little food, I managed to find the energy to fight against the elements. I never gave up on my dream.

When I set off on this voyage in November 2005 I had no idea just how difficult it would be. I had thought a lot about the isolation and loneliness of solo sailing but I never anticipated the degree of suffering I would have to endure, month after month. This became as much a voyage of discovery about myself as a journey round the world. Every day I had to find more strength, and I came to rely on the power of positive thinking. It convinced me that we can all achieve more than we think when we have to face new challenges.

I learned that there is always an end to the bad stuff. Everything is relative to what you have previously experienced. When I faced another Southern Ocean storm with hurricane force winds I consoled myself that I had probably seen stronger winds before, and if that proved to be true then instantly I felt better. I am definitely a glass-half-full type of person. When I can't find something good to focus on, I struggle. If I lose sight of my aim or feel I am no longer achieving it, I struggle. So I had broken my goal of sailing round the world alone into smaller, more achievable targets. If everything was good onboard I made my focus Cape Horn or Cape Leeuwin, the next Great Cape or landmass. When conditions deteriorated I moved the goalposts closer. Sometimes it was to pass the next line of longitude; at other times simply to survive the next four hours and make it to a new weather front. When things were really bad, I concentrated on each small step and gave myself a reward at the end. If I made it through the next few hours I could have a hot drink. If I got through the day I could have a rest or eat my favourite meal. If I got through this storm I would have a shower and change my clothes. No matter how big the challenge you face, every inch counts. The smallest things can make life feel good again.

I have returned the same person I was when I left, but no-one goes through such a journey without changing a little. I am more driven than I was. I no longer understand why people spend so much time worrying about things they can do nothing about. Life is too short for that. It is about seizing opportunities and facing up to challenges. I admit, sailing round the world against the prevailing winds and currents is a little extreme, and many times when I was facing horrendous conditions I wondered why I was doing it.

Sometimes I still wonder how I ended up with the privilege of doing something so special. That is what my story is about. Even when you are out at sea battling against the flow, with your eyes fixed firmly on the horizon ahead, there are times when you look over your shoulder and wonder: 'How on earth did I get here?'

TWO

Dreams and Ambitions

On Monday 22 January 1973, Barbara Caffari drove into work late. The half-hour journey was easier than usual because the traffic had subsided. Barbara's job at All Vacs Ltd on Pinner Road, North Harrow, was to complete the invoices and do the bookkeeping. It was a family business that her husband, Peter, had returned to after national service in Singapore as an RAF engineer. All Vacs sold domestic electrical appliances and had an impressive double shopfront. Inside, rows of washing machines were stacked along dusty wooden floors. It was a child's dream to play hide and seek among them, and a parent's nightmare.

Barbara was 32 and heavily pregnant with her second child. Despite feeling tired and unwell she worked a full day and drove back home that evening to Rickmansworth to cook dinner for her husband before he went out to the Thames Motor Yacht Club in Hampton Court. Peter Caffari was Rear Commodore and there was a committee meeting that night and a long agenda to get through.

By ten o'clock, Barbara was certain the baby was on the way. She called the yacht club and asked Peter to come home. In the background, the news raised a cheer. Their seven-year-old, Jane, was awake and sitting quietly at the top of the stairs. Jane watched her mum pack some bags and they waited together for Peter to get home. When he arrived, they loaded everything into the car and drove as fast as they could to Watford General Hospital.

After a relatively easy delivery, I popped into the world at three o'clock the next morning, a healthy child of 7lbs and 2ozs. My parents were convinced I was going to be a boy and were ready with the name David. After a quick change of plan I was named Denise Helen Caffari.

The weekend after I was born, when I was only four days old, I was taken down to the boat club to spend my first weekend aboard our wooden motorboat *Starlight II*. Countless cups of tea were made and drunk by the wives who came to coo at me, while my father celebrated his new daughter at the clubhouse bar with the men.

Every weekend throughout my childhood we went down to the Thames Motor Yacht Club on the riverfront above Hampton Court Palace to stay aboard the boat. *Starlight II* had been sold and now we had *Louis Philippe*, a bigger 40 foot Bates Starcraft motorboat. The boat was like a weekend cottage to us. In preparation, Mum and I spent Saturday mornings baking and, without fail, would leave with boxes of bread pudding, fairy cakes or rock cakes. As we pulled into the boat club driveway, the gravel crunched beneath the tyres of our car and my sister and I peered out to see what other cars were there, what other families had already arrived. Out on the pontoon, Dad would unlock the boat and we would pass the food and bags aboard. Down below, the smell was always the same: a cold, damp and exciting scent of mustiness and plastic. That was the smell of adventure.

The club was a wonderful place for families; there were always things going on. On Sunday mornings, there were jobs to be done, and if the weather was good I would rush up to help Dad clean or fix things. After that, we'd spend a couple of hours practising mooring or bringing the boat alongside and Dad would repeat everything patiently until we got it right. In the summer holidays, we went away cruising to France, Belgium or Holland for the whole six weeks. As soon as the last bell rang at school I ran home to pack so I could be ready to leave the minute Dad came home from work. We didn't return until the weekend before school started, usually with bags of new school jumpers and shoes hurriedly bought on the way back in Ramsgate.

Mum never missed a weekend or a holiday onboard but she was afraid of the water and couldn't swim. I don't know how she did it, but for 30 years of marriage she put her fear to one side to follow Dad. My father and I loved being on the water. According to family lore, the Caffaris were descendants of a Maltese sea captain who had saved an island from being overrun, and my Dad believed his passion for the sea ran through his blood. He dreamed of retiring to a yacht in the Mediterranean and joked about my mother sending him brown paper envelopes of pocket money each month. It was nothing more than a fantasy but to me it sounded incredibly exciting and I used to imagine what that life would be like. When he was gone, he said, he wanted a Viking funeral with his body sent out to sea on a burning boat.

My parents led busy lives and encouraged my sister and me to do the same. We were brought up to believe that only boring people got bored. There was a constant flow of people through the house and always something going on. Jane and I were expected to do well. My parents wanted us to have every opportunity and if we showed a healthy interest in anything or demonstrated particular aptitudes they were developed. I loved sports and dancing: rounders and relay races, the beanbags and the skittles, the sack race, the flat race and the sprinting. I went to dance lessons nearly every night after school, spent Saturdays dancing and Sundays at the boat club. Even if I had been allowed to get bored, there was never time.

As Jane became an older teenager things changed. She started going to parties and dancing at discos and nightclubs. She spent ages getting ready, a complicated procedure that fascinated me. I would stand next to her and watch intently as she blow-dried her hair and put on make-up, and as she placed the brushes back in their pots I picked them up and copied what I had seen her do. She laughed but if she had time she helped me. Mum and Dad never liked it and I was always told to go and wash my face.

Dad demanded high standards and he was quite old fashioned. He was a man of his generation. He liked Mum, Jane and I to dress like girls. We were never allowed to wear trousers when we went out with him. I don't remember Mum ever owning a pair. My sister and I followed these rules but at least we were allowed to wear jeans if we were out with our friends. Dad didn't understand it. As far as he was concerned, jeans were for convicts serving their time.

A similar rule of Dad's forbade me to have my hair cut short or my ears pierced before the age of 16. That was the birthday that seemed to signal my chance to do all the things that were out of my reach. I was desperate to have my ears pierced like all the other girls at school, but at home rules were rules. No matter how hard I begged, Dad was unmoved. 'If you were meant to have holes in your ears, you would have been born with them,' he declared.

When I eventually turned 16, a few years later, I didn't particularly want to look like everyone else any more and I decided against getting my ears pieced and went to get my hair cut instead. Much to everyone's amazement, as soon as my hair was cut it went curly. I left the hairdresser's in a state of shock. There was no way my father was going to believe I hadn't had a perm. When he came home, Dad looked surprised but said nothing. The haircut was never mentioned, though over the next few years he commented now and then that my hair looked messy these days.

To someone else these rules might have seemed strange but they were because Dad wanted the best for us. I understood that. He was always honest with praise and encouragement, and if he thought you could do better, he'd say so; Dad voiced what a lot of people don't have the guts to say. My friends would often ask his advice because they knew he would be straight with them. He knew I responded to this and he made me feel loved and capable and approved of. The day I turned 16, he sent a bunch of 16 red roses to me at school. As far as I was concerned, no-one could ever be as strong or caring as my Dad.

Boyfriends entered the scene. I was a good test to see how keen they were on Jane. I wasn't the easiest of children, and to guarantee attention I would insist on sitting between Jane and her boyfriend. If they went for a walk I had to go too. If a boyfriend was prepared to go through all this, he definitely liked my sister a lot. Mum and Dad thought I was a perfect chaperone; Jane thought I was a complete pain.

One day the doorbell rang, and the milkman asked to speak to Mum. Nick Hinge worked for Express Dairies and delivered the milk to our door every day. On this occasion he was after Mum's permission to take Jane out on a date. At first, I laughed but when the other children in our close started teasing me about my sister kissing the milkman I didn't think it was so funny. It was serious, though, and from that day in 1982 Nick quickly became part of the family. He joined us on the boat for trips away at weekends and was part of our crew if there were competitions. He and I would practise rope throwing for hours in the garden so we could be better the following weekend. In some ways, Nick and I were competitive for Dad's approval: Nick as a potential son-in-law, and me as a 10-year-old who was eternally anxious to prove herself.

Dad had sold *Louis Philippe* and bought *Tamberini*, a 40 foot glassfibre Fairline motorboat that cruised at a much faster speed than we'd been used to. Jane cried when she heard *Louis Philippe* was going to be sold. For me, however, *Tamberini* was exciting. I was older and able to do more onboard. Unlike Jane, I liked to crew rather than be the skipper; I much preferred being told what to do and I liked it that *Tamberini* was more like home, with duvets on the beds and heating and a kettle and toaster.

Being the smallest and the youngest, I always seemed to be given the worst jobs to do. I was keen to please and wanted to be included in everything, and one of my special jobs was to get the cockpit cushions from the aft lazarette. This was a dark and damp locker at the back of the boat that was awkward for me to move around in, small as I was. I had terrible claustrophobia, and while it was fine as long as I could see daylight, the others had a habit of asking me to pass out the cushions then shutting me in. I would scream as loudly as I could until they opened up the hatch again. It happened every time. I never learned and each time they laughed.

I was 12 when Jane and Nick got married. Jane was 19 and I had never seen her looking so beautiful. In my pink bridesmaid's dress I felt like a doll, and I wavered between tears and excitement. Jane had left home but my view was that I was gaining a friend in Nick rather than losing a sister, and that proved to be true. Nick was an incredibly kind brother-in-law. When I was 14 and Mum and Jane were out at work every Saturday, my job was to wash Dad's car. Nick was then working as a chauffeur and he usually came round and we washed and polished the cars together. If I got bored halfway through, he bribed me by promising to rent out a film or take me on a trip in his car. It developed into our own Saturday Club, and we watched films, recited lines from them and shared private jokes. As I grew older and needed a lift to training, matches or trips away, Nick often volunteered for the job. When I started socialising at the pub, Nick picked my friends and me up at the end of the night and dropped us all home. If I had sorrows, I could cry a little and Nick would stay up with me, listen and say all the right things.

Five years later, in 1990, my sister had the first of her two sons, Alex and Matthew. My parents hadn't really approved of Jane's marriage so young but now my family grew closer again. At Easter weekends, Dad, Nick and I would head off for a cruise to Ramsgate or the Medway, with some navigation competitions thrown in for excitement, while Mum, Jane and the children stayed at home. We always came back with a weathered glow, full of stories; it was almost like a bonding session. It was a life I loved. If you saw *Tamberini* out on the water, it meant I was around somewhere. She didn't move far without me.

Looking back, I can see that in some ways my early career teaching sports was pre-destined. I had gone to university in Leeds to do a degree in sports science and followed that with a teaching qualification. My first placement taught me a tough lesson. Because I enjoyed sport and was reasonably talented at it, I assumed the students would like me and that being liked made a good teacher. I discovered the hard way that it didn't work like that. You have to win the respect of a class and relate to each student as a unique individual.

Schoolchildren are bright and they know that a student teacher is going to be a little naïve in the ways of discipline. It's the perfect opportunity for them to test a new teacher's breaking strain. I was no exception.

The minute I handed out basketballs the sports hall was a deafening cacophony of slapping and bouncing and I couldn't be heard. On a windy hockey pitch it would take me all lesson to round up 30 students, 30 sticks and 15 balls and organise them into groups for practice. Something you think will be easy to do can stress you beyond belief, and the most carefully planned lessons can disintegrate as you speak.

My placement in a pretty rough part of Leeds was with pupils who were not easy to coax into working. Students are the most rewarding part of teaching but they are also the scariest. The first moments with a new class are make or break. You soon learn that you need to start off as a strong character so that you can back off later. If you are too soft it is very difficult to introduce discipline later. Your natural instinct is to be liked but I had already learned to my cost how misguided the nice approach can be too early on. This time I decided to be tough from the beginning.

I couldn't have timed it better as I walked into my GCSE PE class. It was the start of the athletics season and we had to cover some physiology in the classroom before I took them on to the field. If I didn't get control of this class in the first lesson, these kids would be an insane risk when they were throwing javelins later in the week. The entire back row had their feet up on their desks. Everyone was huddled in groups and talking loudly. The girls' skirts were rolled up to make them shorter and some of them were flirting overtly with the boys. The boys were wearing their trousers so far below their waists I knew their taste in underwear before I learnt their names.

I could smell the stale tobacco on school jumpers, mixed heavily with aftershave and perfume. It was all part of the mating ritual of these hot-blooded 15- and 16-year-olds. I visualised the image I wanted to present and sucked in a lungful of air. I pulled my shoulders back, lifted my head up and spoke out in a confident voice. Slow and unfaltering in my tone, I asked for feet to be removed from desks and bottoms to be put in chairs. It worked. I had everyone's attention. I began to feel every part this character I had created.

My second lesson with the class was a practical one concentrating on the history, development and techniques of the high jump. I had been trying not to judge anyone on my first impressions, but having heard about the same students getting into trouble all the time I couldn't help thinking the worst of one boy. The lesson I learned that day will stay with me for ever. It taught me that we all have a talent, though it can take time to identify it and channel that energy in a way that allows it to flourish. This particular student was incredibly hard to deal with but he was one of the most naturally talented athletes I ever had the pleasure of teaching. He jumped effortlessly beyond the benchmark for his age group, he was among the fastest sprinters and he was a superb javelin thrower. If only I could persuade him to train at a club he would continue to develop.

I worked with the school to encourage him. Eventually, he competed in an athletics meet at county level and proudly walked away with a record. I will never forget the smile that spread across his face. Moments like that are what make teaching special. To inspire a schoolchild and encourage and nurture them to face a challenge and ultimately succeed is a privilege.

Teaching practice had taken me to some difficult schools where I had found out that hard work can produce some outstanding results. I felt a great deal of pride in the progress of the less academic students or children who were in trouble in other areas of the curriculum whose talent or determination at sport made them my treasures. However, I was also keen to be able to teach with a little less emphasis on discipline. I decided that I would concentrate on location and let the feel of the school dictate if it was the right place for me.

The school where I got my first job in 1995 was on the edge of the Yorkshire Dales, a 40-minute drive from Leeds. North Halifax Grammar School had football and rugby fields, a full athletics track, a gym and several hockey pitches and tennis courts. There was a tremendous ethos that involved educating children in the benefits of a healthy lifestyle and I was very excited at the prospect of teaching there. At first, life as a proper teacher felt weird. I didn't feel old enough or adult enough to be a teacher. In assembly, I laughed at the same things the pupils laughed at, and I had to practise a stern face to avoid being caught out.

Life quickly fell into a routine. I drove to the school every morning and stumbled into the staff room for a cup of tea before the first bell rang. My tutor group was from Year 8, a bunch of 12- and 13-year-olds with a few wild characters. I had some naturally talented sports stars, some highly intelligent students and a few troublemakers I found myself defending regularly in the staff room. The combination of all these different personalities kept me entertained, while at the same time making me want to tear my hair out. In any other group you could walk away after a class and shake off the frustrations, but the difference with the Year 8 tutor group was that this lot was mine. These guys were as good as I could help them to be.

Year 8 knew exactly what they could get away with; they knew the rules better than me. That year, they taught me what is expected and, more importantly, what is needed from a teacher. I learned not to get caught in the trap of being soft with lovelorn girls whose troubles were all too often a way of getting out of going to assembly. I learned which cries for help were genuine and which were for attention. I had students with special educational needs either because they were exceptionally bright or had learning difficulties. One boy was a particular challenge. He was a great child but constantly in trouble, and I felt it was because he was misunderstood rather than malicious. Some learning difficulty syndromes were just being recognised and acknowledged where, in the past, they had been ignored or put down to bad behaviour. This boy was diagnosed with Attention Deficit /Hyperactivity Disorder, and I got some extra training to help me use a more focussed teaching style with him. That made a big difference and I really enjoyed helping him make progress.

Now I was a fully qualified teacher I could create my own rules of discipline. The school allowed detention as a punishment, but after that you had to find a way to help students, or coerce them, into learning from their mistakes. I remembered school detentions and the silly things we had been asked to do only too well, and I decided I wanted pupils to help out in detention while, of course, keeping them in my sight. So I would run detentions concurrently with practice sessions at lunchtime or after school and set troublemakers the task of picking up all the litter on the hockey pitch or the netball courts. I had all my footballs washed and the hockey sticks coated with linseed oil. The equipment lockers were tidied up and the bibs were sorted and folded. It was great. I also knew that seeing other pupils enjoying a class was a lesson in itself.

I loved the school and enjoyed my job, but towards the end of that term I spotted an advertisement in the *Times Educational Supplement* for a post teaching English and PE at a school in Dorset. It was a very different job, but it stuck in my mind and I found myself thinking more and more about a complete change of scene. Where, a year earlier, it had seemed right to stay in Leeds, close to the Yorkshire Moors and all my friends from university, I now felt I was ready to move on. The job at Harrow House International College near Swanage was near the coast, and the pull of a life close to water was strong. However difficult it might be to leave, I wanted to be within sight of the sea.

THREE

Saying Goodbye

Perched on top of the Purbeck Hills in Dorset, Harrow House is an imposing redbrick building that looks out down to the beach at Christchurch. The college had originally been built as a school in Edwardian times and was requisitioned during the war and turned into a hospital, so there were chilling stories about the ghosts of soldiers haunting the corridors. It was like a rambling stately home, with three floors and a warren of 70 rooms. The first challenge for me was to find my way around without getting lost, and to get to the right lessons in the right places.

Foreign students, adults and children, came to learn English here. The younger students lived in, and part of my job was to teach sports and look after them in the hours after lessons. I fitted into the job easily and naturally, and I loved it. I enjoyed the pressure of the week's lessons and the other social events that we had to organise.

I learned everyone's names, whether they were in my classes or not, and how to say goodnight or good morning to the juniors who lived in college in all their different languages. No matter what language you used, though, bedtimes were quite an operation. You had to visit each room and check that the lights went out at the right time and weren't sneaked back on a few minutes later. Evening activities changed according to the time of year and any new ideas we had, but karaoke was always a favourite. I never dreamed I would sing in public – no-one would if they heard my singing in the shower – but I quickly learned that if you want students to have a go the best way is to lead by example. Karaoke was a perfect way to encourage people to read and sing in English.

Working at Harrow House gave me a buzz I am sure would have faded if I had stayed at a regular school. I loved teaching and the chance to develop skills in young people that they were either unaware of or were untapped. It wasn't a dull routine; it was full of excitement and spontaneity. The mix of cultures and nationalities kept the place alive and it was an ever-changing scene as new students arrived every week, some staying for up to a year and others for as little as two weeks.

In this hothouse world, friendships and romances flourished. Romantic liaisons were hidden from view in odd corners of empty rooms and tennis courts. Promises were made and addresses exchanged as students said goodbye at the airport and as others arrived the process was repeated. Some of these relationships were holiday romances; others made friends for good.

For me, there were close new friendships as well. On our days off, I would go walking on the Purbeck Hills or along the cliffs at Dancing Ledge with some of the other teachers: Toni, Grant, Andy, Terry and Paddy. If it was good weather, we headed for the beach at Studland Bay armed with drinks and snacks, kites, boogie boards, books and sunscreen. It was like a day at the Riviera. Sometimes before going back to the college we would call in at the local cricket ground to see how the home match was progressing or meet others in town for a drink.

My closest friend, and in many ways a father figure to me, was Nick Keeping. Nick was one of the directors of the college, an absolutely charming man in his fifties with an easy way and flawless manners. He was tall and elegant, and even when he dressed to relax at the weekend he wore designer jeans with a pressed white shirt, a jacket, Italian leather shoes and designer sunglasses. Women naturally wanted a share of Nick's attention but what made him special in everyone's opinion, male or female, was his ability to listen intently to everything you had to say.

Nick was often away on marketing trips to promote the college overseas, but when he got back he would entertain us with stories of his visits and the people he had met. He was brilliant with the students and had an incredible ability to read people and understand anyone who was confused or troubled. He could tell if you were unhappy, feeling restless or resented a decision-making process, and he often defended our roles in the running of the college and fought to have our hard work and success rewarded at the end of the season.

Nick had another string to his bow: he was able to speak five different languages. He frequently caught out students who were up to mischief by understanding conversations he overheard, and was able to forewarn us so we could prevent trouble before it was too late. The students were amazed at how shrewd we could be at pre-empting their moves.

When the college manager left, I was promoted to his job and stayed on for another year. It was a far more responsible role. I was in charge of the college accommodation, the arrangements and smooth running of transfer day, when one group of students would leave and another arrive at the airport, and for the health and safety of all the students during their stay at Swanage. It was a big transition from running the sports programme and teaching a few lessons of English as a foreign language.

Nick would usually pop into the college on a Saturday to chat with me. We would catch up on the gossip from the Friday night disco and then look through the arrivals we were expecting. He already knew some of them, perhaps from a marketing event somewhere round the world, and his sympathy and care for the students was an inspiration to me. Once, a 17-year-old Italian student called the school in tears from Heathrow airport. He spoke English very poorly. I couldn't figure out who it was, and there was no-one else to help. I was getting upset myself; there's nothing worse than listening to someone sobbing on the phone when you have no idea how to communicate with them. With perfect timing Nick walked into the office clutching a Saturday paper and a cup of the rich filter coffee he always insisted on. I smelt the coffee before he even opened the door. The feeling of relief was immense. I handed the phone to him and within five minutes Nick had coaxed out the name and nationality of the student. I made some rapid arrangements, and half an hour later a teacher was with the student and the drama was over. For the next three weeks while the Italian boy was with us at the college, Nick checked every single day to make sure he was all right.

Besides dealing with problems, Nick was a fantastic and natural confidant, a father figure I turned to when life got difficult. It felt easy to talk to him about the future and the things I wanted to do. I could tell him anything. When I complained about students or colleagues, when things got me down, Nick would listen, always sympathetically, and offer a different perspective. My love life – or rather the lack of it – was always good for entertainment but he had the patience to discuss all kinds of things. I wondered if I should commit myself to buying somewhere to live and sought Nick's advice. In the end, the step seemed far too daunting.

By far the biggest and most gnawing concern I had was about my Dad, and Nick was there to listen and sympathise. It was a dark cloud that hung perpetually over an otherwise idyllic life at Harrow House. While I'd been at university, Dad had been ill. He had been feeling short of breath and when he'd gone for a check-up, they found an abscess on his lung. An operation to remove it had been a success, or so we thought, and life had returned to normal. Dad had worked hard at walking, cycling and skiing to improve his aerobic fitness and since then we'd had some great skiing holidays together.

I was shocked to hear that Dad was ill again, and this time it was really serious. He had been diagnosed with mesothelioma, which is a rare and virulent form of cancer that affects the lining of the lung, the abdominal cavity or the lining round the heart. It is caused by exposure to asbestos, in many cases 20 or more years ago. How my Dad contracted it we will never know.

The early symptoms of mesothelioma are non-specific and there-fore hard to diagnose. Dad was short of breath and had a persistent cough, a pain in his shoulder and lower back but none of these was severe enough to force him to seek medical help. As the disease progressed, fluid built up between the layers in the lungs, making it difficult and painful for him to breathe, and then the doctors suspected it could be mesothelioma. By this time, however, Dad was a long way down the line.

I desperately wanted to be around to help out during his treatment and recovery and so I began travelling home every weekend on my day off. I felt awful having to work so far from home. The drive home took about two-and-a-half hours and I fell into the routine of going home really late on Saturday night or first thing Sunday morning, returning to Harrow House early on the Monday morning. The journey was often made in tears of guilt and worry.

Back in Swanage I put on a smiling face and got on with my work. When there was a quiet time, Nick would ask how things were. With him, I could let the tears flow for a while and feel better. The worst times were calling home. I hated hearing my mum so tired and anxious but doing her utmost to stay positive and sound cheerful. I felt helpless. Often I spoke to my sister afterwards and she was always reassuring. They were all managing, she would tell me. She would let me know the minute she heard anything important.

Conversations with Dad were brief because he was very breathless but I loved hearing his voice and the warm way he would always ask me about what I was up to. He had another operation to help reduce the pressure from the build-up of fluid in his lungs, and while he was in hospital he contracted the bug MRSA. It turned out to be a long stay that really tested Mum's strength. Every time I visited Dad I had to clean my hands thoroughly and wear a special gown and mask. It was horribly upsetting. It made me feel so distant from him. All I wanted to do was hug him and I couldn't.

Dad's health continued to deteriorate but it didn't fully hit home to me until the weekend I went home and his wound was being dressed. He unbuttoned his shirt and when he took it off I saw that his arms and chest were shrunken and pallid. At first I was shocked. My Dad was the strongest person I had known, a 6 foot tall athletic man full of energy and vitality. As I looked at his emaciated body, I saw how weak and faded he had become and knew that he would never again be that powerhouse of physical strength. I felt heavy with sadness for him and for all of us.

Fatherly as always, Dad wanted to know that I was looking after Mum as best I could. Mum, Jane and I wanted most of all to get Dad back home where we could look after him in comfort. We were scared he would deteriorate faster if he stayed in hospital too long. We had Mum to think of, too. Jane and I investigated the help that was available to Mum for looking after Dad at home, and Macmillan Cancer Support came to our rescue. The charity provides practical, medical, emotional and financial support for people who need cancer care and they certainly helped my parents. Their nurses assisted with daily chores, redressing wounds and medical checks.

Our doctor called in for regular visits and the comforts of home cheered Dad up immensely. Being at home meant he had many more visitors and felt involved in everyone's life again. As far as morale was concerned, it was the best thing we could have hoped for.

My biggest dread as my father fought this terrible disease was getting a call that told me my usual visit would not be enough. That call came one Tuesday just before lunch. Jane asked me to come as soon as possible. I was in work mode and my immediate reaction, I'm afraid, was to wonder if everyone was panicking. Did I really need to come home right now? I think I was stalling. I was hoping the worst was not really happening. As Jane explained, I was already chucking some clothes in a bag. My Dad was dying.

I immediately turned to Nick. I felt the rising panic of despair but I told myself I had to snap out of it. I had to be practical. I had to hold it all together for Mum's sake. She didn't need an emotional wreck on her hands, on top of all her other troubles. And so, like father like daughter, I did what Dad himself would have done: I took care of the practical things. I re-arranged my workload for the weekend and left notes on each section. I packed my bag and Nick helped me take it to my car, making me promise to drive carefully. He said he'd let the rest of the staff and the other directors of the college know what was happening. I assured him I would call when I had more news.

The insufferably long hours of that drive were the worst of my life. I longed to be transported home effortlessly. I was in a panic and constantly had to slow back down to the speed limit. My fear was that I didn't have enough time. I needed to see my Dad before he passed away.

I walked through the back door straight into the arms of Mum. She looked tired and relieved to see me. Tentatively, I walked through from the kitchen to see Dad sitting in a chair in the front room. He, too, looked exhausted but he perked up when he saw me. I hugged him and we chatted. He asked about my work. Then he took a different tack. What were my plans for the future? Did I plan to continue teaching? I tried to bluff through an answer. The truth was, I wasn't sure where my future lay. I still aspired to adventure, but Harrow House was a great lifestyle job that I loved.

Then my Dad said something that changed my life. He said that if I just continued to talk about my ideas I would squander my chances to do anything about them. His exact words were: 'Are you going to talk about it or actually do something about it?' I was kneeling in front of his chair and the instant I heard these words they struck home. I knew he was right. He was invariably right. I vowed then that I would not be all talk and no action, and I said nothing. He knew he had reached the heart of me, that he had said the right thing.

For the rest of that afternoon we made a list of the things that he wanted to happen. There was something about this process of listing practical tasks that made me realise Dad was getting everything in order before he left us. I had to cancel the newspapers and settle the bill. I had to transfer all his shares into Mum's name and then we had to find all his personal documents from the depths of his wardrobe.

That evening Mum and Dad went through the long routine of getting Dad to bed. We weren't long behind him; the strain was taking its toll. Despite being emotionally and physically exhausted, none of us slept. We all lay in bed painfully alert to the slightest noise. The next morning everyone was up early. I sat on Dad's bed to make the phone calls to arrange for his shares to be transferred. One call proved trouble-some; the company didn't want to carry out requests on someone else's behalf. I told them Dad wasn't able to speak. Finally, frustrated by listening to me argue on the phone, Dad took the receiver and rasped excruciatingly into the handset. I could see plainly the pain the effort had cost him and I felt almost winded by it myself.

I set off to tackle some more of the chores Dad wanted done. When I got back I found Uncle Michael, my Dad's cousin Brian and Aunty

Margaret from Australia had arrived. This was bittersweet: it was lovely to see them all and horribly poignant at the same time. I am sure that the gathering of our family and the strength of numbers helped Jane and Mum.

The doctor had a final morphine prescription for Dad, and Jane and I left to collect it. When we got home we announced that the bar was open and gave Dad his medication. Everyone told jokes and stories. Dad checked that I had done all the jobs on the list. I was pleased to be able to say that everything had been done. I didn't surrender to emotion. I was taking over my Dad's role as the practical one and from that we both got great comfort.

Dad looked relaxed. I could see how much he was enjoying all the stories and jokes but by the early evening he was clearly struggling. Mum stayed beside him. He could say nothing. His goodbye to each one of us was with his eyes. There was no frantic fight for life; it was almost as if he felt the time was right and then he passed away. Aunty Margaret, a trained nurse, checked he was comfortable and said prayers. Mum talked quietly to Dad. In our different ways, we were all saying goodbye.

FOUR

Finding My Bearings

I had known my Dad would go but seeing it happen was heartbreaking. At first I felt detached. I needed to be strong for Jane and Mum and to help with all the practical things. We had a lot of help and support, which was sorely needed, but I was really worried for Mum in the longer term. She was now alone. Her husband had been her closest companion for 35 years of marriage. The paperwork she was left to deal with was entirely new and unwelcome, and she was overwhelmed. I continued coming home at weekends to help.

I didn't allow myself a time of grieving. I wouldn't. That was my perverse way of coping. Instead, I immersed myself in work. The summer was busy and I lived by the motto 'work hard, play hard'. However, by the autumn, even I could see I was running on empty. I needed to take a break. Nick understood what was happening to me. He sometimes said I was operating in a robotic fashion. He thought my sparkle had gone. To tell the truth, I was too tired to sparkle. I felt that if I stopped, everything would catch up with me and might overtake and overwhelm me, so I hid. I kept busy. I was terrified to let my emotions out.

After Dad passed away, Nick so comfortably filled the void my father left that I often waited for his guidance before making any decisions. He was a well-travelled, 55-year-old father himself, and I think he quite enjoyed his role in my life, the chance to offer someone guidance and advice. I still wanted to travel and experience new cultures and countries and when, that autumn, I decided I needed a holiday it was Nick who encouraged me. 'Go on,' he laughed. 'Press that "confirm booking" button!'

I wanted to visit somewhere new and indulge a new hobby, scuba diving, so I splashed out and went on a holiday in Kenya, booking a diving and sailing charter onboard a beautiful yacht called *Aristos* moored in Kilifi, Kenya. For the first week we would sail around Pemba Island doing three or four dives a day, and on the second I would explore inland on an African safari.

The owner and skipper of *Aristos* was Steve Edmondson, who worked with Rosie, a divemaster. As a pair they had what seemed like an idyllic lifestyle. They loved every day at work and truly enjoyed sharing the experience with others. I was enchanted by it all. Steve and Rosie sailed, dived and enjoyed the great weather and changing scenery with other people. It was a world of opportunity I hadn't realised existed, and I liked the idea.

Living on a boat felt completely natural to me. This was the environment that I had grown up in. I loved listening to the gentle lapping of the water against the hull and I found the rocking motion of the boat at anchor a wonderfully soothing way of getting to sleep. Living in a relatively confined area requires a certain amount of organisation so that things don't get lost or get in the way of others and I fell easily into the routine of being neat and tidy. I loved the way the days unwound with the daylight and darkness, how we were free to wake at will and sleep when it suited us. My father always used to say that the best way to live is by the sun: when it goes down you should go to sleep and when it rises it is time to wake up. In normal life this is not always practical, but this was the natural pattern onboard *Aristos* and it was perfect relaxation for someone who had been working relentlessly hard.

The mornings were so peaceful and still it was absolutely magical. I would wake and sit alone on deck before anyone else was awake. We had scattered my father's ashes at sea the previous summer but I had never really spent time saying my goodbyes. Sitting on the foredeck watching the sun rise and fish making ripples on the surface I felt at last as if I were close to my father once more. I missed our conversations and I began to talk silently to him and tell him about my work, the summer I'd had and my plans for the year. I promised to take care of Mum. Some mornings, dolphins would swim around the boat and I really felt as if they were taking these messages back to my father.

On the quiet, peaceful evenings after a night dive, we sat on deck under a dark sky filled with stars, the warm wind gently cooling us after a sultry day. Life aboard *Aristos* was touching all my senses, filling up my life again and allowing me to come to terms with my grief. The gap left by my father's death was slowly closing. I remembered conversations we'd had and began to understand why my father wanted me to try to experience new things. I didn't need the safety and security of the known. I could take on new challenges. I could even set off on a new path in life, if that was what I wanted. Change can be a scary prospect but close to the water I felt almost as if my father was helping me.

Rosie was newly qualified as a divemaster and a Yachtmaster. She had done a course at the United Kingdom Sailing Academy on the Isle of Wight and this was her first job in the marine industry. She was incredibly enthusiastic about the training and the job opportunities, and it all sounded fantastic. My father's words resonated again and again: was I going to talk about doing things and changing things, or just get on and do them? I made a decision there and then to investigate courses when I got back home.

After two weeks I returned to Dorset invigorated and much more at peace with myself. I was filled with new ideas and determined to change my future. Although I was excited to be back at work I started to research job options that would get me back out on the water.

Nick was cautious, a realist. He didn't want to see me carried away by fantasy and we chatted about possible career paths. He was so like my father. He encouraged me but he wanted to make sure I had looked at all the options and had decided carefully what would be best for me. He had no knowledge of sailing as a career, so he was objective about it, and I found that a huge help.

Underneath my enthusiasm, I had my own niggling misgivings. Why did I want to give up a teaching job that I loved? I had security, a regular income and 13 paid weeks of holiday a year. Had I lost the plot? Perhaps life in the marine industry wasn't really as rosy as I imagined and, anyway, what made me think I had the ability to turn a hobby into a career? Could I cope away from friends and family, continually setting up somewhere new and making other friends?

Yet the promise of adventure kept tugging at me. The more I looked at the options – teaching windsurfing in Belize; teaching dinghy sailing in the Mediterranean; skippering a charter yacht – the more aware I became of the scope of opportunities out there. In fact, I didn't know the half of it. I was about to make a choice that was to have a much deeper impact on my life than I could ever have dreamt.

In the meantime, the winter season came and went, and I settled back into the routine of Harrow House. Nick would appear in the office every day just before coffee break and we would catch up on the college news. Late that winter, his focus was on marketing and he was often away on overseas visits.

Just before Easter 1999, he went on a business trip to Eastern Europe and we heard that he had been ill. I didn't really think anything of it. Everyone gets colds and infections during the winter, especially when you fly a lot and meet other people constantly, as Nick did. So I was totally unprepared for the phone call I got one Wednesday. I had been preoccupied with trying to confirm the transfer list for a group of new students and book taxis and coaches for the weekend's arrivals. There were bits of paper all over the office and I tended either to ignore the phone or answer rather abruptly.

My curt 'Hello?' met with silence. I could hear a deep breath being taken before the College Principal spoke. In that momentary silence I knew that I was about to hear bad news – news that had nothing to do with work. I held my breath. He told me Nick had passed away in the night in his hotel room. I was stunned, speechless. My mind crowded with questions. How? When? Why?

All these were answered in the next few days, which passed in a blur of disbelief and anguish. Nick's Italian girlfriend told his former wife and eight-year-old daughter in Greece and then we let the students know. It was brutally hard to take in. Nick had never had any health problems and his death felt bitterly unjust. The only good news we could grasp at was the coroner's report that Nick's heart had stopped while he was sleeping. He had made a peaceful departure from the world by going to sleep and never waking up.

Within a year of losing my father I had lost my closest confidant. It felt so unfair. I was angry because I was alone again. I wanted to be strong for my Mum and be a help to her, so I had naturally turned to Nick to help me with my life, and now he was gone. It was a selfish feeling but his death made me feel more alone than ever. It was all such a tragedy.

Nick's girlfriend, the directors of the college and I attended Nick's cremation. We arranged to scatter his ashes in Durlston Country Park, along the coastal path where Nick had loved to walk and look out to sea, facing the elements. It was a blustery day. The wind was sharp and cold, and drew tears that disguised weeping. Nick had been such a dominant character, so wise and full of life. I felt bereft without him in my life. It was as if I was adrift again.

Two great losses in my life in a year took its toll on me. I threw myself back into work and thought seriously about my yearning for travel and adventure. I questioned everything. Was I really doing the two most influential people in my life justice? Were they going to be proud of me? Or should I be asking more of myself? The quest for an answer kept intensifying. I knew I had to find what I really wanted to do in life and follow that path.

One of my best friends from Harrow House, Paddy McMurren, had been thinking of travelling, and earlier that year he'd left Harrow House and set off from Kenya with three of his friends in a Land Rover and a trailer full of tents and equipment. They drove through Malawi, Mozambique and Lesotho, and when they reached South Africa, Paddy sent me an email.

Paddy was as shocked about Nick as I was, and understood what a terrible year it had been for me. So he suggested I took a break and join him and his friends for part of their tour. I jumped at the chance, and in May I flew out to Namibia for two weeks. We travelled into Botswana and through a National Park. The Land Rover struggled in deep sand and my two-week holiday changed to three weeks. During that extra week we drove into Zimbabwe and spent a couple of days at the Victoria Falls. As Paddy and I watched the sun rise over the Falls, I finally made a crucial decision.

With Paddy and his friends, we had explored, we had made our own choices. We had got close to wild animals on the African plains and slept with only a layer of canvas between us and the creatures making noises outside. We had skydived over the vast Namibian desert and seen clearly where it joined the expanse of the Atlantic Ocean. Once again, I realised that life was for living, that we get only one chance at it and we must grab hold of every opportunity.

Paddy and I grew closer. We each confided our dreams and plans. I told him about Rosie and Steve and how I yearned to work in sailing. It was similar, I said, to the travelling we were doing together but in a sense there was more freedom on the sea because there you were less likely to be influenced by someone else. At sea you had to be at one with the natural environment and it was nature that influenced your decisions and actions. A common theme in our discussions was how important timing is to everything we choose to do, and this was a perfect time for me to make a change. I had no ties, no mortgage, no pets, no children, and I had teaching experience to fall back on if I needed to.

I still felt that I needed support or approval, and Paddy gave me that. There were difficult decisions to make but I felt motivated. At the age of 26, I was going to do something completely different. I flew back to the UK and went to see my mother and sister. I explained what I wanted to do, and the reasoning behind it. Understandably, their initial reaction was shock and dismay. They thought I was taking a reckless risk. I wasn't sure if Mum would understand and felt guilty that I was worrying her, so I gave a reasoned argument, presenting both sides carefully and reassuring her that I'd try it for a year. If it didn't work out I could return to teaching. Whatever her concerns, Mum understood my spirit of adventure and gave me her wholehearted support.

So I resigned from Harrow House College and registered with the United Kingdom Sailing Academy for a course in instructor training and skipper training. I started in November and all that winter I sailed and studied. I was in no doubt I'd done the right thing. On a sailing trip in preparation for my final exams we took *Albatross*, a 67 foot yacht that had previously done the Global Challenge Round the World Race, to La Rochelle in France. It was my longest sailing trip so far and I loved it. I felt a great sense of freedom on the open ocean. There was a mixture of exhilaration, fear, serenity and romance. We sailed straight there, ran a watch system, reefed sails and flew the spinnaker downwind, trying out everything we could on this voyage. We were harnessing the power of nature and it was a supreme feeling of independence.

I was under no illusion that the sailing world would require hard work but I was certain that being offshore was worth it. However, I wasn't quite sure what sort of job I might end up with. That turned out to be with Mike Golding Yacht Racing. Mike is one of Britain's most famous solo sailors. He had twice sailed in the BT Global Challenge, a round the world race with amateur volunteer crew organised by Sir Chay Blyth's Challenge Business, had won it outright and gone on to set a record in the same yacht as the fastest person to sail solo non-stop round the world against the prevailing winds and currents. These days, he raced an Open 60, the lightweight Formula 1 machines of the solo sailing world, but he was looking for someone to crew on *Group 4*, his original racing boat.

My initial interview was with *Group 4*'s skipper, Graham Tourell. I was doing sailing training that week and we arranged to meet at a bar in Ocean Village Southampton early one evening. Our crew had been practising sailing in thick fog – or pretending it was fog, anyway. It had been raining hard and we were all wet, cold and tired, plus I was desperate to get to Southampton on time. We moored up with a few minutes to spare. I had no opportunity to dress for the interview, I just grabbed a jacket and ran to the bar. I had no idea who I was looking for.

Within minutes, the door opened behind me, and a group of three young men came in from the rain. They were all wearing jackets embroidered with the logo 'Team Group 4'. I said hello and introduced myself to one of them, and a broad grin spread across his face. This was Graham Tourell. He introduced himself as Gringo, and his two colleagues as

Sparky and Nobbers – Richard Smith and Nick Black. It seemed no-one in the marine industry used their real names.

Gringo was in his twenties, tall, dark and handsome – not the kind of guy who goes unnoticed. We chatted really easily. He told me about the programme for the boat that season, which involved sailing days for clients and races and Caribbean regattas with groups of corporate guests, and it sounded exciting. If I were going to start on the first day possible, I would have to leave Southampton right away to sail to Holland for the North Sea Race. That was exactly what I wanted, to get away and cover some serious sea miles. Gringo assured me that he would call before the end of the week after he had met a few other candidates and spoken to Mike Golding. I had to keep my fingers crossed.

Two days later, Gringo called back. He told me he would happily have me aboard but I needed to come back to Southampton to meet Mike Golding. I asked him what I should wear to the interview and Gringo said, 'To be on the safe side, smart casual, yachtie style.' I had no idea what that meant.

The following week I turned up dressed in beige trousers and a pale blue shirt. When Gringo saw me, he laughed. So far he'd only seen the exhausted, drowned rat version. He took me to a meeting room and there was the legendary Mike Golding. For a relatively short man in his late thirties Mike had a huge presence. All I could think of were his successes and achievements: three circumnavigations against the prevailing winds and currents, and all of those after a career change of his own. Mike had once been a fireman.

I was taken aback at how normal he was. I am not sure what I expected but Mike was a regular guy, he just demanded very high standards from people. He talked about commitment to the job and about what he expected from his crew for corporate sailing. I couldn't quite believe it when he said I could join the team.

From my first day working for Mike Golding Yacht Racing, I understood that to be as successful as Mike, attention to the smallest detail is as important to the bigger picture as the more obvious aspects. We worked from Ocean Village Marina in Southampton and took corporate clients sailing most days. I had a fabulous summer. There were lots of others working in the same marina doing similar jobs on yachts so there was a great social life, and plenty of banter at the end of the day as we cleaned the boats. On *Group 4* we had quite a strict routine and were often the last to finish. We got teased about this but we took a great deal of pride in the boat and loved making her look as good as we could. The difference between this atmosphere and that of the staff room was incredible. Here, we all wanted everyone to do well and we talked about our boats and the weather and sailing days we had just finished. At school the focus had been on the students and the problems we had. I found this environment more positive and I loved it.

I didn't see much of Mike. Gringo dealt with the boat programme, and the mate, Sparky, and I were quite happy with that. We were the less glamorous side of the team. The guys who worked with Mike on his new Open 60 racing yacht were at the cutting edge and when we met for drinks after work, Sparky and I would listen in awe. As a qualified diver, though, I did get asked to do one job on the Open 60: I was to dive down and scrub the bottom of the boat. Being a high-tech racing yacht, the new *Team Group 4* had to have the smoothest, fastest hull imaginable. It was finished to perfection and I had to keep it that way with a soft cloth.

The boat was shaped like a big surfboard and had a large underwater surface, so it was easy to get confused about which bits you had covered and what still had to be done. It was important to be methodical and I was very keen to impress Mike. I was below the hull cleaning it one day when suddenly I heard an engine being switched on. I shot up to the surface, well away from the boat and shouted. Gringo appeared and apologised. It wasn't the engine, he reassured me; Mike had turned on the generator. I was angry and about to complain about the lack of consideration when I heard Mike come on deck, but instead of saying anything I just slunk back under the water and got on with it.

I tried my hardest to learn everything I could from Gringo and Sparky. They made the job fun, attractive and exciting. We made a good team. As a young 19-year-old, Sparky was incredibly impressionable but his talent never failed to amaze me. He was a natural sailor and would take anything on. He was always the first to get his hands dirty to fix a problem and the first to go aloft to sort out a difficulty. He was dark and broad shouldered, small in build but incredibly strong and a great sportsman. He could free climb to the top of the mast on *Group 4* in less than 30 seconds. I learnt a lot from Sparky's energy and enthusiasm. He was never content to sit and accept how a boat was sailing; he always looked for a faster way or experimented with sail trim. I used to feel exhausted watching him but I was always learning.

Sometimes, however, Sparky's social activities got him into deep water with the management. He continually fell in and out of love and kept Gringo and I entertained with tales from his nights out. He had a streak of ill luck and a habit of getting into scrapes and predicaments that required assistance. In the bar, Sparky's party trick was to perform a tequila suicide: snort the salt, drink the tequila and then squeeze the lemon in his eye. Everyone else who tried it suffered terribly from the acidic lemon, but Sparky had a bad eye and he used it, so unlike the rest of us he could still see afterwards.

Gringo encouraged Sparky and me to take on more responsibility. He was incredibly supportive and a fantastic role model. I loved Gringo's way of working, of cracking jokes and creating fun yet still making sure we maintained the high standard of work that Mike demanded. Sometimes it did go wrong. On one corporate day out, Gringo passed the decision-making over to Sparky. We were competing in a fun race with another boat, and in an effort to creep out of a foul tide we cut a corner over the shoal water of the Brambles Bank in the middle of the Solent. It was a bit too shallow for us, and *Group 4* parked inelegantly on the mud. The tide was falling so we were faced with a long wait. We served tea and cakes and kept spirits high.

Sparky was devastated. Gringo joked at our expense but before we returned to the dock he had spoken to the office and smoothed things over with them. Good old Gringo. For Sparky and me it was a great lesson in how humiliating public mistakes are in a branded and sponsored yacht. While we were stuck, I think everyone in the area came to us; I saw faces I hadn't seen for ages.

By the end of that summer I had learnt a lot and at the same time realised I had barely started. I sat down with Gringo and we talked about what was next. This wasn't a conversation I felt I could have with Mike, who was preoccupied with a new Open 60 to race in the single-handed Vendée Globe Round the World Race. What I didn't know was that things were changing anyway, and Gringo was moving from his job as skipper to work with Mike on his new boat.

Shortly afterwards Mike asked me to meet him for coffee. I made excuses but Gringo was having none of it. He was going to make sure I went, even if he had to walk me up to the office himself. I was a bag of nerves. I felt sick and my palms were sweating. Mike asked me straight out if I wanted to leave. I explained that I was grateful for what I'd learned but I wanted to move on. I felt almost as if I was apologising. Mike completely took me by surprise by saying that he wanted to offer me the job of skipper of *Group 4*. I was shocked but I said yes right away. I would have hugged him but he isn't that type of guy, so we politely shook hands and I ran back down to the boat and hugged Gringo. Thanks to

Gringo's support, I was the skipper of a yacht after barely three months in the business.

One thing I soon realised was that I was now set up for a massive fall. So did Mike, and he gave me some wise advice that has stuck with me ever since. He said, 'Out on the water, you can get away with making it up, but as soon as you are in harbour moving the boat, everyone will watch and you need to be confident and able.' With those words echoing in my head I spent hours and hours practising manoeuvring the boat. Gringo was extremely patient as we backed in and out of berths around Ocean Village Marina. We made it fun and eventually I was happy parking the boat everywhere.

One afternoon I was backing *Group 4* between two ferries in a space that didn't offer me any escape if it went wrong. Everything was fine until I noticed that Mike was standing on the wall watching. Once I noticed him I started sweating and getting nervous. Somehow I kept my cool and backed the boat alongside, inch-perfect. Mike walked over. 'That was lucky!' he said. From Mike, that was pretty good. As Gringo reminded me, at least he saw me practising and making the effort. I was taking my job seriously.

Because Mike had such high standards it helped me when I took over as skipper. I tried to emulate the way he ran and managed his Open 60 racing boat and on *Group 4* I labelled and organised everything in a similar way. I often used to look at new designs and ideas and ask if we could follow suit. His usual answer was to remind me that he'd sailed round the world on his own on this boat, so why did I need help to sail it with a crew? That was a fair point. I did often wonder how he had managed to achieve something so amazing alone. I really had no idea how much Mike was influencing me or what lay in store.

My first voyage as skipper was to take *Group 4* to the start of the Vendée Globe Race in Les Sables d'Olonne, France. This non-stop race round the world is considered the pinnacle of solo racing, the toughest race there is, and for Mike it was the culmination of more than four years of planning and preparation. His Open 60 team was already there getting ready and we were to head down to help in the final preparations. Crossing the Bay of Biscay in October can be a tough voyage because the weather is so unpredictable. This was also the handover from Gringo to me, so while Gringo was to be onboard, I was to take the role of skipper, with Gringo and his brother and father as crew.

The weather was kind to us and the trip went without a hitch. I had calculated all the tidal gates and planned our passage accordingly. Apart from a family issue of damp deck shoes and smelly feet we had a great sail. When we got there, my role in the preparations was to dive and scrub the bottom of the Open 60 every day and take a crew of guests out to see the start of the race. Almost as soon as the fleet had disappeared over the horizon we dropped our guests off and set off back to the UK.

We were off a headland when Gringo got an urgent phone call. I was off watch and was woken by him. Gringo's voice was serious. We had to turn back right away. Mike had been dismasted and we needed to get to him and tow him back to Les Sables d'Olonne as soon as possible. It was a terrible time, a shattered dream for Mike, and a challenge for us. Finding a yacht out at sea is very difficult in normal circumstances, but when it is a low freeboard hull with no mast or sails, locating it is that much harder.

Eventually we found Mike and I dropped Gringo onboard and escorted them back to the harbour. Mike had a spare mast and decided to transport it to France and set off again as quickly as possible. Seven days later, he was on his way. In the meantime, I'd become ill, probably from diving in the murky harbour water, so Gringo and I were joined by another sailor, Duncan Maitland, for the passage home to Southampton. When we set off I was tired and weak. We were not prepared for the change in weather that lay ahead.

Before we reached the English Channel we had torn the staysail and ripped the mainsail above the third reef. The forecast was for Force 11 and the sea state was the worst I had ever seen. We stopped in Lorient and assessed our options. The forecast wasn't easing at all. We changed the mainsail to the smaller, bulletproof trysail and rigged up a storm staysail. Gringo had absolute confidence in the boat and I had absolute confidence in him. We all agreed to set out again for home and deal with the weather as it came.

Once we were offshore, I saw a sea that scared and shocked me. Huge waves took complete control of the boat. The wind speed rose until it was regularly touching 50 and 60 knots. As far as I was concerned, we were dealing with survival. The wind was ferocious and freezing and we were constantly being engulfed in waves as they broke solidly over the aft quarter of the boat. One wave swept over and flung me from one side of the cockpit to the other until I reached the full extent of my harness line and smacked into a winch.

Above the din of the storm, I could make out Gringo's voice asking Duncan to get me back onboard. A strong hand grabbed the back of my jacket and pulled me inboard again. I sat down and stared wide-eyed at Duncan. The way he was looking at my forehead made me reach up and touch it. I looked at my hands and saw blood. Dazed, I staggered below deck to check my head and get some warmth into my hands. I remember wanting to go to sleep and hoping it would all go away. I was sure that if I closed my eyes it would get better but I knew that would be unfair on Duncan and Gringo. So we took it in turns to get warm and steer and check the boat. I was not confident at all and struggled when it was my turn. This was not what I had signed up for.

After the worst trip of my life, we moored up in Ocean Village Marina and were met by Paul Bennett and Allie Smith, both former crew in the BT Global Challenge Race, who could imagine only too well what we had just experienced. Paul jumped onboard and made us all a cup of tea, which was lovely. We had not eaten or drunk properly for several days and the tea tasted so good.

At first, I thought this voyage would put me off sailing. I had destroyed sails and been scared. I was sure Mike would be unimpressed even though he was busy racing. What had I learned? Not to go to sea on a forecast as harsh as that or to put three people through such a terrible experience. Yet I had also grown in confidence. *Group 4*'s seakeeping abilities were beyond question and I had learnt that I could take more than I thought I could. You would never choose to sail in such conditions to find out how a boat or an individual dealt with it, and to have got through that was a huge boost to my confidence. I was definitely going back out there again.

FIVE

Turbulent Times

In the winter of 2001 we refitted *Group 4*. I was able to buy a new mainsail for the boat and I spent hours studying manuals learning the intricacies of all the equipment onboard. Together with Allie Smith, who worked in the office at Mike Golding Yacht Racing, we planned the next season. I was excited because it included the Fastnet Race, the famous ocean classic that takes place every other year.

To qualify I had to take part in a series of races that summer, and I began to wonder if this was the path that I should be taking. In June, the latest Global Challenge Round the World Race was ending in Southampton. This was the race Mike Golding had won in *Group 4*. The yachts were newer and different now, but the principle was the same: 17 paying crew and one professional skipper racing round the world on equal terms.

I watched them finish and arrive jubilantly at Ocean Village Marina. They had completed a circumnavigation of the globe, through storms and turbulent times, and were back safely. The celebration of what everyone had achieved was intoxicating. From the minute the first yacht crossed the finish line to the arrival of the last boat, and long into the early hours of the mornings between, the bars were full and emotions ran high. The revelry culminated in a firework display that I watched from the aft deck of *Group 4*. Chills ran down my spine at the thought of what all these sailors had done, what they had been through. I would have loved to be in their shoes. Could I possibly do something as remarkable as skipper a boat around the world?

My time was taken up preparing for the Fastnet Race but by the day of the start I felt very emotional. This was my first taste of offshore racing proper and I was nervous. I checked the weather forecast and studied all the charts over and over before we had even left the dock. We were ambitious and competitive and worked hard to push the boat.

There was one other Challenge one-design yacht in the race, exactly the same as *Group 4*, and though we didn't know where we stood in relation to her crew during the 600-mile race, I was thrilled when we arrived back in Plymouth to discover we had finished ahead of them.

The stakes were rising. Following the Fastnet Race, *Group 4* was entered in the ARC transatlantic race from the Canary Islands to the Caribbean island of St Lucia. I had never crossed an ocean before and the thought of it thrilled and scared me in equal measure. I pushed the worry out of my mind. Working for Mike Golding Yacht Racing, I would surely learn everything I needed to know.

As the time of the ARC approached, I was struggling. I felt I was out of my depth and needed help. In the end I went to Mike. He came down to the boat and walked over it with me, casting his knowledgeable eye over everything. I'd worked late the previous evening to make sure the boat was immaculate. The last thing I wanted was for him to comment on how things were kept or organised; what I needed was hard information on how to sail the boat efficiently and fast.

Mike was reluctant at first but once he started there was no stopping him. He went over every inch of the boat and gave me his suggestions and opinion on everything. I must have filled a whole notepad and suddenly my jobs list was enormous. It was the most feedback I'd had from Mike in 18 months of working for him.

While I was making sure *Group 4* was completely ready, I was also trying to spend as much time as possible with Mum, Jane and her family. It began to get too much for me. I was being pulled in too many directions. Mike knew it too, and he took me to one side. I tried really hard not to let it show, but I couldn't keep it in. I broke down in tears.

'What is the matter?' he asked me. 'Do you need your hand held?'

I couldn't believe what he'd said to me. How could he be so hard and unsympathetic? Pretty quickly, however, I realised that Mike was making me face up to what was ahead. He was saying that he had confidence in my abilities, and that was why he wanted me to get on with it. The only doubt, he was saying, was my self-doubt.

The passage down to the Canary Islands started well but I was worried by some extreme cases of seasickness in the crew. The weather was making recovery difficult and I chose to stop in Portugal for a night to allow everyone a walk around, a good night's sleep and a recharge before we set off again. It made a huge difference. The weather improved and the wind went further aft, making our progress smoother and more rapid.

In the Canaries the reality of what lay ahead really began to hit home. I had a great crew and I got a lot of help from Sparky, who was now working for a different company, Formula 1 Sailing, and sailing on a yacht named *Spirit of Juno*. He was going to be doing the same transatlantic voyage. Sparky shared lots of information with me, including giving me advice on what to buy when you have to shop for 12 people for at least two weeks at sea.

The crossing was fantastic. I realised once again that life out at sea was where dreams come true. Nature really can be your friend as well as your enemy. There is no taming the elements at work out there; your job is to try to make them work for you. When I arrived in St Lucia I was ecstatic. I had crossed my first ocean. I had found the right island in the Caribbean and my crew had all arrived safely with me.

Sparky met me on the pontoon and pointed me in the direction of the bar. The atmosphere was electric and the celebrations went on long into the early hours of the morning. The next day I went to find Sparky. A few days later he would be leaving to sail north to Key West in Florida. On board *Spirit of Juno* was the skipper, Harry Spedding, and we got talking. Harry had sailed in the Caribbean before and he offered to spend a few hours with me talking about the places to visit and where to clear Customs for the different islands.

Harry was tall, with broad shoulders, dark hair and wonderfully tanned, olive skin. He had been a Navy officer before taking up sailing, which I thought explained the short haircut. Now I know better, I realise that it just grows like that, outwards in all directions. Harry was lovely, and I was immediately smitten. He and I were both heading eventually for the Heineken Regatta in St Maarten in March, and I couldn't wait to see him again.

We were to meet up sooner than I had hoped but in the most terrible circumstances. Christmas and the New Year passed and *Group 4* was on her way up to St Maarten in February. I was taking a route on the windward side of the chain of islands, as that was the most direct route, and on the way I received a message from the Formula 1 Sailing team. If I was in the vicinity of Antigua, could I help them? I could easily change my route, and I let the office back in the UK know. Another message came in, this time from Mike Golding Yacht Racing. They had already been in contact with Formula 1 Sailing and, yes, I was to help right away with a search and rescue operation. Sparky had gone missing.

While they were in Antigua, *Spirit of Juno*'s crew had gone ashore to get something to eat. Everyone had different plans: some wanted to go for a drink then come back onboard; others wanted to go on to a club afterwards. A dinghy was left ashore for the last person to come back. When Sparky didn't reappear the next morning Harry raised the alarm. The police established that Sparky had last been seen offering a lift to a woman on another boat. He had dropped her off safely and then had set off towards *Spirit of Juno* but he never got there.

The UK and local Coastguards established a search grid based on how the dinghy would have drifted in the time since Sparky went missing and Harry, who sounded extremely stressed, co-ordinated a search ashore in Antigua. Our role was to circumnavigate the island of Montserrat. At first, taking part in a real-life search and rescue had seemed exciting, but when I knew it was Sparky we were looking for, I felt sick. I sat at the chart table for a while on my own wondering how on earth I was going to tell my crew Andy and Mikey, who knew him well.

I was as matter of fact as I could be. We had no time for tears or sentiment; we were needed off Montserrat as quickly as possible. *Group 4* was only a few hours away and I checked the course and planned the route to the island. We altered course and set the sails, and steadily the tension built. I just couldn't imagine what Harry and his crew in Antigua's English Harbour would be feeling.

We arrived at first light and I let Harry know we were beginning our search. Another Formula 1 Sailing yacht was checking the waters to the north and west of Montserrat in a grid pattern that had been calculated to allow for the current and drift rate of the last two days. We began our laps of the island.

Montserrat is a tall and actively volcanic island that is relatively small in circumference. We had all read the pilot book on our way there and we knew where all bays and towns were on the island. We just didn't know if we were looking for a dinghy, a dinghy with a person onboard, or a body. All we knew was that time was running out if we were to find Sparky alive. On *Group 4* we all prayed it was another of his scrapes, and that we would find him sitting on a beach waiting for us to pick him up.

The height of the island affected the temperature and the wind. All along one quadrant of the island's coast we were in the lee of the volcano and that meant that we were covered in ash still belching from it. We were black: our faces, the decks, the ropes and the sails. It was quite surreal.

As night was falling, we were completing our third lap. I was unsure what we were expected to do next. None of us wanted to stop but we hadn't slept since we had first got the call the day before and darkness was about to make our efforts futile. I radioed in to Harry and expected to be told to anchor and start again at first light. I sensed he wished he could tell me to do that but the word was to sail up to English Harbour, Antigua to help search the coastline there. The yacht to the north and west of us had located the tender. The glimmer of hope that Sparky might be alive was replaced with despair when we learned that the dinghy was untouched, with no sign of any damage or struggle.

Heavy-hearted, we slowly made our way to the rendezvous with the Formula 1 yacht and headed together towards English Harbour. We arrived at two o'clock in the morning in the pitch black and set the anchor. An hour later, we got the message that we would be needed again at seven thirty when we would be split into groups to search the Antigua coastline. I desperately wanted to check that Harry was okay, but that would have to wait until the morning.

In daylight, the harbour looked very different from the impression I had when we had entered in the middle of the night. There were lots of yachts at anchor in the bay and the clifftop hill of Shirley Heights loomed above us keeping watch over the entrance. Even early in the morning, the sun was intense. Ashore, there were volunteers from English Harbour and nearby Falmouth Harbour. The atmosphere was highly charged. Many of us knew Sparky; others were there to help because they understood that the sea was a hostile place. One can forget how dangerous it is even within a foot of the beach, even in a place that is sunny and relaxed. Everyone who was there had made the trip from a boat to the shore many times, and there were at least 50 yachts anchored in the bay. It could have been any one of us.

Andy and Mikey went to the airport to check the coastline from the air. Another group was to use a rigid inflatable boat and check the bays along the coast. Nobody had much to say and nothing needed to be said. It was strange how you could be so actively involved and yet feel so helpless. My heart went out to his family and friends who were waiting for news at home, too far away to join in.

Everyone was bitterly disappointed when the Coastguard came back with statistics about Sparky's chances of survival. They had dropped to less than 25 per cent and the decision was made to call off the search. We were all lost in a world of our own, trying to come to terms with this news. Some held hands, some wept, some just walked off for some private space. The next few days were incredibly difficult. The normal routine of jobs onboard seemed pathetically insignificant.

When you work with someone on a boat you live in such close

proximity that you are like a little family. You share unique experiences with that person, times that are impossibly difficult to explain to anyone who wasn't there. Many of us had, at some time, sailed or lived with Sparky and we each had our own memories of him. It was nobody's fault and every one of us had a new respect for the oceans. On all the boats, tighter rules and procedures were put in place but no one wanted to stay out late or travel alone in a tender. Anything can happen and we had learnt the tragic truth of the cliché that these things happen when you least expect it.

I sought out Harry. I could see he was particularly hard hit. As Sparky's skipper Harry felt responsible for him and I know that he kept running over different scenarios, wondering what he could have done differently. He looked tired and ill. I helped all I could, and everyone arranged a memorial service at Shirley Heights. That evening there was the most wonderful sunset and hundreds of people stood overlooking the bay and the open ocean. We celebrated Sparky's zest for life and said goodbye to a friend who had made a difference to so many of us.

Valentine's Day came round. I hoped Harry would remember the day and maybe suggest dinner together, but he still had a million other things on his mind. I made a casual suggestion that we grab some food together sometime. I still had my fingers crossed. He felt he should stay with the Formula 1 team but to my relief they encouraged him to go out with me. So on Valentine's Day 2002, we had our first date in Antigua.

I was nervous. Harry and I hadn't spent much time alone before. We had always been in a group, even though secretly our attentions had been trained on each other. We talked about ourselves. Harry had entered the world of sailing only recently. He had spent time travelling in Asia with friends and afterwards joined the Navy. I was slightly wary, knowing that sailors since time immemorial are wont to have girls scattered around the world in every port. So I quizzed him a bit, he denied it, and for sheer tolerance of my line of questioning he scored good points from me.

We got on really well and the conversation never flagged. We were served champagne and I was given a rose – by the waiter. What you eat, and how you eat, on a first date is a tricky issue and I felt the safest thing was to let Harry order for me. This completely backfired. Harry ordered sashimi. I had never eaten anything like it before; I didn't know exactly what sashimi was. I like fish – even raw fish – so I enjoyed it, and plainly Harry was very worldly wise.

After dinner, we headed along the shore and chatted as we waited for the tender to pick us up. Just before the others arrived, Harry turned towards me and kissed me. My stomach flipped. When we got back onboard, there was no point pretending nothing had happened: Harry and I were giddy from champagne, and I was clutching a rose everyone assumed he'd given me. Heralded by relentless ribbing, we were officially a couple.

After the tragedy in Antigua, Harry confided that he no longer wanted to sail. We all went together to St Maarten for the Heineken regatta and persuaded him to race. He did it as a tribute to Sparky but slowly and surely Harry got used to running the yacht without him. For us, the regatta marked the end of the Caribbean season and it was time to sail back to the UK. The trip back was far tougher than it had been on the way out.

Four of us sailed *Group 4* back: my first mate Mikey, Gringo's brother Andy Tourell and Paul Kelly, who had raced with Harry in the Heineken regatta. The passage as far as the Azores was fine but our engine was struggling to charge the batteries and was using a large amount of oil, so I decided to stop on the islands. It was a good rest for us. We had a meal ashore, a great night's sleep and a chance to wash and dry some clothes. The next stage, from the Azores to Southampton, however, was the complete opposite. The weather was atrocious. The wind blew from directly ahead at 50 knots. Our course on one tack was taking us towards Spain and when we tacked on to the other hand we were heading for Greenland. The only saving grace was that I had been through worse and had complete confidence in the yacht.

The trip to windward was a long one and our engine troubles worsened. When we finally reached Southampton, it wasn't working at all and I had to manoeuvre into our berth under sail. It was not quite the immaculate procedure I would have liked, but I felt pleased we got alongside without mishap. Mike Golding met us on the dock, watched carefully and invited us all to a hearty lunch.

So much had happened since I'd left Southampton the previous autumn and my sailing career had taken a path that was leading to more racing. I began to think again about the Global Challenge round the world race. When I had watched the finish the year before, I wondered if it was something I would ever be able to do. Now I felt it was well within my reach. I registered for an application form and received it in the post. The shortlist interviews were to take place in May 2003, so I had over a year to bolster my experience. I filled in the application form and sent it off.

Following so closely in Mike Golding's footsteps might have seemed like the right preparation but I was aware that despite having two transatlantic voyages under my belt, I still needed miles and I had to learn much more about how to race competitively. I'd been impressed with the Formula 1 Sailing operation that I had seen in the Caribbean and I thought it would make a great stepping stone to the Global Challenge.

There had been tears and frustrations during my two years with Mike Golding Yacht Racing, but I had learned a great deal about seamanship and developed enormously as a sailor. Leaving was a difficult decision to make. Mike and I went for a coffee and I explained to him what I wanted to do. He understood and wished me luck. I would have his support in everything I set out to do in the future, he said, but as far as he was concerned I was too emotional to be a race skipper. I thanked him for his support but I was stunned he'd been so frank. I shouldn't have been. Mike is not one to beat about the bush; he tells it how it is. And it was true: I could be emotional. I just couldn't help thinking it was working for him that had made me that way. I left even more determined to prove to him that I could make it.

SIX

In It Together

In the winter of 2002 I sailed back to the Caribbean, this time in one of Formula 1 Sailing's racier 65 foot yachts. I didn't give the Global Challenge application form much thought except during a delivery from a race series in Jamaica back to St Maarten. The trip was upwind nearly all the way and it took us ten days. The crew onboard laughed at me: if I thought this was bad, what would it be like as a skipper on the Challenge race, facing a month at a time bashing to windward in the Southern Ocean?

In April, I got an email inviting me officially to the first round of interviews for the race. The timing was awful. The interviews were to be held the following month, at exactly the same time I would be sailing the boat back to the UK. I told Challenge Business that unfortunately I was already committed and I couldn't make it. Their reply said they were inundated with applications and if I couldn't be there I clearly didn't want the job.

It was a fair comment but I felt crushed; I wanted to have my chance. Luckily, fate sometimes acts in mysterious ways. One day during Antigua Sailing Week when I was trimming the mainsail, the middle finger of my right hand got caught in the block of the mainsheet. My immediate reaction was to pull my hand away. It felt as if my nail had been pinched and I clenched my fist hard. After a minute I opened it to look. Doug the Doctor was helming at the time and he told me later that the colour drained from my face.

The top of my finger had been pulled right off. I glanced over to the leeward side of the boat and there, on top of the gas bottle locker, was my fingertip. I grasped it in my good hand and yelled to Doug. He handed over the helm and took me below, where he searched for some of the controlled painkilling drugs I kept in my cabin. That night I flew to Trinidad for surgery with my fingertip carefully packed in ice. The surgeon there examined it, said: 'Do you know what I'm going to do with this?' and dropped it straight in the bin. I'm sure he was right but I was devastated.

When I got back I was frustrated and scared. I wasn't sure how my finger would heal and I had shocked myself. Unable to sail home, I flew to the UK and by this twist of fate I was back in time for the first round of assessments for the Global Challenge. The problem was I was practically useless physically, still heavily sedated and having difficulty doing even ordinary things with my right hand. Challenge Business thought it best that I stayed at home. Ten weeks later I went for my assessment. I was still in with a chance and it was up to me to prove I was suitable.

First, I was asked to attend a sailing trial to whittle 36 people down to a shortlist of 20. I went out for the day with Stuart Jackson, another potential race skipper, the Challenge Business sailing manager, Jeremy Troughton, and a crew of 12 guests. Some of the guests had sailed before and some had never been on a yacht at all. The mixture of abilities was deliberate. Stuart and I were to take turns being the skipper, one of us in the morning and the other in the afternoon, and we had to involve everyone, keep the boat and everyone onboard safe and deal with mock emergencies that would be sprung on us along the way. Stuart had already worked for Challenge Business and knew their boats quite well. We chatted and agreed to help each other as much as possible.

I was asked to be the skipper for the morning so I welcomed the guests aboard and introduced everyone, then one of the crew gave a safety briefing. I asked the people who had sailed before to help as much as possible and added extra information just in case we were tested right away. In fact, the first test had already happened. The safety briefing had mentioned lifejackets but not the harness lines attached to them but I had noticed that and added it without a thought.

We slipped the lines and left. As we were hoisting the mainsail, someone yelled: 'Man overboard!' I got the man – it was really a fender tied to a bucket – back as quickly as possible. Next we hoisted the headsail and I found the sheets had been untied. As we bent them on again, there was another mock man overboard. This time I was under sail and I had to retrieve the 'body' while keeping the boat and guests safe. Finally we got out into the Solent and I was set the task of changing the headsail and shaking out a reef in the mainsail. After that, I was to sail to a specific spot and anchor under sail. I used depth soundings and transit marks to help position the boat and asked the crew to drop the anchor once we had reduced our momentum. Everything went fine.

After lunch it was Stuart's turn. He sailed off the anchor and we stowed it away and hoisted the spinnaker. As we began gybing up a narrow channel, yet another man overboard was thrown. This one really tested us but we got the spinnaker down and hurried back to retrieve the bucket and fender. As we were making our way back to Southampton and helping to tidy and stow, one of the guests suddenly fell down on the foredeck with agonising groans of pain. Stuart and I rushed up and examined the ketchup dripping all the way down his leg and concluded that we had an open fracture to deal with. I got hold of a bunk from below deck to act as a stretcher and Stuart put out a simulated distress call on the VHF radio. Then we lifted the crew member into our stretcher and gingerly took him below for treatment.

A nod from the sailing manager indicated that we had finished for the day. I wasn't confident; I still expected something else to happen. Maybe the engine wouldn't work coming into the marina. But it was over. Stuart and I stayed on for a debriefing and agreed that it had been valuable. The assessment not only proved we were safe but that we could keep a cool head in a crisis. Unfortunately, incidents like these tend to happen at the worst times and can escalate in an instant. It would be all too easy to crack under pressure.

A few weeks later, in September 2003, I was told I had made it to the final shortlist of 20 people. The next stage of selection was a residential week to choose 12 race skippers and two standby skippers, held at a sailing club on Hayling Island. As I listened to the welcome talk by Jeremy Troughton I became painfully conscious that I was the only one who had not taken part in an earlier weekend selection process. I was also the only woman. They were bound to scrutinise everything I did. To explain, I said that I had been out of action for a while. The only comment was from an Australian sailor called Andy Forbes, who commented: 'She's got some balls. Good on her!'

We learned about interview techniques. Our personalities were profiled and we did some psychometric testing. It was an insight into our characters and I told myself it would be valuable regardless of the result. A month afterwards, Jeremy called me again. I was onboard a boat mopping out the bilges, dirty and covered in a film of oil and diesel. When I lifted my head out from the bilge I saw on the screen of the phone that it was from a withheld number, so I knew it was important. I answered and straight away Jeremy told me I was being offered the position as a race skipper for the 2004/2005 Global Challenge Race. I wanted to say something but no words came out. I wasn't sure how to react. I was stunned, shocked, exultant. 'Don't tell anyone yet,' Jeremy warned. 'We'll be making an announcement in November.'

Handing in my notice for a job that I was not able to disclose was a tricky one, but I had a good relationship with Formula 1 Sailing and carried on working for them until I joined Challenge Business. When the new skippers were announced at St Katharine Docks in London in November I finally met my new boss, Sir Chay Blyth. I knew all about Chay. He had been a sergeant in the Parachute Regiment in 1966 when he had rowed across the Atlantic with John Ridgway and five years later became the first person to sail non-stop alone round the world westabout, against the prevailing winds and currents, a voyage that many had considered impossible. He had led crews round the world in two Whitbread races and raced competitively in mulithulls. Sir Chay was a sailing legend.

I had seen him occasionally when I worked for Mike Golding and we had spoken briefly a few times. He was short and stocky, with a head of grey hair and had a big presence that you could feel almost before he entered a room. Sir Chay was renowned for not suffering fools gladly, and my impression of him was that he was not easily approachable but was a great friend to people with whom he was better acquainted.

The 12 skippers gathered onboard one of the Challenge yachts and anxiously waited to meet him. When he arrived he seemed to sense our nerves and broke the silence with a joke. 'Relax. Smile,' he said in his bullish way. 'You're only about to face the firing squad! You might as well get used to it, because it's going to be like this from now until the end of the race.'

It was the first of many meetings with Chay and I got to know him well. He would often try to bait people to get a response but if you had the confidence to answer back he respected that and you would have an interesting conversation. I learned a huge amount from him. He was a captivating speaker, he networked with effortless efficiency, was always looking ahead and planning strategically and he had careful manners. Chay had high standards and he expected the same from us in representing his company. Well, I was used to that.

Our next big milestone was the crew selection, which was revealed at the London Boat Show in January. The skippers had no say in who would be on our teams. Our crews were going to be new groups of people that we would need to get to know and learn about in order to ensure that the next 18 months of commitment would work. Each of the crew members had paid over £20,000 to take part and had made a lot of personal sacrifices for their dream of racing round the world. As skippers, we were being employed to make these dreams come true.

The skippers were ushered into an upstairs room, and five minutes before the crew volunteers were allowed into the room we were handed our crew lists. Six of the skippers had already worked with Challenge Business and had met some of the crews already but for the rest of us the names meant nothing. The six skippers in the know gathered into a huddle and all we could hear were gasps and whoops of laughter. I retreated into my own little world. I was about to become responsible for a group of 17 people that would have to grow into a close-knit team. I was deeply apprehensive.

One of the six Challenge skippers came over and looked over my list and made a few comments. The problem is that other people's opinions can cloud your judgement and threaten to alter your own first impressions. It was kind of him but I didn't listen. I wondered what the reaction of my crew would be to being assigned to the race's only female skipper. To me, it was irrelevant but I wasn't convinced they were going to see it the same way.

The doors opened and the crew volunteers poured in. They were frantic to get the waiting over with and find out who would be taking them round the world. Each of the skippers had been given a different colour T-shirt to wear, and those who had been matched up with sponsors had branded items to hand out to their crews. It was a bitter disappointment to find mine wasn't one of the sponsored boats, and as I watched goodie bags being lined up for other teams I felt I was under even more pressure to even up the odds. When the crew lists were announced, I watched the reactions. Some people were crying, some joked and a few were not even concentrating. It was quite surreal. At the end of the presentation everyone had to go and meet their skipper and claim their crew T-shirt. To an outsider it would have looked like chaos.

My crew mustered around me. I was concerned that I mightn't seem enthusiastic enough. I handed out the shirts, apologising for their drab grey colour and everyone laughed. Afterwards, we went to a nearby bar, where I had organised drinks and snacks for everyone. I had made a big deal about encouraging the crew to invite their friends and family to London, as I knew support from home was going to be extremely important to all of us. In the bar, I explained that we were in this together. We could make it work only if we used the full strength of the team. Everyone was excited, and I was buzzing. Although we didn't yet have a sponsor, I thought it was important for our team to have a name and an image, and within no time at all we had agreed on an identity. From that moment on we became 'The Firm'.

I had a few weekends sailing with my crew before a race round Britain and Ireland. This was a two-week event for a different group of paying crew, and only eight of the 12 yachts were taking part. I wanted to accumulate some miles on my boat, so I volunteered to be one of the skippers. I was lucky that several of my Global Challenge crew also joined for the race. It was going to be a great opportunity to spend some time together and develop a closer relationship.

We set off from the Solent in breezy conditions and rounded the back of the Isle of Wight before heading down-Channel towards the Irish Sea. We had a good start, but as we were tacking to clear St Catherine's Point on the Isle of Wight our mainsail fell down. It surprised all of us and the crews nearby who saw and heard it happen. The webbing strop that attached the head of the mainsail to the halyard block had failed. I asked Marcus, my first mate, to go up the rig and rescue the mainsail halyard, which was still swinging around aloft. This took some time, and it was a rough ride for him 29 metres up in the air while we kept the boat plodding along under headsail alone. When Marcus came back down he was rather quiet.

Kate, one of my Global Challenge crew, had volunteered to be responsible for sails and sail repairs on the race and sewed on a new webbing strop. It was no easy feat while we were rolling heavily in the swell, but before long we were back under full sail again. I was pleased with how we had coped but extremely frustrated at losing such valuable time so early on. As night fell we lost sight of the other yachts and were left to make our own decisions. I chose to head offshore, hoping for a change in wind direction. That was a mistake. The yachts that stayed closer to the rhumb line and took the shortest distance fared much better. We lost out in that decision and I blamed myself for letting the crew down. I resolved to concentrate on making better calls and I left the crew to sail the boat.

By the time we had sailed around the west of Ireland and were heading towards the remote Scottish island of St Kilda, it was very clear that this plan, too, had been a mistake. I made a big decision. It was vital for me to be involved in sailing the boat so that I could help develop the crew's skills and pass on my knowledge. It was no good letting them learn by trial and error. That way we would never win. I know this was a late discovery but from that moment on we began to race more competitively. I enjoyed it more and so did my crew. It was a valuable and timely lesson.

We finished 6th out of 8, so we weren't last. I was glad I'd sailed the race and my crew had done a great job, but I felt I could have done more. Or could I? It was a question that kept echoing in my head. I couldn't decide if I was able to do better, or if I'd learned the lesson that I was out of my depth. I agonised about this and for the next week I went through the motions, wondering constantly if staying on with Challenge Business was really the right thing to do.

The turning point was a skippers' social night, typically full of banter, stories and good humour. Andy Forbes, the Australian skipper of *BG Spirit*, sensed something was wrong. Ever since we had met at the selection week in Hayling Island we had been firm friends and occasionally a sounding board for each other's problems and concerns. Andy is a tall, athletic, easy-going man with a wise head on his shoulders and he frequently seemed like the adult among us. He had been given a heavyweight sponsor yet he had not alienated himself from those of us who were struggling with a lack of support.

He asked me if I needed to chat. We stepped outside with our drinks and I blurted it all out. I didn't honestly think I could take a crew round the world any more. Andy looked shocked for a few seconds and asked me how I'd got that crazy notion. I told him about the Round Britain and Ireland and how scared I was of letting my crew down and coming last. All my life I had aimed to succeed, to make people proud, and now that I had the chance to do that with a crew of people and their families and friends behind them, I was going to disappoint them all. As the tears rolled down my cheeks, Andy listened to my tale of self-pity. 'I think I'll quit now,' I told him.

Andy was firm with me. 'Being nervous and concerned about your performance is one thing,' he told me, 'but doubting your ability when you have as much right to be here as anyone else is ridiculous.'

His words sank in and slowly my spirits began to lift. I realised I didn't really want to throw away such an amazing opportunity. I had to grunt up and get on with it. As my Dad would have said: 'Are you going to talk about it or get on and do it?' Our talk was never repeated and Andy never asked again; he just gave me a knowing look a few days later.

The sponsors for the event signed up slowly and we waited patiently for ours. We were tenth in line and in September two companies, Unisys and EMC, came onboard as a joint venture and the boat was christened *Imagine it. Done.* That was a great morale boost for us all. The identity of a team has a massive impact on morale and the battle of the crews was nearly as fierce ashore as it was afloat. Our last-minute preparations and engagements were particularly testing. There was much nervous laughter as people tried to give the impression of being relaxed but the tension was palpable. This was a huge step in our lives. Everyone was leaving behind loved ones, and I had the responsibility of taking 17 people away from them for ten months on the promise of bringing them back safely.

On the day of the start in Portsmouth, the marina reverberated with the clamour of crowds lining docks. People were cheering, bands were playing and there were long and tearful goodbyes on every pontoon. The Canon of Portsmouth blessed the yachts and all those sailing on them, and HRH The Princess Royal came to see us off and fire the start gun. It was so overwhelming I barely remember saying goodbye to Harry and my family. All I can remember was worrying that I had everyone onboard for the first leg to Buenos Aires.

The rain started and the wind picked up. We lined up in the starting area, the gun was fired and we were off. Support and spectator vessels followed us all the way into the western Solent. We said our last good-byes as they peeled off to return to Portsmouth. Suddenly, it all became real. We were not going to be back here for nearly a year, and none of us knew what challenges or difficulties we would have to face. We waved goodbye, some of us wiped away tears and morale slumped. We were all in our own worlds. Another yacht tacked across us and we scurried to ease sails and bear away behind them. The race came sharply back into focus and within two tacks we had overtaken them again. Here we go.

As we sailed out into the English Channel, the weather deteriorated and the wind rose. We reefed the mainsail and changed down the headsail. As night fell we were pounding to windward in more than 35 knots and very lumpy seas. I was slowly losing crew to seasickness until I was left with only one other person who was well. A huge wave broke viciously over *Imagine it. Done* and washed a group of us into a heap in the cockpit. At the bottom of the pile one of my watch leaders, Sian Hankinson, had been hurled right across the cockpit head-first on to a winch. There was a large lump on her head, slicked with blood. I consulted our doctor, David Roche, who diagnosed concussion and advised me that Sian should stay below deck until we could be sure she was going to be all right.

I looked around at my seasick crew, every one of them probably rueing the day they'd ever joined up, and stared out at the seas building ahead of us. We hadn't even left the Channel. I began to ask myself: 'Do we have what it takes to get round the world?'

SEVEN

Our Little World

We all had different reasons for being there. The 17 men and women who were my crew on *Imagine it. Done* ranged in age from 23 to 60 years old and all came from quite different backgrounds. There were IT consultants, an equities trader, a New York attorney, a doctor, a fireman, a primary school teacher and a housewife. They had all paid a very large sum of money to race round the world but each of them had a different reason for their dream. Some were proving something to themselves; others were proving something to everyone else. Some of my crew wanted to make a change in their lives, while for others it was a way of checking and affirming that they were doing the right things in life. My job was to try to realise as many of my crew's dreams as possible.

I knew from the outset that balancing all these aims while trying to win a yacht race was going to be hard, and it would be all too easy to end up pleasing no-one. My crew were unanimous that they wanted to be competitive, but that meant different things to different people. If you were a natural competitor used to driving hard, being competitive meant winning. If you were aiming for a life experience it was more about testing your limits and doing as well as you possibly could. The two sets of goals weren't necessarily compatible.

Beyond these varying motivations was a mixture of sailing abilities and experience. Some of my crew had sailed regularly before but others had only just completed their Challenge training for the race. Our first long leg from Portsmouth to Buenos Aires in Argentina was all about drawing on people's strengths and developing those with less experience. The more competent we could all become as a crew the better we would perform. We had no illusions: we knew we were unlikely to win this leg, but we aimed to get better and better. To win we would have to improve at a faster rate than the crews on the other yachts.

When you put 18 relative strangers together in a 72ft-long world for a month or more at a time, in an environment where there is seasickness, cold and wet followed by stiflingly hot, sweaty tropical temperatures, you soon learn things about people you wished you hadn't. Inevitably, a watch system that works people hard and breaks sleep into three- or four-hour stints will cause fatigue and sleep deprivation, and that affects everyone slightly differently. Tempers fray. People become stressed and impatient. I was extremely fortunate with my crew. They were a very relaxed and easygoing bunch. They tried very hard to make life easier, not harder, for each other, yet managing people was undoubtedly one of the most difficult and demanding aspects of my job; every bit as hard, and maybe harder, than racing the boat.

We got to know each other and our habits intimately. We soon learned who had poor hygiene and, since I was the skipper, I had to deal with that before everyone suffered. We learned who didn't brush their teeth, maybe because they were suffering from seasickness. We found out who didn't really understand how to flush out the toilet system but was too embarrassed to say so, and then we'd have to sort out the plumbing problem that it caused. One of the most common niggles on a boat where four or five people are sharing a small cabin is smelly feet. Where do you move the offensive boots or shoes when the owner is asleep, and how do you do it tactfully? Another aggravation we had was snoring. That was driving some of my crew to distraction. I solved that by moving all the snorers to the cabins forward of the mast so that the non-snorers could sleep soundly in the aft bunks.

Our watch system on *Imagine it. Done* included a rotating mother watch. Once a week everyone had to cook and clean throughout the day and as a reward they were allowed to have a fresh water shower and a full night in their bunks before going back into a cycle of four hours on and four hours off during the day and three on, three off at night. On a yacht at sea, this is quite a good perk. However, mother watch has some awful jobs to do. You have to clean the heads and cook three meals a day for 18 people, no matter how rough the weather. Some people's cooking skills are better than others and a tired, hungry crew are not the easiest to please, especially if the food is cold, late or bland. We had some interesting chefs who experimented brilliantly with our mainly rehydrated food, while others got it terribly wrong.

As we sailed south, the temperature onboard rose. Being built of steel, *Imagine it. Done* was like an oven in the Tropics and it made cooking in the galley an ordeal. Some of the crew came to me with a complaint. They did not like seeing sweaty, semi-naked people cooking in the galley or at mealtimes. We had already decided that honesty was the best policy onboard, but it was down to me to be the diplomat. I made a ruling that whenever anyone was working with food or eating food at the table, they had to be dressed.

This was only one of many little niggles along the way. As the skipper, one of the hardest things is to decide when to get involved and when to let something sort itself out. Some things are not worth trying to control and other problems, once aired, go away and are quickly forgotten. One irritation that brewed almost to boiling point involved the eating habits of one of the crew. Like most people, he got tired and irritable when he didn't eat properly. His moods were becoming an annoyance for everyone, some more than others; on a yacht with nowhere to hide someone's moody behaviour is pervasive and inescapable. The same crewman also happened to have quite a fussy taste in food and was a self-confessed chocoholic. He craved and snacked on sweet food, left more nutritious main meals uneaten and went to his bunk complaining and moaning. It was driving people mad, and I was asked to do something about it.

I gave a little talk to all the crew explaining that we should try to eat all our food because the calories and nutrition were so important for our well-being but I had to leave it at that. However much I sympathised with the rest of the crew, this guy was 35 years old. If he didn't want to eat, I couldn't make him and I certainly wasn't going to change his tastebuds or his eating habits. So let's live with what we cannot change, get over it and move on, I suggested. It was one of those small things that can get really out of proportion and a lesson on living with others. That gripe was carried all the way round the world but it was never acted on again.

Fatigue and a shortage of sleep had a major effect on people's behaviour and habits and everyone reacted differently. Most commonly, people became less tolerant. Food was such an important focus in our little world that it took on an almost obsessive importance at times, and many of our irritations revolved around it in one way or another. Another of the crew's frustrations involved table manners. During the watch system the crew sailed, slept and ate in a cycle throughout every 24 hours, and people were often grabbing some food quickly before getting their head down, or having a meal before they went on watch. If someone helped himself or herself rather than serving the others who were waiting, however, tempers flared.

On two occasions there were all-out rows about this. It was calmed immediately each time by someone who came straight out with what they were thinking, which is by far the best way to sort out a conflict. My temptation would have been to leave things well alone in the hope they would go away by themselves rather than deal with conflict head on. I learned, however, during the Global Challenge that small irritations can fester and escalate out of control if you don't tackle them right away, and a small annoyance that would have been easy to tackle initially could turn into a really big problem.

However tolerant we all tried to be, and however we modified our habits, there were bound to be conflicts between individuals. The stronger characters onboard sometimes got frustrated with the weaker, less driven personalities. I tried to give everyone jobs that suited their character as well as their abilities, and I tried to play to people's strengths and develop weaker areas. It was tricky. We needed to improve as a team to do better, but some of my crew were comfortable with what they knew; they didn't want to be improved. We all had to learn to compromise. Very quickly we found out what an asset it was to be flexible and how that improved morale onboard. As for a sense of humour, that was essential.

One of the more difficult facets of my job as skipper was managing people whose usual role in life was as a leader. Quite a few of my crew were used to managerial roles in which they were making big decisions every day of their lives. It was not so easy when someone else was managing their expectations and development in a relatively unknown environment. Of course I knew that anyone who had committed themselves to the race was bound to be a highly motivated individual, but during that first leg it was sometimes frightening to have so many dominant characters together in one boat.

I tried to apply some of the lessons I had learned while teaching. I believed that responsibility, or ownership, of a job makes for a more dedicated team. Before the start of the race I offered choices of jobs to the crew to choose, thinking that people would self-select what they were good at. I soon found out that it didn't work that way. Everyone wanted the same jobs because they looked or sounded good, not because they could actually do them well. The crew was not short of enthusiasm and I certainly didn't want to switch it off but I really needed to find the right person for every job. The watch leaders were among the most important, as much for their communications skills as their sailing abilities: no-one wanted to be barked at for ten months. Overall, though, we needed to be sensitive to each other and feel equally important. As a team we would get round. As 18 individuals, we probably would not.

A skill I took from teaching that proved very useful from the beginning of the race was how to make myself properly understood. That is important in any environment but none more so than on a yacht. A delay in doing something would affect our performance but, more importantly, something misunderstood could lead to a mistake and then, perhaps, to an injury. I already knew that if you keep saying the same thing and issuing the same instructions repeatedly, what happens is that the same group gets it and everyone else continues to live in the dark, getting increasingly frustrated. What worked better was to explain something in a number of different ways. We also developed forms of non-verbal communication to relay instructions when it was dark or too windy for a voice to carry from the back of the boat to the cockpit.

The first leg was a learning curve for me as well. I had always been on deck each time we reefed or made a headsail change because the risks to crew and the wear and tear on sails and gear was so much higher. As my crew grew more accomplished I learned to trust them and let them get on with these jobs themselves. Gradually, as my confidence in them grew, my watch leaders took over the role. The turning point came one night when Sian Hankinson came down below to the chart table, where I was sitting, and asked if it was all right to make a headsail change. The wind was rising and the call was perfectly timed. That was the first step for me in learning to trust in other people's strengths and towards getting more relaxation and sleep.

We all got better at what we were doing but so too did the crews on the other yachts, and we knew we were going to be stretched for the entire race round the world. When we reached Buenos Aires, however, we thought we had a better measure of what this challenge was going to take. We were wrong. The leg ahead of us across the Southern Ocean to New Zealand was to test us in ways we never imagined. There is no time for trivial irritations when you are struggling to survive day by day, and the personal ambitions that have motivated you amount to very little when you are faced with a decision that could mean someone's life or death.

EIGHT

What a Result

Everyone was nervous when we left Buenos Aires for the leg to New Zealand. In port, each crew had practised setting up their storm trysail and had talked over heavy weather procedures in preparation for our first experience of the Southern Ocean. We had all read accounts from the previous races and knew of the hardships previous crews had endured. We had seen graphic photographs of injuries sustained down there and had watched over and over again the footage of these 46-tonne steel yachts, normally so safe and solid, being tossed on to their sides by ferocious waves. We had contemplated all this, and we had seen winds of 50 knots ourselves before, but we knew that what was to come was beyond our comprehension.

As we raced down the coast of Argentina and passed the Falkland Islands the weather began to change quickly. The sea temperature dropped and as the following winds were replaced by a chill south-westerly they forced us to add layers of thermal clothes. After a week of hard racing the fleet converged at the Le Maire Straits, a narrow and fiercely tidal channel 120 miles from Cape Horn. The middle of the fleet – including us – and the backmarkers piled in behind the leaders, and as we entered the Straits we were able to count ten other Challenge masts. This compression of the fleet was deeply disappointing to some crews and a bizarre gift to others. Either way, as we closed in on Cape Horn the race was starting afresh.

As we approached Cape Horn the mood onboard was a potent mixture of excitement and fear. Not only did we have this infamous landmark to pass but there was a deep low pressure system closing in on us fast and threatening very wet and extremely windy weather. From the nearby land, we could smell vegetation and a tang of seaweed. We got closer and the wind increased, keeping us busy reefing and changing sails. In the afternoon the wind backed, forcing us on to a more southerly course, and the visibility closed in so that when we finally passed the longitude of Cape Horn all we could see from the deck was spray and an ocean of grey.

The evening light faded. We pushed onwards to below 56°S, and when the final tip of the South American landmass was east of us, the swell increased appreciably. We were now rising up on huge waves and dropping down into deep troughs. On top of the deep ocean swell, the wind-driven sea state was rising and in the inky dark of our first night in the Southern Ocean we fought on in drenching conditions. *Imagine it. Done* bucked over wave crests and crashed down, on and on, sending waves over the bow that tumbled along the decks, washing away anything or anyone that was not tied down. This was the furthest south I had ever been and it was scarily exhilarating. We were still on the continental shelf and the sea was short, angry and confused. *Imagine it. Done* felt minuscule and irrelevant in this maelstrom.

The earlier excitement had dissolved and now I noticed how quiet and subdued everyone had become. No one was sure how long this storm would last but one thing was for sure: from here on for the next 6,000 miles we were going to go through storm after storm, that was the certainty of the procession of intense low pressure systems that circulate ceaselessly round the bottom of the world. I didn't know what the boat could take, what we could take or how much worse conditions were likely to get. It was down to me to decide where to strike the balance between safe seamanship and competitive racing. As the wind rose, the first hard decision had to be made. If we reefed and changed down early it would be difficult work and involve some risk for the foredeck crew but the boat would be safer and the sailing less stressful. On the other hand, these conditions might not last, in which case we should save the effort and personal risk and stick it out. It was a tough choice and I was worried that anxiety would make me too cautious. Weighing up both options, I chose to be safe rather than sorry. I assigned jobs to everyone we needed to help prepare the storm trysail. We got it on deck ready to be hoisted on its separate mast track and sat ready and waiting.

The seas breaking over us were bitterly cold. It was not easy keeping blood flowing to the extremities and I varied the watch system to allow the on deck watch to rotate below deck to get warm, or at least to feel their fingers again. Everything we had to do, above deck or below, was more difficult. As the boat pitched and plummeted, you needed acrobatic skills to shuffle and swing, handhold to handhold, the few feet towards the heads or your cabin. Seasickness returned to crew who had not suffered since the first few days of the race. Cooking in the galley and heating large pans of boiling water was a test of organisation and perseverance, and when a meal was ready it was not an event many people looked forward to.

I wondered how we could cope with this life for the next month. Yet what amazed me most as the days and weeks wore on and we went through gale after gale, was my crew's ability to adapt to it all. The Southern Ocean was a frightening, bitter, hostile and desperately desolate place. The weather changed frequently and unpredictably but the bad bits didn't last for ever. Although it was grey and forlorn, sometimes the sun did break through.

We were down to the last 1,000 miles of the leg when, on 22 December, the Global Challenge race changed for us. There was a very large and confused sea and we were hanging on grimly as the boat was flung around like a cork on each successive wave. As we were eating breakfast a colossal rogue wave picked us up. We rose up steeply and when it passed beneath us we went into freefall into the trough behind. The boat landed with a jarring crash that was followed at once by a loud clattering from one of the cabins and a howl of pain.

The cry from John Masters was answered by Ray Davies, who was the closest as he was cooking breakfast for the off watch. He went forward to check and came back out of the starboard forward cabin saying ominously: 'You'd better come and have a look, doc.'

David Roche was our doctor on board, a GP from Sussex in normal life, and he had just saved his bowl of cereal from capsizing. He rushed forward. John had been standing at the base of the mast between the forward two-man cabins, and when we crash-landed he had been launched into the air and flung bottom-first through the rails of one of the pipe cot bunks. His injuries appeared minor, just a bruised ankle and painful ribs. I let him skip a watch to rest, after which he came back on and seemed fine.

However, 12 hours later, John's situation had changed dramatically. His lower abdomen was painful and he had lost his appetite. When the doc examined him again, he was very tender. The next day he had developed a fever and things were not looking good. We were deep in the Southern Ocean, 1,500 miles from the nearest land. This was not a good place for something to go wrong.

David called up our fleet doctor in the UK, Dr Stuart 'Spike' Briggs, who suggested that we start John on intravenous antibiotics. We informed the Challenge Business race office that we had a medical

Me in the summer of 1973, aged about 6 months, while on holiday in Malta visiting my Dad's side of the family.

At nursery school at the age of 4, wearing my favourite T-shirt.

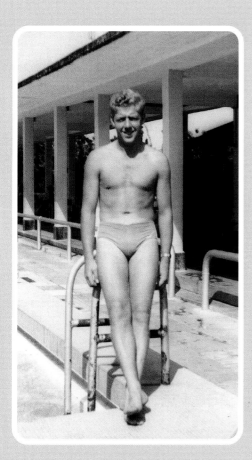

Above: My Mum, Barbara, in 1973, the year I was born.

Left: My Dad, Peter Caffari, aged about 18, by a swimming pool in Singapore during his National Service with the RAF.

Dad, my older sister Jane and I on holiday in Holland on our motorboat *Louis Philippe*. I was aged about 6.

Our 40ft wooden Bates Starcraft motorboat *Louis Philippe* on the River Thames. We spent every weekend and every school holiday aboard.

Crewing under the supervision of Mum in 1983. We are going into a lock and I'm starting to learn how to handle the lines.

A hug for my Mum aboard *Louis Philippe*, during a weekend on the water, aged 5.

Dressed as cat for a dance show called *Façade*, from the musical *Cats*. I was 9 and dancing gave me the opportunity to perform, which I loved.

My Form 8 class at North Halifax Grammar School in July 1996 - a great bunch.

My last day as a teacher at North Halifax Grammar School before leaving to go to Swanage.

In the sports office at Harrow House International College, filling in the timetable. Andy Croft, in the background, was my boss at the time but left the next year and I took over as the College Manager.

Nick Keeping in September 1998. Nick was a colleague from Harrow House, a great friend and mentor to me. He opened my eyes to the fact that there was a lot of world out there to go and experience. I was devastated by his death the following Spring, but it spurred me on to go and do new things.

Paddy McMurren and I on our trip by Land Rover in Africa. Paddy was a fellow teacher at Harrow House and romance blossomed when we were in Africa.

I was made skipper of Mike Golding's 67ft yacht after three months working for him. This was taken during the Royal Ocean Racing Club series in 2001, when I was qualifying for the famous Fastnet Race.

With my boyfriend Harry, a fellow yacht skipper who I met at the end of the ARC rally in December 2001, at his sister Jo's wedding.

Richard 'Sparky' Smith aboard *Spirit of Juno* at Christmas 2001, weeks before he was tragically lost in the Caribbean.

situation onboard and were starting their standard crisis operation plan. For now, our assumption was that John had an infection in his abdominal cavity, perhaps an abscess on his appendix, but his fall meant that other possibilities needed to be considered as well.

When John began vomiting I was really worried. Keeping him hydrated was going to be a problem. We moved him towards the back of the boat where there was slightly less motion and where we could keep an eye on him from the chart table, and began giving him intravenous fluids. This was not easy. We had all grown used to the pitching and sometimes violent motion of the boat but it made it difficult to insert a cannula into a vein and set up the fluid bag and the tubing at an angle that would not be knocked by crew shuffling past.

The doc was still sailing the boat with his watch and trying to treat John, who was getting sicker as every hour passed. I was doing the same, as well as my regular routine of overseeing both watches, navigating, receiving and analysing weather data, and keeping the daily fleet radio schedule. Without regular rest when we were off watch, fatigue and stress were wearing us down. The doc was becoming distracted. I asked Gary, a fire fighter, to help take care of John as well. As John was unable to move from his bunk, everything had to be done for him, from keeping him clean with bed wipes to emptying the pee bottle he was forced to throw out in the direction of the chart table. The crew carried on racing the boat as hard as they could but my mind wasn't on the race any more. I felt torn. It was no longer all about performance and yet we needed to hurry; we were still far too far out at sea for any kind of rescue to be carried out.

On Christmas Eve, we sang carols on deck and tried to be as festive as we could. Father Christmas delivered some secret Santa presents to everyone onboard but it was difficult to lift the spirits. For some it was a day to remember for ever, while others were gloomy at spending their first Christmas away from home. Either way, emotions were running high and everyone was sad and deeply worried by John's rapid deterioration. He had developed a heart arrhythmia and his fast, irregular heartbeat sometimes soared to 140 beats per minute. He had an intermittent high fever and his abdomen was swelling out alarmingly from his pelvis. I took the doc to one side and asked him what he thought was happening. What was the worst case diagnosis? His answer shocked me. David said that if the internal abscess burst it would be a matter of hours before John died. There was absolutely nothing we could do and there was no way of knowing or controlling whether or not it burst. We were relying on God.

I was determined that somehow I would make something happen. We badly needed to get John off the boat. His life might depend on getting proper hospital treatment, possibly surgery, as soon as possible. Nothing could happen where we were, so we sailed on. Helicopter rescue is limited to 200 miles from land and the nearest land was the remote Chatham Islands of New Zealand, much too far away from us for a medical evacuation.

Our supplies of intravenous drugs were running low. I sent a message to the Challenge Business race office to ask for a ship-to-ship transfer of medicines to be arranged with another yacht. Paul Kelly's crew on *Save the Children* was the nearest, about a day's sail to the north, and the race office diverted them to rendezvous with us on a converging course. I was impatient to get it over with and nervous at the same time. It wasn't going to be easy. However skilled you are at boathandling, it is a very different matter in the huge swells of Southern Ocean when you haven't seen another boat for weeks. Trying to manoeuvre close enough to another 46-tonne steel yacht to transfer a small watertight container was a real challenge and I was very mindful that the contents of that container represented life or death for John. After two attempts, we passed it between the two yachts and Paul Kelly and his crew bade us farewell. We were left alone again to deal with our troubles. That was a choking moment. Still, we had more fluids, more drugs and some chocolate to help.

We sent a message to race headquarters stating that we were turning on the engine and retiring from racing and we pressed on, motorsailing to make the best speed possible towards the Chatham Islands. Until this moment I had never heard of the Chatham Islands and had no idea where they were. Now they were the most important place on Earth.

John stabilised with the extra fluids and drugs. The doc was working hard but when I told him our calculated ETA given the weather forecast he looked at me, tired and ashen, and shook his head. 'We don't have enough drugs to get there,' he said. The situation was getting more serious and I immediately told Challenge Business that we needed another ship-to-ship transfer, preferably from a yacht between our position and the Chatham Islands so that we would not lose any time getting to land. They asked *Samsung* to turn around to help us.

Another email from the Challenge race office told me that the rescue services had suggested an airdrop of extra drugs as we neared Wellington. That was 800 miles and probably five days away. I thanked them politely and replied that we would probably not have a living patient to adminster them to by then. We needed to get John ashore at the earliest possible opportunity.

At the time we had no thoughts beyond our own troubles and had no idea what else was happening in the world. Unknown to us, a tsunami in Asia had devastated large parts of the coast of Indonesia, Thailand and Sri Lanka and killed hundreds of thousands of people, and New Zealand had sent many rescue and medical experts to help. In the midst of this massive catastrophe, Challenge Business put me in touch with the New Zealand Maritime Rescue Co-ordination Centre, which advised me that a Mayday was going to be sent out to see if there were any other vessels in the area that could assist us. Shortly afterwards, the message flashed up on our computer screen. Seeing a distress message for the vessel you are sailing is a very strange feeling. The reality of our dire situation sank in further. The New Zealand rescue centre called again later to say that the only merchant vessel in our vicinity was a long way off and no better equipped with IV drugs and fluids than we were. There was nothing to do but continue towards the Chatham Islands and, in the meantime, the rescue centre would try to see if an airlift was possible.

On day six of our crisis, *Samsung* appeared on the horizon. The transfer between the yachts went perfectly and as soon as it was done *Samsung* altered course and sailed away from us. Our engine was working hard as we tried to motorsail into more than 30 knots of headwinds and a lumpy sea. Progress felt excruciatingly slow but my crew were doing a fabulous job, watch on, watch off, as we slogged to close land. John and the medical team hung on. Yet I was filled with dread. What if the abscess burst?

Sailors often talk about the consequences of injuries and illness at sea but very few people have to deal with them. My engine was still going but that worried me, too. We'd had a series of engine problems throughout the summer and the engine was due to have a replacement fuel pump fitted in New Zealand. Here I was relying on it to save someone's life. The pressure was unbelievable.

What if the engine broke down? What if we didn't get there in time? These were not questions I wanted to answer, but it is the skipper's job to plan for every eventuality, however unpleasant.

What if John died? According to the crisis plan, there was to be a burial at sea in the event of a death unless we were close to land. I was trying to think of what we would do if we had to sail with a body aboard until Wellington. I knew that not everyone would be able to deal with it psychologically and I didn't think I could manage this scenario on my own. I confided in Darren and Andy, who were two of the toughest of my crew physically and mentally, and on whom I thought I could rely should the worst happen. We tried to make light of it but it was not an easy discussion.

Ashore, arrangements were being made for an airlift for John as soon as we got close enough to the Chatham Islands. A helicopter and a spotter plane would be needed for the rescue and had to come from New Zealand. John would hopefully be winched into the helicopter but first a spotter plane had to pinpoint us quickly as we would be at the very edge of the helicopter's fuel range. There would not be much time to get it right.

It looked as if the rescue could be possible on New Year's Day. Then we hit a problem. As we got closer to the rendezvous it was obvious we weren't quite going to make it. I calculated that no matter how hard we pushed *Imagine it. Done* we would still be 210 nautical miles from the Chatham Islands by the time darkness fell, just out of helicopter range. The rescue could not be done at night, and the tiny Chatham Islands didn't have enough supplies to refuel the spotter plane and the helicopter once they had landed there.

Undefeated, the New Zealand rescue centre arranged for a Convair flight to pick up fuel from Wellington on New Year's Eve and deliver it to the Chatham Islands to be ready for the helicopter and spotter plane. The same day, the Westpac rescue helicopter and a Vincent Aviation spotter plane took off from Wellington airport and headed south-east to the Chatham Islands, some 500 nautical miles away, on what was to be New Zealand's biggest maritime rescue in a year and the third longest distance mission ever.

Everything was on hold until first light. The following morning the flight crew woke to find low cloud cover and rain. The departure time was pushed back by a further hour.

Eventually the cloud cleared and the spotter plane and helicopter crews took off. We established communications with each other relatively easily and I gave them our latest position, course and speed, sea state, wind speed, wind direction and cloud cover. The spotter plane appeared and flew overhead. We received a detailed brief about how the 100 foot hi-line rescue would work. I gave each of the crew a task and took the job of helming the boat myself, as it was going to be critical to maintain a constant course and wind angle when the helicopter was overhead and the rescue was taking place. Everyone got into position. I kept reminding myself that my only job was to concentrate on the compass course and wind angle display.

We were 100 miles from the Chatham Islands when the helicopter arrived overhead, less than an hour from land for them but easily another 24 critical hours for us in strong headwinds. John's abdomen was getting larger all the time, and on the morning of the rescue he began to vomit once more. David the doc was nervous. He inserted a spare intravenous cannula in John's arm and helped him into his dry suit. Once out of his bunk, John's blood pressure dropped alarmingly and the doc confessed that he was worried John would lose consciousness on the hoist up to the helicopter.

In a 6 metre swell and 35 knots of wind, the hi-line was passed down from the helicopter and a paramedic was lowered to the boat. The crew pulled him aboard. John was attached to the same harness as the paramedic and they were snatch-lifted from the yacht and winched up. I had assigned a rescue swimmer to stand by in case John fell from the hoist and ended in the water but he wasn't needed, and a few minutes later we received a thumbs up and the spotter plane and helicopter flew off.

The relief on board was colossal but there was silence as everyone wrestled with different emotions. Now that John was in safe medical hands, one of these emotions was a deep and contrary sense of disappointment. We were out of the race. Since each stage was scored on points, retiring from this leg dropped us down almost to the bottom of the results table. All our hard sailing in the last three months counted for nothing, and no matter how hard we raced round the other half of the world we could never hope to win the Global Challenge.

I was overcome by tiredness after John was airlifted off. I set a new course towards Wellington, we made sail and I turned my poor, exhausted engine off. A wonderful quiet filled the boat. The doc and I said goodnight to everyone and went to our bunks. I fell immediately into the deepest sleep of the race. When I woke it was like being on a different boat.

In the Chatham Islands, John and his wife, Lorraine, were flown to Wellington by the New Zealand Air Ambulance. It was an instant relief for him. He could stop being strong and let the doctors do their jobs. By midday the same day, he had been admitted to the intensive care ward at Wellington Hospital and was about to undergo surgery. His illness was every bit as serious as we had feared. The fall a week earlier had caused a perforation to part of his large intestine and he had a huge pelvic abscess. Part of his colon and a section of his small intestine had to be removed, and he had septicaemia despite all the antibiotics we had given him. This was one lucky man. Someone was watching over John, and for that I am eternally grateful.

When we arrived in Wellington we all wanted to slip into our berth quietly. We were not prepared for the huge reception we got. The crews who had previously arrived all turned out, and so did many members of the public who had been following the rescue on TV or in the local newspapers. The best feeling, though, was the news that John's operation had been successful and he was recovering well. I rushed ashore, had a shower and went to the hospital with the doc and Gary to see our patient. When I saw him plugged into a bank of machines I was hit again by the seriousness of our situation. John was thin and wan but in good form. The surgeon came to see us and thanked us for our part. A day later, he said, and it would have been too late for John.

In the next few days, we met some of the people who had been involved in saving John's life. 'Rescue Dave', the helicopter winchman David Greenberg, is a legend and became a lifelong friend to the crew, and he joined us in John's place for the next leg to Sydney. He told me off because I'd reported the sea state as moderate. I guess it's all relative.

My crew did a superb job. I am proud of how they handled a difficult time. They were focussed and professional. You never know what life is going to throw at you, but it's true that you do become stronger with each experience. John's letter to us summed it up beautifully:

'The race has been a shining example that you have to take what is thrown at you, and it has been far more than I expected in the beginning. We all began with high hopes of not only finishing the journey but also winning. I didn't complete the race but I consider I was the biggest winner, having become a famous almost-halfway-round-the-world-sailor and returning after amazing care from scores of dedicated people with my life intact. What a result.'

Sir Chay Sets a Challenge

In New Zealand everyone took a holiday while service work was being done on the yachts. After such a difficult leg, we all needed to get away and deal with the disappointment in our own way. Harry flew out and we went travelling. It was fantastic to see him and have some time alone. When we returned to get *Imagine it. Done* ready for the next leg we had a team meeting and decided to change our goals. Since an overall win was out of the question we would take each leg at a time and aim for a good result in every one.

In a crew of 18 people everyone's priorities are slightly different, but we all wanted to make a difference, to make a statement. Personally, I wanted to make my crew proud and I felt I needed to prove my abilities to myself. My self-esteem had suffered on the leg to Wellington and I lacked conviction. We felt we were doing it for John, too, because we knew his dream had come to an end.

The leg across the Tasman Sea from Wellington to Sydney was a relatively short sprint for us and the fleet was close together. For a week, we were rarely out of sight of another yacht. Things were going well and we were lying in second place midway through the leg when I made a crucial decision to go north, a course that took us away from the others. It was the wrong move. First, we ran into light airs and then into a southerly 'buster' that brought 40 knots of wind. By taking a different route the other yachts rode round the same weather system and straight into Sydney Harbour. We went from hero to zero in less than 24 hours. In the end, we limped dismally into one of the most spectacular harbours in the world in last place. It took us an hour-and-a-half to drift across the finish line and all we wanted to do was drown our sorrows.

From my earliest days with Challenge Business, my worst fear had been coming last. My crew were frustrated, unhappy and distant. I felt sick. I didn't want to see or talk to anyone. Harry was standing on the dock as we came in. It was Valentine's Day and he was clutching three red roses, one for each year we had been together. I just wanted to be hugged and be comforted but the dock was full of photographers and other crews, drunk and happy. I hid below for a while, going through checklists with the Australian Customs and Immigration officials until I could no longer put off going ashore. As I came on deck Loz Marriott, the skipper of *Pindar*, put his arm round my shoulders and led me to the bar for a quiet drink with Harry, well away from questions and curious stares. As always, the skippers had a sixth sense for how each other was feeling. Someone had to finish last on every leg. This time it was me.

The stopover in Sydney was short, and I had an early debrief with the crew. We acknowledged two things. We knew we could sail the boat fast but to finish ahead of the others we had to stay with the fleet. I promised not to take any fliers and to try to sail the shortest possible distance on the leg to Cape Town.

We left Sydney in sunshine but as we headed south the temperature dropped steadily. It looked like a depression was going to meet us as we turned the corner south of Tasmania and headed back into the Southern Ocean. The strange thing was that by our second day at sea the position reports indicated we were lying second. I plotted the positions, checked them all again and stared at the computer screen. I had lost so much confidence I didn't think it could possibly be correct. Still unsure, I asked Kate to come and check. Her grin said it all. The crew were as surprised and thrilled as me. Since the beginning of the race we had dreamed of being at the front. Now we were here, all we had to do was stay there. Suddenly there was a new mood onboard. The atmosphere of concentration was intense but everyone was smiling.

Back in the Southern Ocean, storms built and rolled over us again and again in the weeks that followed. We returned to a remorseless life of beating into waves and wind and each day's progress took us further out into the biggest, emptiest, most remote ocean on the planet. We got news of another serious injury, a fractured and dislocated hip that a crew member on *Save the Children* had sustained in his bunk as the boat crashed off a wave. He had been dosed up with morphine and Paul Kelly's crew were heading back to Hobart. It reminded us how hostile this environment was and how easily accidents could happen. I cautioned my crew for the umpteenth time to look out for each other and take care. There is no room for heroes out there. The ocean isn't fussy about who it hurts.

Everyone in the fleet was having a difficult time. When you are racing to windward in big seas, everything onboard becomes an obstacle and movement is restricted to short manoeuvres between handholds. You hang on to whatever you can find as the boat lurches or plunges violently. Waves blindsided *Imagine it. Done* and we fell on our side into troughs. It is impossible to describe how unnerving it is to watch the top of the mast disappear under the water of an approaching wave. Crash landings became a daily fact of life again; the yacht would drive through the top of a big wave straight into fresh air and freefall momentarily, lifting us off the deck and suspending us in mid-air until she landed again with a thumping crash.

At the front of the fleet, our close battle with two other boats continued. We passed our mid-ocean waypoint in first place and celebrated. We believed we could hold on until the end; after all, from this point onwards we were heading north-west and gradually leaving behind the cheerless, grey cold of the Southern Ocean. We tried to keep our focus. A couple of times while changing headsails on a foredeck continually awash with breaking seas crew members were washed overboard to the end of their lifejacket harness lines and quickly retrieved. We had to be careful but we were determined to maintain the fight.

After 7,500 miles in the Southern Ocean, the coastline of South Africa took shape on our approach charts. As we reached the warmer waters I began to think about celebrating with my crew. I was going to tell them how proud I was of them and we were going to enjoy the well-deserved feeling of euphoria as we drank our first cold beers.

Only 40 miles from the finish line we lost the wind and sailed into a hole. Our nearest rivals, *Spirit of Sark* and *BP*, came up behind and sailed into it with us. We spent a day in each other's company until a fourth yacht, *Stelmar*, came storming up to the same windless zone and we all bunched up. We trimmed to coax every last fraction of boat speed from *Imagine it. Done* and sidled to where we thought there was likely to be more breeze to keep the chasing pack at bay. We spent our last night trickling along in thick fog, and as it lifted just off Cape Town we could see the three other yachts ahead. After more than a month of relentless, hard sailing we hadn't even made it on to the podium. My crew was aghast. In an instant, morale collapsed and the cheerfulness and determination vanished. Suddenly, they were tired, resentful, cold and miserable.

When we arrived in Cape Town, our disappointment was too difficult to hide. We barely spoke to each other. I couldn't even bring myself to berth the boat. I persuaded Sian, my watch leader, to steer alongside while I coached her and controlled the throttle. The other crews were there to cheer us. Crates of hot food and cold beers were carried aboard, but for the first time ever my crew didn't step off of the boat. They drank and ate and were subdued. We were all beyond words. The Challenge technical team were on the dock and none of them knew what to say to us. I was asked for an interview and as I described what it was like to have led the most difficult leg of the race right up until the final few miles I cried.

I had never been this close to winning and I felt shattered. I just couldn't imagine how we would bounce back from this. Over the next two weeks, we did a good deal of soul-searching but we were not alone. It was a time of mixed emotions for everyone. On the next 7,000-mile leg to Boston we were all going to sail back into the northern hemisphere and cross our outbound tracks. At this point we would technically have circumnavigated the globe. In a sense, everything we did from then on would be surplus to requirements and so everyone's thoughts were starting to turn to life after the race.

Sir Chay called the skippers to a meeting, a shock tactic to remind us all that the Global Challenge should be a stepping stone and that we should be planning our next moves. I hadn't given much thought to what I would do next and I wasn't alone in feeling that it was all still a long way off. Afterwards, Chay circulated among us and chatted about our plans. I was candid and told him I didn't know, but despite our recent downfall I was enjoying the race and wanted to do more sailing. I think that surprised him.

The following day, Chay asked for a quiet word. While we walked, he came straight out with it: he thought I should have a go at becoming the first woman to sail single-handed non-stop round the world against the prevailing winds and currents. In the 34 years since his voyage in *British Steel* in 1971, only three other people had followed in his foot-steps: Mike Golding and two Frenchmen, Philippe Monnet and the current recordholder, Jean-Luc Van den Heede. No woman had ever achieved it but Chay thought that was only a matter of time.

I laughed politely at his suggestion. I had never even considered solo sailing, and I couldn't imagine doing anything as extreme as Chay was suggesting. He looked at me shrewdly and said: 'Give it some thought.'

When we left Cape Town I again promised to stick with the pack and concentrate on sailing the boat fast. After the cold and wet of the Southern Ocean the warmth of the South Atlantic was welcome at first, but before long we ran into a large high pressure cell where our boat speed dwindled and the temperature rose. The equatorial sun burned all day and there was no shade to hide in. Inside the steel hull, it was insufferably hot. As we coaxed every fraction of speed from the boat we hoisted spinnakers, dropped them and hoisted them again.

Progress was mind-blowingly slow and our frustrations grew. I watched the boatspeed display register a row of zeros. The mood on board was volatile. Patience wore thin and it led to misunderstandings and a disagreeable pressure cooker atmosphere. I wrote in my diary:

'I think I am probably as low as I have been on this whole race and I have an outer ear infection so I am taking drops. I think I would like solo sailing . . .'

I started to think of Chay's idea from a practical point of view. I had the experience to do it. I was about to complete the same route round the world so I knew a little of what to expect. If I were to sail in the same type of yacht I would know exactly how to sail her, how she would behave and I understood all the systems aboard. Could I do it? I thought I could. Did I want to? I turned the idea over and over in the final weeks of the race and came to the conclusion that I did want to attempt it. I wasn't one to turn down a challenge.

We arrived in Boston at the end of a frustrating 7,000 mile fifth leg within minutes of two other boats and we were exhausted. Nevertheless, we worked hard during the stopover to get *Imagine it. Done* ready for the shorter and even more intense legs to the finish in Portsmouth, and when we left again we were a committed and focused crew. We raced hard and tried not to let our minds stray too much. At times when a watch was on deck and struggling to stay awake and concentrate, however, some odd conversations took place. People's thoughts were turning outwards. I instigated one such conversation. My crew had sailed for 33,000 miles on this yacht. What did they think could be done to improve her?

'Power winches, a huge engine for the calms and indestructible spinnakers that never need to be repaired,' they replied, laughing. There were useful suggestions as well. I liked the idea of a grinding pedestal that gave the sailor more winching power and the suggestion of a mainsail with fixed tack lines for each reef so that you wouldn't need to go forward to the mast when reefing in heavy weather. I took the conversation on a slightly different tack. What did they think could be done to make the boat suitable for solo sailing? The crew laughed even more.

At first they thought the idea of sailing a boat designed for 18 people single-handedly was absurd, but slowly as we sat on deck trying to urge *Imagine it. Done* onwards the concept took root.

Throughout the next few weeks I thought more about the changes I would make, and how I would cope alone. Sometimes I was sure I could do it all myself. At other times I would look at the crew in action and realise it was impossible. Every time we dropped the spinnaker we had a team of seven, at a minimum, and I didn't see how I could ever manage this manoeuvre on my own. One dark night we were roaring downwind under spinnaker, with a strong wind behind us. We could see a mast light ahead and another abeam of us to the north. Astern, I counted nine other lights as the fleet made an assault on the finish. Everyone was sailing as close to the limit as they thought the boats could take. Kate had been helming as we surfed down following waves, the log clicking up now and then beyond 20 knots. She handed over to Pete to drive. I was trimming the spinnaker. Suddenly a big gust took us. We barrelled down a wave and watched the speed go up . . . 25 . . . 26 . . . 27 knots. Everyone on deck cheered and the boat carried on like a freight train until it hit the bottom of the wave and the spinnaker exploded with a huge crack. As our speed faltered, the boat began to broach. Pete fought the wheel madly. I called down for all hands. If I could, I wanted to rescue the situation without having to put the deck light on – we didn't want to let our competition see we had a problem.

Within minutes the foredeck was crawling with people pulling frantically at the torn sailcloth to get it back on deck so we could hoist a headsail and continue our fight to the finish. It took a good 20 minutes to sort out the mess. I looked over my shoulder and in the distance off to port I saw the bright light of another yacht's deck floodlight. Our nearest rivals were having a few spinnaker troubles of their own. We had made a foolish mistake. As they say: more haste, less speed. I resolved not to push things so hard again. I told my crew how pleased and impressed I had been by their teamwork but at the same time I was worrying about the predicament from a different point of view. I had needed every last crew member to tame a spinnaker the size of a tennis court. How on earth was a solo sailor to deal with a ripped spinnaker in the same frantic situation?

When we crossed the finish line off Portsmouth in July 2005 at the end of our ten-month odyssey in tenth place overall, it was a hugely emotional moment. This was the end of a journey round the globe the hard way. We had finished it only because we had helped each other and worked together as a team. There had been sleepless nights, restless days in the Tropics, dramas and disappointments on every leg and we had coped with illness and injury. David Roche, David the Doc, had sailed round the world and done much more besides. I had watched him put stitches in Andy's chin, he had inserted cannulas and run drip lines in the most challenging conditions, and he had given us innumerable drugs for aches and pains and ailments along the way. If I were to take on the same adventure alone I might have to do all this myself. I would have to do everything without help. There would be no grabbing a few hours' sleep safe in the knowledge that I had a watch leader keeping an eye on our progress and the safety of the yacht. For 24 hours every day, for months on end, I would be solely and entirely responsible for everything that happened, foreseen or unforeseen. It was almost impossible to imagine but the one absolute certainty was that it would be an even more gruelling feat.

TEN

Ready to Go Again

After the race ended in the summer of 2005 I carried on sailing for Challenge Business until the end of my contract in September. Sir Chay and I had regular chats and he was full of encouragement. I had to find a sponsor to fund the solo voyage and Chay gave me advice about business meetings and how the world of corporate sponsorship worked, all areas that were new to me.

The crucial thing is to reach the people who take decisions and can make things happen. I wrote to directors of successful companies I had sailed with before or during the Global Challenge seeking their advice and sent them an outline of my plan. Everyone was very positive. The trouble was I had a deadline to meet. If I was to give myself enough time to sail across the Southern Ocean in the months of longest daylight hours and least risk of ice, I had to go that winter. If I waited another year, I would lose momentum and I feared I might talk myself out of it.

Quite by chance during the summer I got chatting to Patrick Snowball, the Executive Director of the insurance and investment company Aviva plc. I had first met Patrick a few years earlier on a corporate sailing day. A tall man and a big character, Patrick had been a Major in the army before going into business and was a great communicator. He loves sailing, has his own yacht and I had seen that in a race environment he was naturally competitive.

We had headed out in perfect sailing weather with warm sun and a steady 15 knots of wind that allowed the 12 Challenge yachts to set a course and have a short race. The racing was close and although I had manoeuvred us into the lead the other crews were hard on our heels as we passed the entrance to Cowes on the Isle of Wight. As we passed the next mark we sailed past Ellen MacArthur's trimaran *B&Q*, in which Ellen had set a new solo round the world record earlier in the year. There were guests onboard and as we sailed by we all waved.

Late the same afternoon as we were motorsailing up Southampton Water a rigid inflatable boat came alongside. Patrick and his son Tom were onboard. They had been sailing on *B&Q* for the day and had come along to say hello and congratulate me on finishing the Global Challenge. Patrick, Tom and I chatted away, and I mentioned to them my plan to sail round the world. Patrick promised to get in touch when he got back. I knew immediately that he was going to be invaluable and that he was the perfect person to advise me on how to realise my dream.

A couple of days after our chance encounter, I emailed Patrick and said how jealous I was of his day's sailing on Ellen's trimaran and told him that although I had only recently returned from the Global Challenge this new idea had been suggested to me by Sir Chay Blyth. If I was successful, I would become the first woman to sail non-stop alone round the world against the winds and currents. I imagined the idea would come as a surprise, I added, but Chay and I felt it was only a matter of time before a woman attempted this feat. I asked for his advice on how to raise sponsorship and to whom I should talk. I was sure Patrick would laugh but there was no harm in asking.

About a week after that, Patrick rang me and suggested we meet to discuss my crazy idea. As he hadn't used the word 'no' I was immediately excited. When we met he made it easy for me to convince him there and then and offered to take the plan to Aviva's directors.

Sir Chay Blyth knew of all these discussions and was right behind me. He briefed me on how the meetings should run, what I needed to prepare and what I should wear. I was given a crash business course. Chay said that the average was a one-hour meeting, and if I was kicked out after 20 minutes things were not looking good. If a drink was offered, take it, he said, because that way you'll get to stay in the meeting for at least the length of the drink. I was to exercise my ability to listen rather than interrupt and, like my father, he told me I should dress like a girl but not as if I were pretending to be a City power player.

Armed with a new notebook, a pen that didn't leak and several copies of my presentation, I set off to meet Patrick and Stephen Pain, Aviva's group corporate affairs director, in a skirt and jacket, my hair carefully tied up. I turned my phone off, tuned in my listening skills and kept my fingers crossed. I wanted to get the right result and to make Sir Chay proud of my efforts.

I was about to learn that when it comes to getting sports sponsorship, timing is everything. Fortunately for me, the project I was proposing coincided with the launch of Aviva's new marketing campaign, called 'Forward Thinking'. The aim of this was to increase awareness of the company's new name. I hoped that would help me with the board decision, but all I could do was make my case then get back to work and wait.

On a sunny day in early September I was out on another corporate hospitality sailing day in the Solent and was working on the foredeck when the phone rang. It was Patrick Snowball. 'Are you sitting down?' he asked me. I crouched down on one of the spinnaker poles and held my breath. 'You're going off round the world again!' Patrick said. He was delighted for me. I was almost delirious. Suddenly flustered, I asked my sailing mate to take over running the boat and started making phone calls. The first was to Sir Chay, who sounded even more excited than me, if that were possible. The next, and probably the most important phone call, was to Andrew Roberts.

Andrew was the Project Director of Challenge Business. He had owned a boatyard in Dartmouth and had prepared a series of race boats for Chay and other top multihull sailors, and in 1989 he and Chay had started the Challenge Business. Andrew was the man behind the design and build of the 49 yachts that had raced round the world on the crewed Challenge races and two solo voyages, including Mike Golding's record-breaking circumnavigation. A patient and precise man, Andrew will spend any amount of time planning and checking to ensure everything is done to the best possible and safest standard. My impression of him was of someone who would leave nothing to chance and he was the natural linchpin of this project. I had enjoyed working for him during the Global Challenge and I knew his experience, patience and enthusiasm could get me round the world.

This project was new and exciting and I got the feeling Andrew was enjoying getting his teeth into it. I was immediately inundated with spreadsheets detailing time schedules and jobs lists. We decided that I should do the voyage on the same Challenge 72 yacht I had raced on the Global Challenge. I was pleased, as we had already spent a year together and I knew her inside out. Andrew worked back from the target of getting to Cape Horn and the beginning of the Southern Ocean by Christmas and calculated I should leave the Solent on 20 November, on a spring tide that would propel me westwards towards The Lizard on the Cornish coast, the official start line of the round the world record.

The big difficulty would be getting the boat modified for single-handed sailing and ready to go in time. She had been designed and was set up to be sailed by 18 people and many of the sailhandling systems required the horsepower of a crew. There was a limit to what we could change in the time available but at a minimum we needed a new suit of sails of a different design, furling gear to reduce the sail area in strong winds and a grinder winch to handle them, and autopilots. Everything had to be checked, changed or serviced, the hull had to be painted and branded and we had to carry out intensive sail and equipment trials before I set off. It was a project with a precariously tight timescale. Andrew estimated that 1,800 hours were involved for his technical team alone, all to be shoehorned into only eight weeks. We were at full steam ahead, yet in the weeks ahead Andrew never lost his cool, no matter what the setbacks or how high the piles of paper on his desk grew.

I visited Mum and Jane, who listened to my news with stunned silence. I had only just returned home after sailing around the world and here I was, at the beginning of September, planning to go round again for the second time in a year. To fill the silence Mum asked in a whisper: 'Alone?' I nodded. Jane said: 'So soon?' My nephews Alex and Matthew grinned and exclaimed: 'Cool!'

Emotions were mixed. My family would never say no to my dreams but they were worried. As I told them more and the plan sank in they were also excited, and they felt very reassured and comforted that I was working with the Challenge Business team. They knew I was in good hands and every risk involved would be eliminated if it were humanly possible.

A little over two weeks after Patrick Snowball had called me with the good news, I was in Plymouth with Andrew and his team, deep in discussions about logistics, supplier timescales and load calculations. Alistair Hackett was responsible for the logistics and spares onboard while Matthew Ratsey was involved in the technical requirements of the various modifications, which took much more patience than I had first imagined. I realised I was out of my depth. It finally hit home as I helped the rigger, Neil Gledhill, take measurements for the furling gear from aloft. I sat on the middle spreaders and shut my eyes. What the hell was I doing? What would it be like being up the mast at sea on my own? A wave of panic surged through me. There was so much to learn and to organise. Maybe this project was bigger than me.

Harry's enthusiasm and encouragement bolstered my confidence. We went down to Plymouth together and I showed him the yacht out of the water. The mast was lying on trestles next to the hull, the rudder was out and in another corner of the shed. The insides were stripped bare and stored away in a container and the headlining was down, exposing frightening lengths of wiring loom. Even the hull had been cleaned and polished. *Imagine it. Done* was gone and we had a blank, white canvas ready for the new image of *Aviva*.

Over the next few weeks a routine developed. I spent several days a week in Plymouth and would start the days there talking to Andrew, catching up with what had been done and deciding what should happen next. We started our discussions at nine o'clock in the morning and by half-five we were still there and my brain was aching with an overload of information. The container became my sanctuary; it stopped me getting into trouble by talking in circles and by retreating there to itemise the boat's inventory I felt as if I was being productive.

There were meetings with sailmakers, sparmakers and electronics specialists. Andrew and I walked the bare deck of *Aviva* and began planning how I would handle various sails. It was difficult to imagine the size, weight and volume of sails that I would have to manhandle on deck from the sail locker, and the prospect of the boat bucking beneath me as I hoisted them, and the power of the wind filling them as I was trying to furl them, was alarming.

Then for the first time in ages, I had a whole free day to myself. There were not going to be too many of these before the start in November, and I spent the time shopping for personal items: medication; toiletries; underwear; a bikini. It is a tricky job trying to work out how much deodorant and toothpaste to take for six months and I really didn't want to run out of toothpaste. I also had a list of appointments to keep with the doctor, the bank manager and the dentist. The dentist observed that I had a tendency to grind my teeth under stress. I told him I thought it would get worse.

I went to see Dr Spike Briggs, an intensive care doctor who had sailed on the Global Challenge and had been our fleet doctor during the last race. We discussed the medical kit I would need and what each ointment, tablet or cream would do for me and I wrote notes about each that I would be able to understand no matter how tired, ill or in pain I might be. We talked about the medical risks and some of the ailments that could get seriously out of hand unless I could help myself.

We decided the biggest risk we could do something about was a fall that resulted in an open fracture, which could rapidly become life-threatening in a remote part of the ocean. I felt physically sick at the thought of it. After getting myself below deck somehow, I would need to inject myself with morphine. The morphine in the medical kit was contained in ampoules. How on earth was I to prepare a syringe if I had broken my right arm? Spike decided that, without the luxury of time to prepare a custom medical kit, the best solution was to take an Epi-pen auto-injector. Then he took me through each procedure and suggested how I should attempt everything and where I should position myself for each process, bearing in mind that if I fainted I didn't want to hit my head or end up out of reach of medicines. I had never even thought about these possibilities before and shivers ran down my spine. Three hours later I left Spike's house feeling as if I ought to sail in a padded suit.

Autumn gales hampered our work. Launching *Aviva* in Plymouth had to be delayed because of weather and I spent some time talking on the phone to Sir Chay. He gave me a bit of a pep talk, reminding me that I had the opportunity to set a world first and sail into the history books, just as Roger Bannister had done, and Neil Armstrong and Sir Edmund Hillary. That cheered me up. He also advised me to take plenty of video footage, as it was something he greatly regretted not doing on his pioneering voyage.

Eventually, when the gales abated, *Aviva* was lifted into the water. The mast was stepped without too much trouble and I asked Neil to place a coin underneath the mast heel, a sailor's superstition that is supposed to bring you luck. There she was afloat, my home for the voyage. There was no backing out now.

The autopilots were wired up, the new mainsail and furling stay-sail were bent on and we were ready for trials. We spent the next week testing and calibrating equipment. Secretly I was getting very nervous about going out on the water on my own. I knew what conditions to expect on the voyage. I knew that if things got really bad all I had to do was point *Aviva* in the right direction and she would get through it and all I had to do was stay onboard. I was nonetheless worried that it would all prove too difficult on my own. As no-one had ever sailed a Challenge 72 single-handed, our assumptions were theoretical. But on the other hand, I was also quite excited about the chance to find out if I could do it alone. What I badly needed now was some practice.

At the end of the first week in November Harry and I had our first opportunity to go sailing alone. It was my chance to see how – and if – I could handle *Aviva* with the security of knowing there was someone else to help out if necessary. As we left Plymouth Sound I reminded myself that nothing onboard, not a single thing, was ever going to happen without my effort or involvement. The first job was to hoist the main-sail. Hoisting a 190 kilo sail all the way to the top of a 29 metre mast is exhausting. The head of the sail was still a long way from the top when my lungs felt as if they were going to explode and the muscles in my arms and shoulders burned, but I told myself that nothing is impossible if you set your mind to it. I just had to allow longer to do all these jobs.

I set a reef in the main and unfurled the headsail. *Aviva* responded, heeled and we surged away. In the gathering darkness of the late afternoon, the reassuring lights of land faded out behind us. Beyond Plymouth Sound we left the lee of the breakwater and shelter of land and the wind increased, settling at about 25 knots with gusts of 30 knots. I returned to the pedestal grinder and wound another reef in the mainsail and furled more of the headsail away to get the balance right. *Aviva* was sailing along beautifully, carving her way into the seas and tracing a confident, bubbling wake astern. She felt fantastically assured. I, however, was not. By 0200 I was in despair, worn out and ready to get off the boat.

I thought the whole idea of solo sailing was awful. I didn't see how I was ever going to be able to cope with sailing solo overnight, let alone around the world. It had taken me until midnight to summon up the courage to leave the deck, even momentarily. I was so used to handing over the deck watch to someone else that leaving *Aviva* sailing along with no-one up there watching over her seemed a completely alien and crazy thing to do. When I tacked the boat an hour later, I was surprised at how smoothly it went, but I suspected the pitch darkness helped. Had I seen the headsail flogging until I winched the sheet in for the new course I would probably have been more stressed. I had never had to trust electronic alarms before either, and it took me a long time to feel happy with the radar guard and wind instrument alarms. Eventually I was satisfied enough to close my eyes warily for an hour. It wasn't real sleep but it was something. Catnapping was another thing I had to practise. Little did I know that for the next six months most of the sleep I was going to get would be essentially the same quality of 'pretend' sleep.

As day was breaking, Harry and I sailed back towards Plymouth. In the twilight hour before dawn I practised the art of single-handedly tacking the cutter rig with three sails: mainsail, yankee and staysail. With the new day, my earlier desperation gave way to determination and a fresh self-confidence. I was so pleased we had made the effort to go out on an overnight sail and that although Harry had been onboard I hadn't needed his help. I had done everything alone. I felt then that when I cleared the English Channel and its busy shipping lanes I would be able to settle more easily into a routine.

We delivered *Aviva* east to Portsmouth and a berth at Gunwharf Quays, where a symbolic leavetaking was planned. The idea was for me to have a public send-off at a weekend and sail away alone before Harry and Neil came onboard to help me as far as Plymouth. The start line for the record is off The Lizard so there was no need for me to sail all the way down there single-handed, and with so much shipping in the Channel it wouldn't have been sensible. A final stop in Plymouth would also give me a chance to top up fuel and water tanks one final time.

In the last days before setting off from Portsmouth the team worked frantically through the remaining jobs. Andrew Roberts was like a man possessed. When I came down to *Aviva* he was toiling away re-organising and labelling the boxes of spares and methodically working his way through a huge checklist. It was an essential job and I was extremely grateful, but watching him was beginning to stress me out. With so many people aboard doing different jobs there was a great deal of rubbish and equipment everywhere. Slowly, as we cleared it all away, I started to appreciate how much space I would have to myself. I was still used to getting the boat ready for a crew of 18. One person living here for six months wouldn't use anything like the same amount of room. There would be no trouble finding room in the lockers for Christmas presents, no matter how many I was given.

In the afternoon we took *Aviva* out and did some final checks. We calibrated the spare autopilot and I tried out the method I was going to use should I encounter extreme heavy weather and need to hoist the trysail, the tiny heavyweight sail that I would set instead of the mainsail in a violent storm or if the mainsail tore beyond repair. The trysail was small but it was made of extremely stiff, thick orange cloth that was heavy and hard to handle. We had used the trysail on *Imagine it. Done* in the Southern Ocean but it had taken several crew to haul it up on deck and attach it to the separate mast track. On my own, it was bound to be a struggle. The windage of a 29 metre halyard alone is incredible and it's hard to keep hold of in strong winds. In 10 knots of breeze in Portsmouth Harbour I had no problem, but we looked a sight and were drawing rather a lot of attention; other boats pottering by were plainly wondering what on earth we were up to.

There were more checks and a few additional jobs to do next day but when at last we were finished and nothing more could be done, Harry and I went back to our flat in Southampton. Mum, Jane and her family had come down and we exchanged presents and went out to dinner. I had been away on long voyages so often in the last few years that we had established a new family tradition: our final meal together before I left to go sailing was always a pizza. Unknown to me, my Global

Challenge crew had come together too, and were in a Chinese restaurant next door, so we joined them for a drink. I was given more cards and presents. When we said goodbye the mood was festive, but everyone's hugs were tighter and longer than usual.

On Sunday 20 November I woke early. I lay there for a minute, savouring my last morning in a proper bed. I was about to set off on my second circumnavigation in less than a year. Then I was up and feeling worried. Until this moment, I had been so preoccupied by getting *Aviva* ready that I had never stopped to reflect on the enormity of what I was taking on. I had never actually sailed solo before, not for a single minute, not in any kind of boat. Now that the day of departure had arrived and there was no going back I turned that over in my mind. Did I doubt I could do it? No. Handling the huge sails on my own might be more difficult than I imagined but I never for a second doubted that I would find a way and would adapt to it. At the back of my mind I wondered how I would deal with being on my own for so long but I put that worry aside, too. I couldn't imagine any emotional reason why this project would fail. No matter how hard it was, I would find a way to cope. The process of giving up starts with dwelling on the negatives, worrying and finding reasons not to do something, and I wasn't going to start my voyage with that attitude.

Harry was fussing and I could sense his nervousness. He made a cooked breakfast for us both and we waited for the taxi we had ordered the previous evening. The arranged time came but there was no sign of it. We waited. I began to get jumpy. Damn. I was going to be late for my own departure. After the longest imaginable half-hour, the taxi rolled up outside. As soon as it drove off we realised that with all the fuss we had forgotten to take the food we had bought for Harry's and Neil's delivery to Plymouth. One thing was for sure: they were not going to eat my food!

At Gunwharf Quays people were milling around, and already a crowd was forming on the dockside. The sun was shining and there was not a breath of wind but it was bitingly cold, a perfect late winter's day. The entire technical team were there and we jumped up on to *Aviva* and went below, out of the public view. Andrew, Alistair Hackett and Matthew Ratsey, Keith Baxter the electronics wizard, riggers Neil Gledhill and Peter Lucas, Peter Pearce the engineer and the boatbuilder Paul Tanner all stood round, joking and smiling. These were the people who had got *Aviva* perfectly prepared for this day and ready for anything the world could throw at us in the next 29,000 miles. They understood better than anyone what was likely to lie ahead, what a toll it would take on *Aviva* and me, and their smiles told me they believed I could do it, that I had what it took. They presented me with an all-singing, all-dancing multitool and a card signed with messages from them all. I was touched by the gift and I fixed it straight on to my belt.

The Global Challenge skippers had all turned up and so had many of the crews, their friends and families. There was an air of reunion and lots of photographs, speeches and farewells. Sir Chay Blyth spoke. He explained how it was 35 years earlier when he had been in exactly the same position as I was now. He said I was the right person for the job but that a monumental adventure lay ahead of me and at times it would get really tough. At that point I looked at Mum and saw tears running freely down her cheeks. She was squeezing Jane's hand so hard it was white. Seeing Mum crying, I felt my heart wrench painfully for her and fought back tears of my own.

As I stood at the top of the gangway leading down to the pontoon I was met by a phalanx of cameras. I was surprised and quite embarrassed but there was no-one to hide behind. By the time I got to *Aviva* and stepped onboard, there were hundreds of people on the dockside. It was overwhelming.

Silence fell as Canon David Brindley of Portsmouth blessed *Aviva*. I hugged Mum, who was in tears again. Jane was wonderful, telling me how proud of me she was and hugging me for so long I thought she wasn't going to let go. Captain Andrew took the helm and Harry, Neil and the boys slipped the lines. Once we were off Southsea Castle, they hopped off on to a rigid inflatable boat and I sailed on alone for a bit, a symbolic solo voyage that lasted only until we were clear of Portsmouth. Then Harry and Neil were brought back out to *Aviva* and we headed west, next stop Plymouth.

As the three of us sailed down-Channel, I made some last phone calls and checked the weather forecasts with Mike Broughton, the shore based meteorologist who was to send me weather files and routeing suggestions every day. I was excited now. In Plymouth, I topped up with fuel and water and headed out into Plymouth Sound. The boys helped me hoist the mainsail and I thought: this is the very last time I will have another pair of hands to help me. They took some pictures then said goodbye. It was an emotional moment. I found it difficult to say goodbye to Harry and was thankful we were in company but as I saw him turn to leave I sobbed. I steeled myself with the thought that I was going to make them all proud of the work they had put into the project and, ultimately, proud of me.

Aviva settled to her course towards The Lizard and as the land behind us receded to grey the realisation of everything I had taken on sank in. I was now truly alone for the first time in my life. For a while, I wasn't quite sure what to do with myself. I didn't want to leave the deck. I was too fretful to relax and too nervous to occupy myself. In true British style, I made a cup of tea. I wrapped myself up warmly and sat in the cockpit with my drink as I headed for the start line.

ELEVEN

Going It Alone

On 21 November 2006 at 13.49, I sailed across the start line. I was buzzing with happiness and excitement – it was real, the voyage was finally happening. With the big Code 0 headsail set I pointed *Aviva*'s head south-southwest and she accelerated purposefully until we were creaming along at 10 knots. Land soon vanished astern and we sailed throughout the day under a clear sky and a watery sun. I was feeling pretty good. The forecast was excellent, promising following winds to speed us across the Bay of Biscay. A few days of this weather and *Aviva* and I would be off to a sprinting start.

Everything was going really well until around 1600 when the tack line of the big Code 0 headsail blew. With nothing to keep the forward bottom corner of the sail tight to the bowsprit any longer, the luff shot upwards into a concertina of wrinkles. This was one eventuality I hadn't planned for; the Code 0 had been delivered only five days before I left and this was only the second time I had flown it. For the next hour I tried to wrestle the huge sail on to the foredeck, fuelled by adrenaline and a bit of cursing. I was trying to control the halyard at the same time as the sheets but as I tamed one piece of flogging sail the wind would fill another corner and wrench it out of my control. This wasn't going to work; I had to find a different method. So I decided to drop it in the more confined space of the halyard pit area where I could trap it more easily. Finally, I managed to gather the cloth in bit by bit and then I booted the whole lot down the companionway.

To keep our progress up, I unfurled the smaller yankee and stay-sail and took a breather. Then I set to work on the Code 0 again. It was almost as hard trying to haul the sail through the saloon into the forward sail room where I could spread it out ready for repairs. When it was all laid out I fixed a new webbing stop along the last half metre of the luff, made three holes with a hot knife and fixed the strop on with nuts and bolts. All I had to do now was wait for flat calm weather to get this beast of a sail up and furl it back on the drum. It was another two weeks before that chance came.

I was exhausted but relieved to have recovered the sail in one piece. When I settled the boat down again, I saw from the boat speed display that *Aviva* was going as fast and occasionally slightly faster with this new, more conservative sail plan. That was another useful reality check for me. Maybe these things all happen for a reason, I thought. Maybe it was nature's way of telling me to change down early while I was still learning.

I didn't sleep at all during that first night; I was busy doing something every hour at least. I wasn't worried about this. The wind was increasing and I was so nervous that I couldn't have rested even if I'd had the time. At about midnight there was a loud bang and I looked forward to see the yankee headsail unfurling. The furling line had snapped. I dug out a spare line, grabbed my head torch and made my way forward where I sat on the bow in the dark while a good 30 knots of wind just aft of the beam sent *Aviva* plunging through the waves at full speed. With my head torch trained on the furling gear, I fed the new line round the drum, went back and furled the sail in.

From that moment on I was paranoid about the line chafing through again and I must have gone forward every half an hour to check it. At first light the next day I investigated the cause of the problem. Whenever the sail was partially furled the line had been rubbing on the corner of the furling drum, so I added another turning block aft to alter the angle. Then I collected the two parts of the broken furling line and set them out to dry so I could splice them back together to use again.

When I checked the charts again I was cheered by the fantastic progress *Aviva* and I had made. It was only day two and we were already off the Portuguese coast and still marching southwards at 10 knots. With the unpredictable Bay of Biscay safely behind me I was happier, though the fast progress was making life onboard uncomfortable. As *Aviva* ran before following seas her rolling motion was lively and unceasing. Everything took longer to do and I found it difficult to settle into a routine. Sometimes I still felt swamped by the enormity of what and I had taken on and the immense number of miles ahead. I hoped that as the weather calmed and I got used to the idea of what we were doing, *Aviva* and I would both settle down.

I had not been able to get much sleep since leaving Plymouth and was running on adrenaline. I didn't feel like eating, and as the fresh food went bad I threw it overboard. Towards the end of the first week, however, I started to feel more relaxed and more at ease with the routine of life at sea. The weather was definitely getting warmer and as we rolled down the latitudes I was able to discard my fleece mid-layer. Even the milk was going off, which made me smile. I was starting to enjoy myself.

As I settled into the routine the daytime flew by yet the night hours dragged endlessly. It was odd. I was always busy during the nights reefing or making sail but even if I lay down to sleep or rest for a while I had fallen into the habit of waking every hour. I would get up, write in the logbook and check the sail trim and deck gear. It had been the custom on the Global Challenge to make a log entry on the hour, every hour, and it was a habit that I couldn't shake.

Many people who sail solo spend time beforehand with a specialist in sleep patterns to figure out the best times of the day and night for them to snatch some sleep. I hadn't had time before I left so I was making it up as I went along. It wasn't working out the way I had imagined. For one thing, I didn't feel comfortable getting into a proper bunk. When we had been getting *Aviva* ready to leave we had removed all the crew bunks onboard to fit extra fuel tanks so that I could run the generator to power my navigation, communications equipment and autopilot 24 hours a day, and made a bunk in the saloon where I could lie down and still be within sight of the instruments and the radar display at the chart table. This bunk was a perfect fit and I thought I would easily be able to rest here. The reality was very different. I rarely used it, preferring instead to lie in a foetal position at the chart table and catnap, covered by a fleece blanket. If the weather was harsh and I might need to get back on deck in a hurry, I took off just my foulweather jacket and lay down in the rest of my clothes. If conditions were better, I might discard a couple of layers and – the ultimate luxury – take off my boots for a change.

I was learning that when you are on your own, your alertness to different sounds intensifies. When a yacht is sailing hard it is very noisy but out of this commotion you can detect when something is not right and very often identify what is happening. If, for any reason, the normal pattern changes or you hear a new sound you know something is wrong and you need to get up and check what it is. Together with changing weather, it was this background of noise that shaped my sleep rather than the cycle of day or night. I would lie down at the chart table, shut my eyes and tell myself I was asleep but really I was lying listening and waiting for a different noise.

In these first few weeks, every nap I had was of this pretend variety but slowly I fell naturally into a routine of catnapping for 20 minutes at a time, sometimes 40 minutes. I catnapped when things were quiet and settled and dozed until something woke me, either a strange noise, the radar guard zone alarm or an instrument alarm that was warning me the wind had changed or the autopilot had strayed off course. Now that I had a 24-hour day this ability to sleep at short intervals was fantastic. Quite often I felt recharged by only a brief amount of sleep. When I couldn't doze I might walk around on deck for a bit, fill in the logbook and then nod off. The secret was to trick your mind into thinking you had taken a break. When I needed to, this routine of snoozing and mental self-deception allowed me to stay awake for long periods at a time. I was to find out very soon how valuable this skill could be. Sometimes conditions are so horrendous that no matter how tired you are the movement and din of the boat makes sleep impossible.

The first weekend at sea was a milestone for me. I hadn't eaten all the calories I needed but I decided that if I threw the last sliced loaves of bread away it would stop me making Marmite sandwiches to eat and force me to cook some proper food. I ate properly, celebrated my first week with a shower, put on a pair of shorts and felt like a new woman. I looked again at an email from Mike Broughton advising me of a tropical low that was moving east quite quickly. Mike expected it to pass to the south of us by lunchtime the following day and suggested it might even be possible to hitch on to favourable winds in its north-westerly sector and get a slingshot towards the Tropics, though he warned: 'There are some gale force winds associated with the low.'

I was not especially worried about this low, though I knew that any tropical depression was a volatile and fast-moving phenomenon. The night that followed was nothing like I expected. Mike's message was the king of all understatements – I was about to face the biggest storm of my life.

The wind rose steadily throughout the day. I reduced the mainsail reef by reef and furled the headsails, then sat and waited, glancing nervously at the wind instruments as the figures ticked up, each sustained gust exceeding the last. When the wind rose above 60 knots I knew that if this continued I would have to get the mainsail down and sail on under staysail alone. The last thing I needed was a torn mainsail to deal with or a hand-stitched repair for the next 28,000 miles, yet I knew that hauling the mainsail all the way down the mast track and lashing it securely was going to be a great fight.

The wind speed climbed relentlessly beyond 60 until I had 76 knots across the deck. Colour seemed to have been completely washed from the scene. The seas were pitch black and scarred with vivid, pale streaks of white spume as the wind sliced off the tops and vaporised them, or drove them back down the wave faces in angry veins of foam. As waves broke over us, tons of water crashed down on *Aviva*'s deck and sent a river of white water cascading down the sidedecks and into the cockpit. The wind screamed through the rigging. It was so ferocious and so chokingly dense with salt spray that even with jacket hood done up tightly and the face flap fixed firmly across my face I was fighting for breath.

Aviva careered onwards into the darkness, corkscrewing mercilessly on every wave. The mainsail had to come down. I clipped on a harness line and got ready. It was a struggle to stand up so, for safety, I crawled forwards towards the mast on my hands and knees. I was uneasy; I wanted to feel the security of wearing a lifejacket as well. So I came back, put on a lifejacket and went forward again. I grabbed the halyard just as *Aviva* tore down a wave and the momentum swung it away. The windage of the rope was so powerful that I had to open my hand and let go. In these conditions, my grip was not strong enough to hold on to even one piece of rope. The monstrous force of the wind was impressive. To stop the halyard going anywhere, I lashed the block down.

For the next hour-and-a-half I clung on to the mast, tugging with all my might at the take-down line attached to the head of the mainsail. The friction and windage was so great that the head of the sail would not budge – but I couldn't give up. Little by little I hauled it down, grabbed the end of the halyard and lashed it. Then I tied the sail up as tidily as I could to prevent it being damaged by the waves or the wind. I was thoroughly soaked. So much for my freshwater shower earlier on. The only comfort was that the waves surging over *Aviva* felt quite warm – warmer than the heavy rain that was now falling. If I had to do this in a Southern Ocean storm – highly likely, I thought – it would be a different game altogether.

As *Aviva* surged down enormous, steep waves the autopilot struggled to keep her on course, and I noticed that one of the two interchangeable units had emptied itself of hydraulic fluid and the slippery liquid had run all over the cockpit. I steered for a while until I felt the autopilot could cope with the sea state and switched to pilot 2, which took over with a comforting drone. After such a long period of effort, my hands and legs throbbed with pain but I was absolutely buzzing. There was no way I could snooze. Now that the sails were protected from harm all I had to do was hang on for the ride. I clipped on with two harness lines, one on each side so that I couldn't fall far in either direction.

At last, dawn came, revealing the wild scene. It was shocking and exhilarating; there was something intoxicating about seeing nature at such an extreme and surviving it. Yet in the space of four hours that morning, the storm dissipated. By midday the wind had died away, leaving behind a large and extremely uncomfortable sea. It was weird. *Aviva* had been sailing in one direction as the storm was tearing the opposite way. One thing about a tropical storm, I reflected, is that it is over very quickly. It wouldn't be like that in the Southern Ocean either.

An email arrived from Mike Broughton. '*The capricious tropical storm system . . . ! It looks like you had quite a night,*' it read. '*A tropical system is a rare feature in this area and its speed of movement to the east is pretty amazing.*' I could vouch for that. I looked at the weather reports with fascination as the low pressure continued to hurtle eastwards un-interrupted, filling ever so slowly. I could see that I had only clipped the edge of it. I had been lucky. Things might have been very different if my course had intercepted the storm cell upwind on its eastern side.

I was impressed by *Aviva* and myself. I had managed the storm all on my own, my sense of humour and sanity were intact and *Aviva* was in perfect shape with all her sails in one piece. For a few hours, I didn't rush to put up more sails; and instead I took it easy and allowed myself to recover while the seas subsided a little. Gradually, as the adrenaline wore off, I started to ache all over. By the afternoon the barometer showed that the pressure was starting to rise and more stable conditions were establishing themselves. I hoisted the mainsail back up as far as the third reef and *Aviva* steadied to it. After that I gybed the boat and unfurled a cautious portion of the headsails. It had been as tough a night as I ever remembered but I knew it was good practice for the Southern Ocean. I believed I could deal with a 70-knot storm if one came again.

A kind of uneasy normality returned to *Aviva* and as it did I was overwhelmed by the desire to tell someone what we had been through so I called Harry on the satellite phone. He was surprised and secretly horrified but he listened sympathetically and the reassuring sound of his voice was wonderful to hear. I missed him terribly and had to fight to control my emotions. We agreed that a quiet 24 hours would be the best thing for me and *Aviva* and I confessed to Harry that although I thought the voyage was a bit insane after all, I was sure there were parts I would love and I was still pretty positive I could complete it. It was talking therapy for me and when we finished the call I felt much better.

By midday the next day, I had made full sail and *Aviva* was sailing like a dream, making effortless progress south. The motion had eased and was quite comfortable so while the going was good I decided to get the watermaker started and top up the tanks. I switched it on and waited. Nothing. I checked and double-checked everything I could think of. I couldn't believe it – there is always something! Every time I turned the watermaker high pressure pump on, the generator would turn itself off. I emailed the shore team in Plymouth and awaited instructions. Shortly afterwards, a set of instructions was sent through from Peter Pearce, the engineer. I read through the message. Great. It looked like a fairly easy job that I could get on with that evening.

By 0200 the following morning, the watermaker still was not working and I was losing my patience. In Plymouth, the shore team had taken an identical watermaker to pieces to describe the process of getting the pump to turn over, but although I followed these instructions carefully neither the main pump nor the spare pump would work. At the end of the day, I emailed them again. *'Dear all,'* I wrote. *'I would call you, but I am currently crying. I now have two high pressure pumps in pieces that do not turn anywhere. How the hell did we end up with two on board that don't work?!'* I threw a few tools around in frustration but there was nothing to do but wait until morning and call the shore team again.

On the following day I phoned Andrew Roberts as soon as I could. With a sixth sense, Andrew had anticipated my call and had already spoken to the pump manufacturer and worked out the solution for me. It was so simple. When the pumps had been serviced, the pump housing had not been torqued down uniformly. In a split second, my hard won confidence shattered. I felt like a fraud. I couldn't get a simple high pressure pump to turn over. How on earth did I expect to get around the world?

I went back to the oilskin room where the watermaker was fitted and sat with tools and pump parts all round me, frustrated and soaked in sweat as the day grew hotter and the little cabin more and more stifling. At last, in the middle of the afternoon, after a full 24 hours of watermaker maintenance, I was able to call Andrew to let him know it was running and the tanks were being filled. By the time I tidied up, I was starving and I set about cooking a monster-sized tuna and pasta meal.

By the end of the second week I was getting closer to the Tropics. The signs were there. As I toured the deck in the early morning light, checking for chafe or signs of anything awry, I found flying fish that had been unlucky enough to land on *Aviva* as they tried to escape a predator. I absolutely hate the sight or feel of fish and I felt sick removing them. The worst thing about them was their sinister, prickly dorsal fin and the way they shed their scales when you handled them. When they are soaring between the waves they look incredible, but it's a different story when they are lying on your boat, dead and dry.

The days were wonderful. *Aviva* ran on contentedly in perfect tradewinds and whenever I could I sat on deck and soaked up the sun. The sea all around was deep blue and capped with an occasional white crest. Once or twice a pod of curious dolphins came up for a closer look at us and sported in the bow wave. As we passed the Cape Verde Islands I was happy with our progress south, maybe a little worried I wasn't working hard enough, but enjoying the chance to eat and sleep well and take care of myself before I reached the Doldrums. This band of very light and variable winds is punctuated by strong and unpredictable thunderstorms. The frustration of calms and the hard work of continuous sail changes wasn't far away.

At the beginning of December the Open 60 yachts that had raced to Brazil on a big French race, the Transat Jacques Vabre, were starting their journey back to Europe. Mike Golding had raced his boat *Ecover* and I learned that Gringo was nearby on his way back to Southampton. I called him up on the radio. Gringo said that they had made a quick Doldrums crossing and carried wind most of the way across, so that cheered me up. We had a laugh and talked about his mum's shortbread. Mrs Tourell had sent me off on my adventure with boxes of her home-made shortbread and I hadn't eaten any yet. We agreed that it was crazy to think that we were going to pass so close yet not actually be in sight and we wished each other well.

My chat with Gringo brought back to me how much I was missing other people. This was only my second week at sea and there would be at least another 20 weeks to go. I wondered if I would continue to miss company or harden into a strange and isolated state. I browsed through my diary and saw how factual it was and how careful I had been to hide my emotions. The descriptions of *Aviva* romping along in these beautiful sailing conditions were insipid and unexciting. My observations were dispassionate. I decided I needed to be more honest and expose my feelings a little more.

Mike Broughton continued to send weather information and analyses every day and his prognosis for the Doldrums looked quite good. Gradually I ran out of the tradewinds and the weather became

Me and my crew on *Imagine it. Done* racing out of the Solent in 2004 on the first leg of the Global Challenge Round the World Race; the wind and seas were beginning to build.

At the helm of *Imagine it. Done* on the Southern Ocean leg of the Race to Wellington, New Zealand. We were down at nearly 60°S – it was freezing cold and snow was lying on deck.

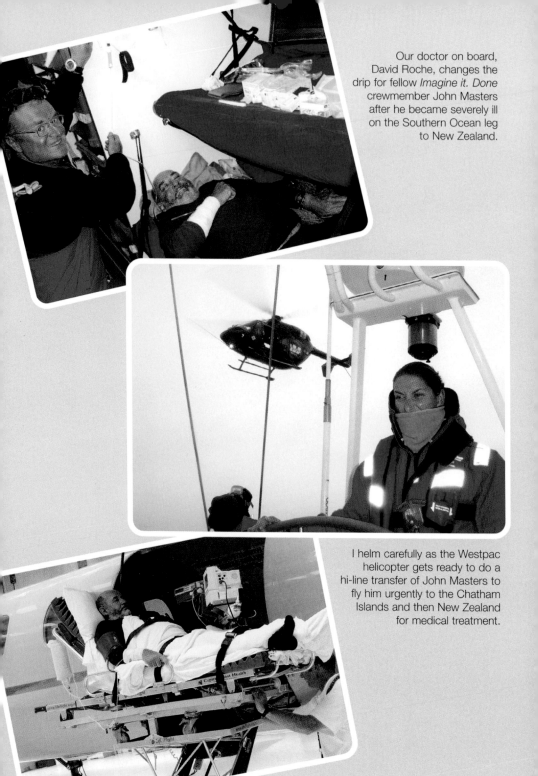

Our doctor on board, David Roche, changes the drip for fellow *Imagine it. Done* crewmember John Masters after he became severely ill on the Southern Ocean leg to New Zealand.

I helm carefully as the Westpac helicopter gets ready to do a hi-line transfer of John Masters to fly him urgently to the Chatham Islands and then New Zealand for medical treatment.

John Masters is transferred to a plane for the next leg of his journey to hospital to be treated for suspected peritonitis.

Sail trials off Plymouth in *Aviva* in the late autumn of 2005 as I got ready to set off on my singlehanded round the world voyage.

Me with the Aviva Challenge shore team. From the left: Andrew Roberts, the project director; Mike Broughton, my weather router; and Harry Spedding.

Aviva well reefed down in heavy weather in the South Atlantic, plunging to a crash landing in a large trough.

A grey but thrilling day as I overcome my autopilot problems and finally round Cape Horn and head for the Southern Ocean.

In heavy weather, *Aviva* lies over on her side in the Southern Ocean, with the whole side decks awash.

Taking a nap at the chart table seat of *Aviva*. This was my favourite place to rest as it was so close to everything important. I only lay down on a bunk a few times in the whole voyage.

So many presents! Christmas Day alone aboard *Aviva*, trying to put a brave face on and make the best of the day.

Back down on deck, exhausted, tearful and defeated, after a frightening and unsuccessful mast climb.

My badly bruised left arm after the mast climb, which was extremely painful.

A huge iceberg in the Southern Indian Ocean, an exciting and terrifying sight for me.

A green foredeck. So much water had come over *Aviva* so continuously in the weeks sailing across the Southern Ocean that a thick weedy growth had sprouted on her.

Overwhelmed by emotion, I fire a flare as I cross the finish line of the round the world record at The Lizard in Cornwall at 17:55GMT on 18 May 2006, becoming the first woman ever to sail non-stop round the world against the prevailing winds and currents.

Jubilation at the homecoming reception for *Aviva* and me in Ocean Village Marina in Southampton.

Face to face with people in Southampton after six months alone at sea.

more unsettled. Squalls appeared randomly and I was woken regularly at night by the alarm as the radar picked them up. I was waiting constantly for a change in the wind and getting tired and hot. Meanwhile, the jobs list lengthened. As I sponged the bilges I found a fuel leak, a small one but it was hard to trace and the little diesel that had leaked had spread an awfully long way. Every time I ticked off a job I was adding more at the bottom. '*There is a long way to go*,' I noted enigmatically in my diary.

I called Mike and spoke to him about the weather ahead. The Doldrums is a fluctuating band that encircles the globe between the tradewinds of the northern and southern hemispheres and it is constantly on the move. Where there had been wind a few days before there were now very changeable conditions and I was just going to have to live with it.

On 6 December I was definitely in their grip. I had a night of endless squalls and when they abated I was becalmed for ten hours. It was deeply frustrating. The only good thing about it was that the flat calm gave me a chance to bleed the air from the hydraulic system of my dodgy autopilot pump. It was messy and time consuming, the type of job for which you really need another set of hands and eyes, but with a little patience and a lot of contortion, I succeeded in getting the system to work again without any alarms or errors. Straight after that, the wind filled in from a new direction and I held my breath. I was hoping the new breeze was the precursor of the south-easterly Trades, the sign I had made it through the Doldrums. I didn't want to get trapped if it wasn't, though, so I hitched a lift on the new wind to make as much progress south as possible as fast as I could.

I crossed the Equator on 8 December, Mum's birthday. The south-easterly tradewinds were established and *Aviva* was sailing beautifully in 15-20 knots of wind. With the new wind direction we were hard on the breeze and well heeled over. Sailing at an angle once more took some getting used to.

As I crossed into the southern hemisphere I toasted Neptune with champagne and chocolate and took some photographs. My next milestone was Cape Horn, 3,600 miles ahead. I talked to Mum on the satellite phone and a little later in the day the phone rang again. It was Nick Moloney. The Australian solo sailor was sailing his boat back to France to complete the route of the Vendée Globe Round the World Race, which he had been catastrophically forced out of earlier in the year when his keel had fallen off. I knew all about Nick but we had never met. He spoke about many emotions I had been feeling. We chatted about solo sailing, the isolation of it and the demands it makes of you physically and mentally. It was wonderful to know there was a kindred spirit out there. When he rang off Nick said: 'Phone me any time. If you need a chat when you're in the Southern Ocean or you just want to cry at someone, give me a call.' It was a fantastic boost.

The wind backed and freed us. *Aviva* picked up speed but the motion was still uncomfortable. I didn't mind much because I would have chosen speed over an easy time anyway; the quicker we went, the quicker I would get home. I had ticked off three weeks and progress was good. I hoped I could keep it up in the deep south. I didn't have long to dwell on my loneliness, however, because a little later the watermaker failed again and I was back in the oilskin room surrounded by tools. Alistair Hackett and I talked about the problem and our troubleshooting developed into a long chat. We had a gossip and a laugh about all the things going on back at home, 'the real world' as we referred to it, and it was great to feel how much Alistair cared. Encouraging emails kept coming in from Andrew, which were so lovely they made me cry.

These tumultuous emotions were getting out of hand. Happiness could give way to utter despondency in an hour. It wasn't like me at all. I couldn't control it, and I couldn't understand it. It was only much later in the voyage that I came to realise how deeply sleep deprivation affected my mood. No wonder it is used as a form of torture. That evening my lonely world was inexplicably charged with melancholy again. I called up Harry and wept down the phone. Poor Harry, there was nothing he could do or say so he listened. I felt much better afterwards and I thought: there's nothing wrong with me. I can cope. I'm being productive around the boat. It's just that it won't be long now until Cape Horn. Part of me was dreading what lay beyond.

TWELVE

Crossed Wires

Aviva and I made slow progress southwards. I was learning all the time but at a price. The weather was fickle, and as I reacted to every alteration in the wind I seemed to be making a sail change or adjustment of some sort every five minutes. I decided I couldn't live this way and that it might, ultimately, be just as fast to set *Aviva* up for the averages and let her sail. So I backed off a bit and we began to make better progress despite the light winds. Once I had lightened my workload I tried to get to the bottom of my autopilot problems.

The shore team sent me a series of emails with instructions about the tests I should carry out. We knew that the alarms were going off because of aeration in the hydraulic system; we just didn't know exactly where the air was getting in, or why it was affecting one autopilot ram and not the other. I was to bleed the system from top to bottom and carry out some response tests on the electronics. So I worked my way through the list, releasing various pipes and bleed screws, noting down the results and sending them back to the shore team. The autopilots seemed to work again afterwards. The alarms were silent and cautiously we all began to feel more optimistic.

Little by little I was leaving the Tropics. For now the weather was still hot with occasional tropical squalls. When a squall overtook us and torrential rain pelted down on *Aviva* I was able to stand on deck and enjoy the luxury of a long and cooling shower under the dark sky, and when the rain stopped I soothed my sunburnt skin with moisturiser. It is not always easy to keep dry and clean on an ocean voyage, and although I washed salt out of my clothes regularly there was so much sitting around in these steamy, sweaty, salty conditions that I had fallen victim to the dreaded gunwale bum, a painful and unpleasant skin rash. We had seen lots of it the year before on the Global Challenge. The remedy was not glamorous: fresh air and nappy cream.

Often the sailing was magical. Out at sea where the horizon is endless colours appear to develop a special intensity. The backdrop of blue sea and sky is somehow richer and more dramatic. Each sunset and sunrise is burnt with a vividness you seldom see on land, and the deep hues of amber and red made it seem as if *Aviva* and I were sailing into infinity. Every sunset looked as if it had been painted from a different palette, and every evening this glorious show changed with the sudden tropical nightfall into a black canvas spiked with diamonds. With no ambient light to poison them, the stars in the night sky were opulent, the planets and constellations dense and pin-sharp. In quiet moments I tried to identify the few I knew, always wishing that my knowledge of space was better.

Sometimes during the day, and occasionally at night, I had company. Dolphins swam round the boat again – a sign, I believed, of good luck. No matter how tired or stressed you feel, the sight of a pod of dolphins fills you with a great sense of well being. I loved to sit on the pulpit and watch them darting and weaving around each other and playing in the bow wave, perfectly synchronised with *Aviva* as she surged on or dipped in the waves. Their gracefulness and timing made it look as if we were all moving through the water with a deliberate choreography.

Every few days, a batch of messages was sent to me from viewers of the Aviva Challenge website. Messages of support had been left by people all over the world, and I was amazed at the amount of interest the voyage had aroused so far. Reading these gave me such a lift; I don't know what I would have done without them. The smallest comments made a huge difference to my morale, and as I read them I felt that all our efforts so far were worthwhile.

While the winds were light, I wrestled the repaired Code 0 head-sail on deck from the sail room and hoisted it. The repair seemed fine, which was a relief because I needed this larger sail to maximise our speed. We gybed often as I tried to shape the best possible course towards the tip of South America but it was frustratingly slow going. One of the autopilots still wasn't right and I could not shake off a feeling of disquiet. I wished I felt more confident but I had a nasty suspicion that I wasn't going to be able to rely on them.

The wind shifted to the south and that brought a sharp temperature change. For the first time I was feeling a chill wind straight from the Antarctic and the increase in apparent windspeed made it feel colder than it really was on deck. I had already added a fleece but the cold worked its way through the extra layer. At its warmest, near the Equator, the sea temperature had been 32°C; now it was cooling rapidly around *Aviva*. There were some advantages. The water in the tanks was colder as well, so when I made up powdered milk it tasted better, and a bowl of cereal was something to look forward to again. It was better to focus on these small benefits than to think about the life of numbing cold ahead. I wouldn't be properly warm again until I returned to the Atlantic, and to do that I had to survive the Southern Ocean.

Just before Christmas the wind dropped away completely and it gave me the chance to tackle a job I had been putting off. To be ready for the hard weather ahead, I had to lower the big yankee and replace it with a smaller, heavier duty sail. This procedure would normally take five crew. After three hours of brawling with sails I was bruised, if not beaten. First, I had to get the replacement headsail out of the sail room and up on deck, then I had to lower the 90 kilo yankee down on to the deck, flake it out and fold it into a sail bag before hoisting the smaller sail, which still weighed in at 70 kilos. I was exhausted by the effort, and the planning needed for every stage of the task tested my patience, but when I was done I looked up at the sail with a sense of relief and accomplishment, knowing that another preparation had been made for the Southern Ocean.

On Christmas Eve, strong and very gusty weather arrived and the wind fluctuated wildly from 10 to 40 knots. The range covered all of *Aviva*'s sail combinations and it made me work hard. In between sail changes I sat down at the chart table and looked at our position. We had covered 6,000 miles, the equivalent of three transatlantic crossings, but it was still only a fraction of the journey. The distance didn't scare me – it was the time stretching out ahead that made me feel so dejected. It was bad enough being on my own at Christmas; I didn't dare think of how many more months it would be before I saw my family and friends again. I tried to keep driving myself on because when I stopped and thought about it I got emotional. Right now, people would be driving home to see their parents, or they would be going out for a drink with friends. All I would have was a few minutes of crackling, alien-sounding conversation over a satellite link. In the midst of this sadness an email arrived from Sir Chay. His message read:

25 December 2005
1234hrs GMT
Christmas is almost upon us and I am quite sure you will get a little emotional and melancholy. You are anything but alone. I, for one, will get melancholy

thinking of you out there and recounting my times single-handed at sea. I will be thinking of what you will be doing.

See it this way, it is only once on your own and it will cement your future. As one mile passes you never have to sail that mile again. Have a great Christmas. People all over the world will be asking: 'I wonder what Dee is doing?' I know what Dee will be doing – she will be doing her job and making a fantastic effort to be the best.

On Christmas morning I woke to the worst possible present. It had been a stormy, tiring night and at first light I found that the pump set of the active autopilot was squirting hydraulic fluid everywhere again. I immediately changed to the other pump set to stop the leak worsening. It took a fair time to clear up the spilt fluid and top up the system, and it was as bad a start to Christmas Day as I could imagine. I was crushed that the pump had failed again; I was sure we had fixed it. We are going to be plagued with this problem, I thought dismally. Sometimes it's hard not to despair.

I had never spent Christmas alone before and I kept breaking down in sobs of self-pity and bitter frustration. Although I had no-one to share the day with I had a compulsion to follow at least some of the family traditions I had grown up with. The saloon of *Aviva* was decorated with tinsel and balloons and I had put up a miniature Christmas tree and arranged the Christmas cards people had given me before I left so that I could see the wonderful messages that were written in them. On Christmas Eve I had taken all the presents out of a locker Harry had so carefully stocked so they would be waiting for me on Christmas morning. Now it was time to open them. The sense of excitement and antici-pation was every bit as strong as I remembered from childhood, though my presents were mostly sensible and grown up. I had hand repair cream to moisturise my dried-out, salt-pickled hands; a couple of books; a DVD of *Sex and the City* – perfect escapism for 40 minutes at a time – and lots and lots of chocolate. For once I felt as if I was having a normal day. I dug out a CD of Christmas carols and as I trimmed the sails to keep *Aviva* moving I sang along at the top of my voice.

When I was happy with how things looked on deck, I made the special Christmas dinner meal that Allie Smith, a friend and colleague from Mike Golding Yacht Racing days, had prepared for me. Allie used to victual Mike's boat for round the world races and had chosen and packed all my food. She had considered the different climates I would be sailing in, how many calories I would need during each part of the voyage and organised the meals into ten-day boxes so that there was variety and some choice for me, but arranged in a way that deterred me from plundering all the food I liked at the beginning.

Since my daytime and night time patterns were mixed together and continually interrupted, Allie had arranged the food in small portions that I could eat often to keep up my sugar levels. There were cereals for breakfast and boil in the bag or freeze-dried main meals that were simple for me to prepare on *Aviva*'s single-burner expedition stove. Most of the meals could be made in 10 minutes and required nothing more than boiling water and some stirring. When they were ready, I served them in a bowl so the food wouldn't spill and ate with a spoon; you don't need a knife for rehydrated meals with the texture of baby food. They didn't always look appetising, and eating them was a necessary function rather than a pleasure, but the point was that eating properly was easy and my food contained all the nutrients I needed.

For Christmas Day, Allie had done me proud with a special package of food that for once I really did look forward to eating. There were tins of roast chicken and mixed vegetables, dauphinoise potatoes, and a Christmas pudding with brandy sauce and custard to follow. For once, I tried to take my time over dinner and savour it. It tasted delicious, and afterwards I felt much better. Meanwhile, outside the weather was gradually moderating and *Aviva* sailed along without complaint. It was almost as if someone was looking down and allowing me to enjoy the day after all.

As soon as Christmas Day was over, however, our problems returned. On Boxing Day the wind came ahead and increased to 30 knots, with gusts of 35 knots. *Aviva* and I were hard on the wind again and back to the uncomfortable motion of pitching into head seas. No sooner had I finished reducing sail than the autopilot alarm went off again, indicating a new fault. I walked back to the pushpit where the autopilot pump units were mounted only to find the active pump unit, the one that had been fine, squirting out hydraulic fluid. Now both autopilots were faulty. This was a disaster! If I had to helm *Aviva* instead of leaving it to the autopilot I would not be able to do anything else around the boat – not sail her properly or communicate with anyone. When I changed the two autopilot pumps back and forth I found each would operate for a short period of time before cutting out, so while one of them was working I dashed below to make a few calls and get more instructions from the shore team.

By a slow process of elimination we were able to prove, late on Boxing Day, that air was being dragged into the hydraulic system through the reservoirs. We concluded that while pumps worked in a moderate sea state the aeration problems began when the boat was heeled right over and the motion was violent – in other words, the times when *Aviva* was at her hardest to steer and in need of incessant rudder movements. We had not experienced these conditions during our autopilots trials.

This was a worrying discovery bearing in mind that *Aviva* and I were shortly going to face 12,000 miles beating to windward. My other concern was about how much hydraulic fluid I had used topping up the system. Nearly half of my spare fluid was gone and I now had only eight bottles left. There was no way I could continue with that kind of consumption. I simply could not afford to lose any more fluid from either of the pumps.

In any case, without two fully functioning autopilots it wouldn't be safe to round Cape Horn and go into the Southern Ocean. *Aviva* was too big to steer herself safely in difficult conditions, and if I had to leave the wheel to carry out a sail change or a reef or go up the mast to repair something aloft, she would be out of control. My sponsors were very nervous and extremely concerned for my safety, and although I didn't know it at the time they sought an assurance from Andrew that it was safe for me to continue. They wanted to know what the risks were, and when any decision to abort the voyage would have to be made. One of the options discussed was to stop at the Falkland Islands and anchor or pick up a buoy so that I could try to fix the autopilots while the boat was at rest before carrying on, but the bottom line was that if the autopilots couldn't be fixed neither the shore team nor the sponsors wanted me to continue.

Late that evening an email came in advising me that a press release had gone out explaining the autopilot problems I was having and stating that my record attempt was in jeopardy. I was stunned when I read this. I had never failed at anything in my life and I never for a second imagined not being able to complete this round the world voyage, let alone calling it off before I even got to Cape Horn. I struggled to understand the reason for the press statement and as I did I became angry.

As far as I was aware, the worst case scenario was that I would have to stop at the Falkland Islands. I simply could not understand why the PR agency was promoting the idea that my adventure might fail. At the time I was so focussed that I couldn't appreciate they were erring on the side of caution. I believed the message underlying this statement was that my backers and the shore team had somehow lost confidence in me. But why, when we were all still working so hard to resolve the problems? What made it even more disappointing was that this wasn't a personal failure but a technical issue that was absolutely no fault of my own. We had to find a solution.

I read and re-read the email and then tried hard to forget it. I busied myself by working through my jobs list and then cleaned *Aviva* furiously to tame my anger. I was even more determined than ever to fix the auto-pilots and turn my fortunes round, if only to prove wrong those with such little faith. With constant communication and advice from the shore team, I worked through a series of tests to try to find the source of the problems. Eventually we identified the cause as the small size of the hydraulic fluid reservoirs. When the boat was pitching and rolling, air was being drawn into the breather pipes and causing an air lock. When the autopilot was under pressure an alarm would sound and the fluid was then forced through the breather pipe, until it spilled over. Somehow we needed to find a way to expand the tank and raise the breather pipe to allow air to escape without dispelling the oil.

Andrew and his team were busy throughout Christmas and New Year trying to find the answers. It was like the Apollo 13 mission. The manufacturers had made a mock-up version of my autopilot system and were running through potential solutions, while Andrew, Alistair and Matthew were trying to think of parts of the boat that I could canni-balise to make repairs. I was emailed instructions that read like a treasure hunt, sending me to various corners of the boat to remove items.

I understood what we were hoping to achieve: I needed to find a pipe nipple with the right thread to make an attachment breather pipe for the reservoirs. Andrew suggested where to look, and after removing quite a few pipe connections round the boat I stumbled, more by chance than anything else, on the right sized pipe on the boat's oven. Removing it meant I would not be able to bake bread for the rest of the voyage, but I was only too happy to trade bread for two working autopilots and the chance to carry on.

I disconnected the oven and used the pipe fittings and some plastic hose to make a breather pipe. Then I drilled two holes in the lid of the box that housed the pump units and ran the pipes directly upwards to the aerial frame at the stern of *Aviva*. When that was fixed in place I covered the end with the finger of a rubber glove. What I had now was a watertight breather pipe that allowed the hydraulic oil level to rise, while stopping any air or spray being drawn in. I was so pleased with my creation that I took a photograph to send to the tech-nical team for their approval. All I needed was some rough weather to test the new modification.

Although the autopilots settled down and began working again, maddeningly the alarms continued to sound. I was beginning to be driven crazy by the endless high-pitched screeching, particularly below deck. I was exhausted and getting more overwrought by the day. I sat on deck and felt leaden and heavy-hearted with despair. I knew I had to snap out of this way of thinking. It was better to do something than to well up with negative thoughts so I got up, took a sponge and bucket and started to mop out the bilges. This dirty and disagreeable job was therapeutic; I was improving *Aviva*. Gradually I felt happier. I wasn't going to give up and neither were Andrew's team of detectives. The shore team reckoned that the hydraulic problems had been masking another fault, possibly a defective sensor, and the answer was to hard-wire the pilots so they operated separately.

Keith Baxter, the electrician, patiently talked me through the complicated process of rewiring the box at the back of *Aviva*. One of the annoying rules of yachts is that something you really need to fix will always be somewhere extremely difficult to reach. While trying to get to wires in the box at the stern I scraped the skin off my knuckles, cut my fingers, slipped in hydraulic fluid and dropped countless screws but I wouldn't give up – I couldn't. Eventually the job was done and we had a result. For the next two days *Aviva* and I sailed on in wonderful peace and quiet, and although I checked constantly and expected the worst, the alarms stayed silent.

Aviva and I were now three days from Cape Horn. A final decision had to be made about whether or not I went round the corner and into the Southern Ocean. We believed we had finally fixed the problems. Andrew sent me an email on New Year's Eve saying he thought the chance of one autopilot failing again had dropped to about 30 per cent, a risk he considered acceptable, but what did I feel about continuing? Later in the day we spoke on the phone. It was great to talk to him. We were going to succeed. We both promised to speak more often and from that day on I called Andrew every week for a chat, to check in and let everyone know what was going on. It was good for everyone's peace of mind.

On New Year's Eve, Alistair sent me a message that extinguished any doubts I had about the shore team's wholehearted support. '*Go for it,*' he wrote. '*I think you are really struggling with being by yourself and it has surprised you how hard it is but I really believe you can do it.*' Reading that email I knew I had made the right decision. I had a superb team behind me and the strength I gained from their belief in my ability was enormous. So much of overcoming any challenge is about self-belief and self-confidence.

The other decisive conversation on New Year's Day was with Mum. She was with Jane and her family and a house full of guests, and I was able to join the party briefly by speakerphone. Everyone was having fun and the air of optimism about the year ahead was infectious. Mum was positive and encouraging; she told me I should seize my opportunity. She believed I could keep going round the world and she told me that she loved me and she would see me again soon.

After the call home I spoke to Harry and thanked him for listening to me so patiently through all the excitement and tears. As everyone else celebrated the start of 2006, I watched the hands on the clock above the chart table overlap on the stroke of midnight. I wished *Aviva* and myself a Happy New Year and I smiled. This was the first day of another year and time for fresh resolutions. I had conquered all of the challenges so far and I was going to round Cape Horn and overcome whatever troubles lay ahead. I was determined to make this my year, whatever it took.

THIRTEEN

Welcome to Cape Horn

Aviva was barely moving across a glassy sea. We were only 165 miles from the Le Maire Strait, the gateway to Cape Horn and an area infamous for savage winds and tides, and here we were ghosting along in 10 knots of northerly wind. The temperature had continued to drop. It was serene and crisply cold, a perfect winter's day with a pure blue sky and crystal visibility. I had my fingers crossed that these conditions would last until I rounded Cape Horn. I had passed without seeing a glimpse of this famous landmark last year and this time I badly wanted to take a photograph of *Aviva* and me with Cape Horn abeam.

Keeping the boat moving in these light winds was incredibly difficult but it did allow me to get some other maintenance jobs finished and tick them off my list before the Southern Ocean. The time had come to service my generator. This was an important task that I was going to have to do several times during the voyage. I was happy enough about changing the oil and fuel filters but I had never changed injectors before and I was a little nervous about it. Like the autopilots, my generator was a vital piece of equipment onboard. It charged my batteries and provided power for all the navigation and communications equipment as well as the watermaker, so it was absolutely essential to the success of the voyage. I was about to take it apart and hoped that when I put it back together again it would still work. This put a lot of pressure on me.

Before *Aviva* left Plymouth, we made a video of the mechanic, Peter Pearce, doing the same job on my generator. We laughed about it and called it my idiot's guide. It was a comprehensive, step-by-step illustration of precisely what I had to do and what size spanners I should use on what bits of the generator. I watched it again nervously, and while it was still flat calm I got stuck in. It was a messy job but it went without a hitch. When I had finished I went back to the switch panel and pressed the start button with some trepidation. Hearing the generator roar into life again was a wonderful moment.

I arrived the next day at the entrance to the Le Maire Strait. There had been little change in the weather but I was feeling frustrated. I couldn't wait to get to Cape Horn and these light following winds were making our progress infuriatingly slow. The tide in the Strait had turned strongly against me. We fought the current and *Aviva* plodded on.

At the southern end of the Strait we were only seven miles from the nearest land. I studied our position and the ragged edges of the coast-line on the charts with a mounting sense of excitement. This was the closest I had been to the land since passing The Lizard six weeks ago. It felt quite strange to me. I had become used to the open ocean and the endless horizons. I didn't feel any safer near the coast; I felt slightly confined by the hazards in this weatherbeaten and changeable place. Cape Horn was only 120 miles away and it was my second visit in as many years. I said to myself: 'Please let me see it this time so I don't have to rush back again.'

We gybed repeatedly through the night to shape a course clear of land and I got no sleep. As daylight flooded back to fill the void of night I had my first glimpse of Tierra del Fuego, the rocky land at the very tip of South America. I was astonished by the rugged, craggy scenery, which reminded me of the west coast of Scotland. The hills and cliffs were scarified by the endless punishment of harsh weather and I felt incredibly fortunate to be seeing it on one of the few days when it would ever be possible to appreciate the impressive beauty rather than to fear it as a deadly lee shore.

I stayed on deck and watched the land as we passed until I was interrupted by the VHF radio squelching into life. I turned up the volume. It was Cape Horn Radio and they were calling me on channel 16. 'Welcome to Cape Horn,' they said.

The radio operator asked me for some details. What was the name of my vessel and what was my last port of call?

'Charlie, Alpha, Foxtrot, Foxtrot, Alpha, Romeo, India,' I said. 'The name of the vessel: Alpha, Victor, India, Victor, Alpha. Last port of call: Portsmouth, UK.'

Cape Horn Radio confirmed this and asked: 'How many people are on board?'

'One person.'

'The captain of the vessel and one crew.'

'Negative, Cape Horn Radio. One person.'

'And what is your next port of call?'

'Portsmouth, UK.'

There was a long delay after this and some minutes later the radio operator came back and asked me to confirm that I was one person on board sailing from Portsmouth, UK and heading for Portsmouth, UK. There was a smile behind the polite voice as he asked: 'Are you lost?'

I laughed. No, I wasn't lost, I explained. I was on a westabout circumnavigation of the world. Cape Horn Radio acknowledged this. They confirmed to me that I had rounded Cape Horn at exactly 0940 UTC on Wednesday 4 January 2006 and they wished me well on my voyage.

I received a message from Sir Chay Blyth congratulating me on becoming a solo Cape Horner and reminding me how few people could claim such a feat in a westabout direction. So far only four men and one other woman had passed it along the route I was taking. I looked out at Cape Horn again with a feeling of euphoria. I could smell the land and see small drifts of seaweed and occasional flocks of penguins weaving through the water next to *Aviva*. This fearsome point of land, Everest for any sailor, is truly a monumental landmark. If you can get past here safely, I thought, you have conquered one of the biggest hurdles of a round the world voyage.

After 46 days alone, I had company on the water for the first time. A cruise liner that had been hugging the shore close to Cape Horn was on the move and, hearing my conversation on the radio, the captain called me up. He told me that they had been on a cruise along the Antarctic Peninsula and were on the way back to Ushuaia and wanted to say hello and good luck. Then he said he had guests on board and would I mind if he circled around so they could take photographs? I said that I didn't mind; I wasn't going anywhere fast as the wind had almost completely died away. The ship closed in and I could see the decks crowded with people waving. So many faces! I laughed excitedly and waved back.

It was turning out to be a busy day. The next voice on the VHF radio was the Chilean Navy, out on patrol and also calling up to say hello because they had heard about my voyage from Cape Horn Radio. They asked me for the boat's call sign and MMSI radio identification number. They came over as well. It was fantastic to see other faces and talk to people, but strangely I found it slightly claustrophobic; it was too busy all at once. I got some good photographs of Cape Horn at last and was basking in the excitement of the moment when, very gently, the wind began to fill in. I was well aware that the light airs would not last, but as the first puffs of new breeze fanned out across the gloss of placid water I started to think seriously about the speed of the approaching depression. I could find myself in very severe conditions if I was still on the continental shelf when it hit at full force.

Curiously, I felt relieved to be in the Southern Ocean. Just a few days earlier, my record voyage had been in jeopardy and my worst fear had been that my dream of sailing across the Southern Ocean would be stopped before I even got there. Now that I was here, about to strike out into the most remote and hostile ocean on earth, I was pleased. This was the beginning of the second chapter of my voyage. It was going to be long and tough but the sense of achievement would be immense. When I compared my progress to those who had gone before, I could see that at the same stage Mike Golding had been one day ahead. I wanted to mark *Aviva*'s progress against Mike's track to have something to motivate me, but what happened in the next two months in the deep south was in the hands of the Gods. It depended entirely on what the Southern Ocean delivered.

As darkness engulfed us, *Aviva* and I headed just south of west to clear the continental shelf as fast as possible. The breeze built and I reduced sail progressively until I was heading into 45 knots of wind. It was a stark contrast to the morning I had enjoyed. I was now rearing up on steep waves and plunging back down into dark troughs. We were hard on the wind once more and back to life at a 30° angle. It was all horribly familiar. We'd had only one storm that touched 50 knots on the Global Challenge but somehow that had been different. Now that there were no other people onboard or conversations to distract from the punishment the boat was taking, the sound of *Aviva* crashing upwind seemed fiercer and more frightening. The decks were sluiced by breaking waves and I hung on for the ride. During the night, I passed south of the tiny Islas Diego Ramirez, which lie right on the lip of the shelf. This was the last piece of land I would be near until New Zealand, 6,000 miles away.

As we sailed over the edge of the shallower water and out into the deep ocean I could feel a transition. The sea state changed dramatically and the short, sharp, steep waves transformed into large and long waves that rolled *Aviva* up to the tops and let her slip down into the troughs rather than tipping her into potholes with a crash. The aggressive pounding eased and the motion became easier and less jarring. It was much kinder to the joints and it made sleep a little easier. I was so tired. I hadn't slept at all the night before because we had been navigating close to land, and all day afterwards I had been urging *Aviva* on through calms and concentrating on getting around the Horn. I estimated that it was a good 36 hours since I had last shut my eyes for a rest. Now that I was well away from land with no traffic around and only waves and wind to deal with I desperately needed to sleep.

The Southern Ocean is fierce and fast moving, but storms often pass over as quickly as they arrive. My first night of 45 knots was little more than a brief reminder of what was in store, and a day later *Aviva* and I were bowling along in 20 knots of wind and magnificent weather. The wind had freed us and we were tracking along in the right direction. It felt odd after weeks of heading south to be sailing west at last.

I was so elated at getting through our first Southern Ocean bruising that I decided it was time for a celebration. There is no better reward out at sea than a long-awaited hot shower and a change of clothes. Afterwards, I felt like a new woman.

For the first few days, the Southern Ocean was gentle with me. It was only an introductory offer – the lull before the real storm – and I was unaware of what was to come, but I revelled as *Aviva* sailed along under bright skies, with the sunshine brilliantly lighting up huge slabs of blue sea and occasional white wave crests. I was enjoying being so far south and getting to know a few new companions. Sometimes, a Wandering Albatross flew by, soaring effortlessly on its huge wings and skimming within inches of the surface of the sea. I marvelled at how close they could fly over the water without ever getting drenched by an oncoming wave.

Although the wind was relatively light the big ocean swell rolled on regardless. In the Southern Ocean, the seas are never flat. No matter how calm it is there is an underlying swell that circulates without end round the bottom of the world. The uninterrupted ocean is funnelled through the narrow gap of the Drake Passage between Cape Horn and the Antarctic Peninsula, and is pinched by the Cape of Good Hope but out in the open ocean, where there is no resistance and nothing to stop the build-up of waves, the swell rolls on ceaselessly, overlaid during gales by wind-driven waves that crest and crumble from their tops.

Despite the continual pitching, *Aviva* was quiet. To my great joy, I had not heard a single screech from my autopilot alarm for days. That was unheard of; all the way down the Atlantic I had never had more than a few hours at a stretch without the sound of one alarm or another. The difference that made to my sanity and sense of well being was unbelievable. The alarm was meant to sound only if *Aviva* headed off course, and I hadn't fully realised what a draining part of my daily existence the endless noise had been or how it had eaten away at my trust in the boat's equipment. I switched back and forth to check them and as each of the pilots worked away quietly in the background I couldn't help feeling as if the faulty ones had miraculously been replaced and I was starting my voyage afresh. I began to think I could put all those horrible times behind me and forget them.

While things onboard were going well, I concentrated on eating some good food and getting rest as often and for as long as I could. I was able to see from the forecast that another depression was approaching, and as well as preparing *Aviva* for heavy weather, I wanted to prepare myself with reserves of sleep and energy. My little happy bubble was about to burst, and I was soon to learn again how fierce a Southern Ocean storm could be at the latitude of 59°S.

The first sign of the approaching storm was a change in the wind direction. As it backed to the west I was forced to sail hard on the wind in either a southerly or a northerly direction. Either course was far from ideal, but I could not afford to be driven further south because the risks of ice would increase dramatically. So I chose to head *Aviva* to the north. The wind rose and I gradually reduced sail by putting reefs in the mainsail. The waves began to wash over the deck, and each time I went up to reef the mainsail I was drenched by water and frozen to the core. There was no warmth in the air, and as the wind speed increased the wind chill reduced the air temperature to well below freezing. A wave of freezing water hit me square in the face as I battled with reefing pendants in the pit area, making me gasp for breath. No matter how hard I winched, my fingers remained numb with cold.

As soon as I finished, I went below to warm up and get the blood circulating back into my hands and feet. I struggled out of my sodden foulweather jacket and clenched my fists inside my fleece. The pain of the blood flowing back was excruciating.

The barometric pressure dropped swiftly and I knew we were in for a battering very soon. That night the first real storm hit *Aviva* with a shocking intensity. For eight hours we had wind speeds in excess of 50 knots. Throughout the night, as *Aviva* reared and bucked on vicious cross seas, the autopilot alarms went off no less than five times. In fairness, I can't think of how any machine could have kept fighting the rudder so hard in those conditions. Each time I reset the alarm I prayed that the pilot would work just a little bit longer. The worst of the storm came in the early hours. I was so far south that there were only five hours of darkness now, but in the pitch black before sunrise the sound of waves breaking over the boat and the wind howling through the rigging was terrifying.

The autopilot lost its bearings again and the alarm went off. With no resistance from the rudder, *Aviva* was shouldered aside by a huge wave and tacked herself. By the time I had got on deck we were fully aback, heeled over and completely pinned down on our side. Waves were coursing along the side of the coachroof and everything below it – the sidedecks and the stanchions and guardwires – was submerged beneath frothing water. I looked up to see the mainsail bearing down on the running backstay, the part of the rig that supported the mast and prevented it bending forwards out of column. I had furled the headsail away much earlier, but the smaller staysail I was using to help drive *Aviva* onwards through the waves was aback against the babystay and putting even more pressure on the rig. This was bad. This could go horribly wrong, I thought, as I scrambled to release the runner tail and the staysail sheet to release the pressure.

The cockpit was deeply awash and all the ropes were streaming out behind us in an almighty tangle. It was so windy I couldn't even stand on deck so I crawled around on my hands and knees, urgently hauling in the lines I needed. I grabbed the wheel but *Aviva* was heeled so far over that there was no steerage and she slid sideways at an alarming rate. When I had the runner tail, the mainsheet and staysail sheet back onboard the next challenge was to get the sails in on the new side. Each was loaded up with the pressure of 50 knots of wind and was straining under massive loads.

As soon as I released the staysail sheet the sail flogged violently. I heaved on the new sheet but my weight was so insignificant and pathetic against the force of the wind that it would not budge and the sail continued to shudder uncontrollably. I got to the pedestal winch and began grinding, winding the handles with all my might. Slowly, inch by inch, the sheet came in and the staysail filled. I wound in the new runner the same way and *Aviva* settled down and took off on the new tack. I was breathless and jumpy with adrenaline. The sea was still extremely rough and now I was faced with having to tack the boat back once again to get on to the right course. I rested for a couple of minutes to get my breath back and try to get some feeling back into my fingers.

Sailors often describe big seas as mountainous and this is just what they looked like. The seas are the only contours in our world, our only landscape, and these were the highest I had seen. When we rose to the tops it looked and felt as if we were at altitude and I could see the seas around and beyond to the horizon. As we crashed down that wider world was shut off again beyond the next approaching range of peaks. Every wave blocked out progress like a wall.

I gathered my strength and set up to tack again. After a few attempts I managed to swing the bow of *Aviva* through the eye of the wind and rushed for the sheets to tame the sails before they flogged themselves to destruction. The muscles in my arms burned. Three quarters of an hour after setting up for the tack, *Aviva* was finally back on course and I was sitting in a heap at the bottom of the companionway, freezing and exhausted. When I took off my foulweather gear I found I was soaked by a mixture of salt water and sweat. This was one long, long night. How much longer was the storm going to last?

The answer, unfortunately, was much longer than I thought. After daybreak the wind subsided and I had a brief respite with only 30 knots before another front caught up with us. The wind speed indicator clocked upwards again until we had 45 knots of wind once more. I had only just started across the Southern Ocean; there were another 12,000 miles to go until the Cape of Good Hope and my exit. Already I had experienced far worse weather than we had encountered on last year's Global Challenge. I felt tired and battered by the pounding and after only one week, which included a few days of pure enjoyment, I was already starting to count down the days until I could leave behind the stress and isolation. I knew that the weeks ahead would be as much a test of mental stamina and fortitude as they would of physical endurance.

Aviva was showing some signs of wear and tear. I kept an eye on the deck gear and equipment, and I could see some new signs of chafe on the headsail furling line. As soon as conditions allowed and before it reached breaking point, I would have to end-for-end the line or replace it with the one I had spliced in November. I didn't want a repetition of the dramas of that first night at sea. I also spotted a small hole in the staysail that would need to be patched. For that, I would have to drop the sail completely. It would not be an easy or quick job and I needed better weather to carry it out. Until that day arrived I would have to look after the sail and prevent it flogging, possibly even furl it away earlier than normal and break out the yankee headsail instead when the wind rose. We could not sail on to windward bareheaded; *Aviva* needed some driving force at the front to keep her pushing on through the waves.

I was puzzled about the hole. I didn't know what had caused it and I wouldn't be able to prove anything for sure until I got it down and inspected it. I ran over various options for repairing it in my mind. I knew from past experience that if I stuck a Dacron patch on the salty, damp sailcloth it would last only as long as it took to hoist the sail again. I could try to dry the sail but no matter what I did the chances were that an adhesive patch would soon peel off, and I'd have to go through the process of lowering the sail and rehoisting it all over again. The only sure way to repair it was to hand stitch a patch over the hole using a leather sailmaker's palm to punch the needle through the thick, heavy 9oz sailcloth. It would take tough hands and a lot of patience and I would need to do the repair sitting on the foredeck. This was not a job to rush. The Southern Ocean is a relentless succession of storms and the secret was to get all the jobs done I possibly could as soon as the weather allowed so that when the next storm rolled over us *Aviva* would be in good shape to look after me. Until the next lull I had to wait and hang on again for the ride.

In the worst of weather, I tried to concentrate on getting some sleep. Once I had reefed down and checked that *Aviva*'s sails and deck gear were ready for the weather in the coming front, there was nothing more I could do except prepare myself. If I rested then, I would be in good shape to deal with a crisis if it arose and be ready to make sail again as soon as it had passed through. So by getting my head down in the storms, I was helping to speed up my progress through the Southern Ocean. The difficult part of sailing through storms is not reefing in time but having the confidence to make sail again at the earliest possible opportunity. Changing up a gear efficiently afterwards is what wins miles and I was keen to be fit enough to maximise our speed in that phase.

So much for the theory. In reality, it was often impossible to sleep at the height of a storm. Riding it out was becoming a mental test, a battle of wills between me and nature. It had become a habit to sit at the chart table staring at the numbers on the instrument displays as the wind speeds rose. If I concentrated really hard I believed I could stop the figures ticking upwards. I knew this was ridiculous but I couldn't stop. I would sit mesmerised by this futile game when there was nothing else I could do, and when I gave up trying to control or appease the wind I lay down and closed my eyes in a vain attempt to convince my body that I was sleeping.

FOURTEEN

The Loneliest Place in the World

It took me an hour and a half to repair the tiny hole in the staysail. With the lull in the weather the evening sun broke through and I sat on the foredeck with music at full blast, practising my karaoke skills at the top of my voice as I sewed patches on the sail. Using pliers to pull the needle through the tough fabric took patience and I cursed as I punctured the flesh of my hand with the heavy sewing needle. Once I had finished sewing one patch I had to start a second on the opposite side because the two plies of the sailcloth were slightly out of line with each other. It was a tedious job but essential to preserve the life of the sail, and in the end I was so proud of my repair that I took some photographs of it to send back to the shore team and to the sailmakers in the US.

The weak sunlight washed over the sea surface and although it was bitterly cold it was dry on deck and I was able to keep warm. I couldn't have been luckier with the weather and I looked to the skies and said thank you. I had never really been religious but when you are deep in the Southern Ocean you look for help from anyone who may care or listen.

The break in the weather was short-lived. I hadn't long finished the sail repair when the wind increased and we were back to the business of crashing upwind. *Aviva* settled at about a 33° angle of heel and I wedged myself into corners to avoid being thrown around below decks. The effort involved in doing even the smallest, most everyday job in rough weather is very tiring. The pitching motion was regular, every few seconds, and every now and again *Aviva* fell off a wave and lost contact with the ocean below her.

It was all so familiar. For a split second we were airborne, waiting for the almighty crash and shudder of the impact to reverberate through the boat from the top of the mast to the stern and, as we landed, for the sound of the wave breaking over the foredeck. Your muscles tense as you become airborne and when the boat meets the next wave the vibrations that shudder through the boat travel through your body as well so that your brain feels like it's being shaken inside your head. The force of impact is so brutal that you expect something terrible to happen every time. You look around frantically to check that everything is still stowed away and hasn't broken free. You hope nothing has been damaged on deck or, worse, in any part of the boat's structure that you cannot see. In heavy weather this state of stress and worry was normal life for me and I had no choice but to adjust and get used to it.

There was no forgiveness in the weather as *Aviva* and I gradually got further and further away from land. The week before my birthday in January we were close to what is known as Point Nemo, the most remote spot on the planet, the furthest from any kind of civilisation. The nearest land was approximately 2,000 miles from us and the closest human being to me was a Russian cosmonaut on the International Space Station. In a jokey email, I was politely informed that it would be quicker to send someone to rescue the cosmonaut than it would be to help me. More than anything, that brought it home to me how wild and isolated this stretch of ocean was, and how important it was for me to stay safe. If anything were to happen to me down here, I really was on my own.

I was feeling dejected and utterly worn out, and I wrote in my diary:

'Feeling quite down today. Have had 30-40 knots for two-and-a-half days and massive seas. I'm tired; relentless beating is wearing me down. Another low pressure to pass on Thursday as well. Cried a lot today. Can't be bothered to do anything, just tried to sleep with no joy. I cried at my messages, so I opened a feelgood card and cried again. Got to snap out of it. I am just feeling so downhearted. Such a long way to go! Have just got the weather through. There is another front of plus 50 knots. Please give me a break!'

My thoughts were scatty and difficult to put in order. I was suffering badly from sleep deprivation and I knew it, but that awareness was of no help in dealing with the effects. When I was tired, emotion welled uncontrollably. I would cry in frustration at the weather or at a job that needed to be done – things that would never trouble me at any other time. I was worn down by the incessant clamour of the wind and waves on *Aviva*. When it was really rough, the noises were loud and frightening: the inexorable wind howling through the rigging, the percussion of creaks and groans from *Aviva*. These were all normal sounds but they were disturbing nonetheless. Even the regular and most familiar noises are disconcerting in severe weather. The sluicing noise of running water as waves rolled along the deck or broke over the foredeck made me worry that the sea was running into the boat somewhere and I would go around *Aviva* lifting the sole boards to check the bilges.

Even when it was very rough, I was still sailing the boat as hard as I could. As time went on I got better at adapting to heavy weather sailing. Strangely, one of the hardest aspects was adjusting to the change when it stopped. When you are in consistent conditions you get used to them; that is what you know and you quickly forget how things once were. Somehow you become inured to the difficulties. A simple thing like going to the heads is a perfect example. On *Aviva*, the two toilet compartments were forward of the mast, where the pitching was greater. If we went into freefall and crash-landed, the sensation of weightlessness and the impact that followed were exaggerated. So to go to the toilet, I first had to perform acrobatics to get from the saloon, through the central corridor to one of the forward compartments, usually bouncing off the walls as I lost my footing. Once outside the heads I had to brace myself while I struggled out of several layers of clothing. I usually went right forward and sat in the sail locker because it was the safest place to prepare for the next stage of the operation.

By the time I was down to my final layers of clothing I was bitterly cold. I needed to ration my fuel to last all the way round the world so I had to limit the time I ran the heaters. I always chose the downhill toilet for comfort and hoped that I would be able to get back out before *Aviva* made another crash landing. The process of flushing a marine toilet involves opening valves, pumping the water in, closing the valves and pumping the water out, then repeating the whole process. There is no point in cutting corners because fixing a blocked toilet is one of the most miserable and unpleasant jobs onboard. Once I had finished, I had to manoeuvre back out of the heads, clamber uphill to the sail room and wrestle back into all those layers of clothing. It all took time, and while I was about it I just had to hope that nothing happened on deck that required me up there in a hurry. The business of going at all was something I put off if I possibly could.

Back home, Mum must have sensed how tired and dejected I was feeling because she sent me a message that I will never forget.

'I have a glow of pride. So many well wishers giving encouragement and support every inch of the way. It is a long voyage so remember and treasure all the yesterdays then stretch out your arms and grasp with both hands all your tomorrows. You are doing fine . . .'

I was so touched by this email that it changed the way I looked at my world. Yet again Mum had known exactly the right thing to say at just the right time. However hard it might be, this experience was unique and special and I needed to remember every bit of it. I smiled. There were no tears this time, just a focus on what I was doing, and why, which grew from that day on.

I celebrated my 33rd birthday within a few miles of Point Nemo. I was the most isolated person on the planet in an empty place that bore comparison with the void of outer space, yet I was in the midst of an immensely rich environment. The ocean around me was a special place untouched by humankind. There was no pollution. I knew that the sea life beneath was plentiful, there were birds fishing ahead of the most extreme weather fronts, and I had this whole view to myself. My spirits were lifted even further by the realisation that I was celebrating the day with more people than ever before. The messages of support for *Aviva* and me had grown beyond my hopes. People were following my adventure from all over the world and I had scores of birthday wishes. This was probably the most original celebration I would ever have.

Among my presents was a small birthday cake. I ate it with real pleasure. I was enjoying myself, and in a mad moment I even began to worry about how quickly the voyage was passing and wonder about the mixed feelings I might have when it came to an end. How quickly everything changes in the Southern Ocean, I reflected – even my own state of mind.

A week later, I had another celebration. A special meal, some music, poems and a costume had been put aboard *Aviva* at the request of Sir Chay Blyth. He was going to be celebrating Burns Night and he wanted to make sure I could do the same. The party box contained a Tam O'Shanter, a tartan tie, a Robbie Burns poetry book and some Scottish tunes to sing. The meal was a traditional Burns Night supper. I was not too sure about whether or not I would like the haggis but I had never tried sailing single-handed before this either, so I reckoned I ought to give it a try. There were tatties and neeps, haggis, cheese and biscuits, rice pudding and a wee dram of Scotch whisky. I sampled the haggis but I must admit I shared a good portion of it with the fish.

I had a go at reciting some poetry in a Scottish accent. This made me laugh. It was a good job Sir Chay wasn't able to hear it; he would have shuddered. I loved the evening; it gave me something to enjoy and was a variation to my routine. The change of menu, too, was perfect timing and it brought home to me how much I was missing different types of food. I had a real craving for fresh fruit, particularly apples to crunch into or a juicy orange, and I would have done anything for a Diet Coke.

Conditions did not improve. For six days in a row we sailed in winds of 30 knots or more and when I looked at the forecasts I could see no let up ahead. Life onboard was hard and monotonous. *Aviva* was driving on with three reefs in the mainsail and the yankee and staysail part furled. I based my decisions on whether or not to roll out more headsail and power up *Aviva* as much on the increases in sea state as on wind strength. We had been sailing in a gale for so long that it seemed uncomfortably normal; I had trouble recalling what anything else was like. I was used to the Southern Ocean, to its monochrome grey and overcast skies. One of the Global Challenge skippers used to remark that he had seen every shade of grey down here, and I knew exactly what he meant. It was as if only grades of black and white belonged here, as if this world was somewhere so ancient that it preceded colour. Everything was washed out and faded, and no matter how positive I tried to be about it I longed for variety, a small break in the skies.

I was at the point of no return. *Aviva* and I were closer to New Zealand than to Chile, although New Zealand was a long slog uphill. In terms of the overall voyage I was still a long way short of halfway but I had no wish to look closely at the distance. To me halfway round the world was the International Dateline, and that was what I focussed on. When you are sailing the wrong way round the world you have to sail so many extra miles on an upwind course to try to find the kindest route round oncoming depressions that my course was making a laborious zig-zag around the bottom of the planet. These deviations are part of what makes a westabout crossing of the Southern Ocean so incredibly challenging and they meant that I spent a large portion of my time sailing away from where I really wanted to go. It could be quite demoralising and I tried not to count up the extra miles we were sailing.

As each depression approached from the west, every three or four days on average another one was brewing. As they rolled over *Aviva* and I we went through the same familiar sequence. The wind rose as the low pressure system got closer and that would be followed by a wind change when we reached the front, sometimes marked by a distinct line of cloud overhead. To avoid sailing too many extra miles I needed to keep *Aviva* on the favoured tack heading, if possible, slightly north of west, so the timing of our tack on this front was important. As a front approached,

I was generally hard on the wind on a south-westerly heading. When it passed overhead and the wind backed, I would tack over to the north-west and gradually be lifted on the new tack. We would continue until the advance of the next depression, when I would be headed and tack to the south-west, and the whole process would be repeated all over again.

This was the pattern of Southern Ocean lows. In reality no two depressions were exactly the same and the general rule was always subject to change. The biggest variation in the conditions we experienced happened if the low pressure system had spun off a secondary low. I came to dread those two deceptively innocuous words. A secondary low is a newly formed, smaller depression that rides on the back of a larger and older system, and I soon learnt that they had a much bigger kick than their precursors. These were like booby traps in our path, and we had to be extremely careful to sail a course that dodged their most vicious winds.

The most dangerous quadrant of a secondary low is usually north-west of the centre, where at times there can be winds in excess of 70 knots. Twice already on this voyage I had experienced winds this violent, and I was not in a hurry to repeat the experience. Back in the UK, Mike Broughton kept a sharp eye out for signs of these developing new lows because it is in their nature to spring up with sudden and unexpected ferocity. Each day he would send me forecast information, estimated timings of the wind shifts I might experience, and suggested the best route for me; the safest compromise between the shortest route and the safest course. I was happy to tack and head further south, adding extra miles to the voyage, if it meant we would dip below the centre and the north-west quadrant of a secondary low. The problem was that *Aviva* was not quick, not in relation to the speed of the depressions tearing across the Southern Ocean, and getting out of their path was always a race against time.

While the Southern Ocean was grey by day, once or twice the sky was lit at night by the most extraordinary display of spectral light. One evening, the clouds cleared away and the sky was illuminated by shifting, ghostly beams from the Aurora Australis, the Southern Lights. It was an absolutely mesmerising sight. The sky was filled with stars, and shafts of colour danced across them. The scene filled me with a feeling of purpose. It was, quite literally, like seeing a sign of light at the end of the tunnel.

We continued beating to windward in strong winds that never seemed to let up. Every day there was 30 knots, sometimes a little more but seldom much less. An email came in from Mike one morning that advised me of an approaching cold front and gave me some estimated timings for its arrival. It would bring extra wind, he forecast, but it would be short-lived. I wasn't worried about this, but when I read on I saw with alarm that Mike had added a note of warning about the weather a few days ahead. I sat bolt upright at the computer and re-read the email. I was heading straight for another tropical storm.

I could not believe it. How could I possibly be in danger of meeting a tropical storm at 45°S – what part of my latitude down here was tropical? It was bitingly cold outside. Regardless, the tropical storm was approaching at great speed, so fast that I would probably not be able to get out of its way. I had a sinking feeling of déjà vu. Mike kept tracking it. He named it Chatham, after the nearest point of land, quite unaware of the bad memories that name conjured up for me. The irony was not lost on me, however. I was going to be facing another test of tenacity not far from those rocky islands where we had carried out the rescue of John Masters.

Mike sent me a QuikSCAT file, a depiction of real-time winds over this part of the ocean observed from a satellite. It was clearly showing a vortex exceeding 70 knots. The chances were that Chatham would hit me with the same sudden ferocity I had experienced during the tropical storm in the Atlantic, and there was a chance it might be even more severe. My inbox filled with new emails from Mike. A tropical storm is hard to forecast because its path and intensity can change so swiftly. Although Mike was giving me his best guess about the weather forming ahead there was no way to know for sure what we would get until the system caught up with *Aviva* and me. All we knew for sure was that it would catch us. By the tone of the messages, I could tell Mike was worried for me. Until now he had known I could cope with the storm force winds, even if I didn't enjoy them much, but I sensed that he believed this time was going to be different.

There was no obvious way around this system. At first, Mike looked at the possibility of heading south to try to get underneath the centre of the storm and away from the worst of the weather, but on reflection he felt it might not be quite as bad as he had feared and the safest thing would be to head closer to the centre to reduce the amount of time I spent at the mercy of the storm. So I was encouraged to ease the sheets a little and come off the wind a touch. *Aviva* loved sailing freer, and as I bore away those few degrees she accelerated easily and we surged on, hurrying towards our fate.

The plan was for me to sail right into the middle of the depression and tack when I got there so that I could reach out the other side of the maelstrom of winds. After I tacked and was freed on to a reach, I would be on a much faster point of sail and that would help slingshot me out of the worst winds and seas. The inherent disadvantage with this strategy was that sailing fast in the storm brought its own hazards. The risk of damage to *Aviva* was much higher. The beating we would take would be shorter but it would be more savage.

I checked everything on deck carefully and made sure that all the sails were in order, the ropes were neatly and securely stowed and everything was set up properly. I rigged everything I might need if the worst were to happen. I lashed down the excess material of the reefed mainsail to make sure the winds and breaking seas couldn't flog it to shreds, and emptied the water that had collected in its folds so that the extra weight wouldn't damage the sail or add any unnecessary extra load on the boom.

Once I had finished doing everything that could possibly be done on deck, all that was left was to prepare myself and wait for what came. I ate a meal to give me a boost of energy, stowed a few energy bars and other snacks that would be quick and easy to eat later and filled a Thermos flask with hot water so that I wouldn't have to try to light the stove and boil a kettle in heavy seas. I had made the mistake of not preparing in advance in previous storms and found I was cold and thirsty for a long time as a result. When you become dehydrated you feel the cold much more, and I remembered feeling chilled to the bone and much more drained than I should have done. I was now applying all the hard-won lessons from my weeks in the Southern Ocean. I always say that every day you are at sea you learn something new, and on this voyage I had gained knowledge with every experience, no matter how hard it had been.

When *Aviva* was prepared and I was organised, only then did I begin to feel apprehensive. I couldn't shake off a feeling of foreboding. I went up and down on deck, checking and rechecking, and I tried in vain to rest. No matter how hard I tried not to think about it, I couldn't take my mind off the imminent weather. I kept remembering the last tropical storm, the spume-filled air and canyons of water, the deafening wail of the wind and the overwhelming sense of being minuscule and irrelevant in the midst of this unleashing of raw power. I had no idea how that would compare with what was in the offing now, but this time I had a fatalistic sense that a tempest was hunting me down. It was surreal. In the midst of such a vast ocean my little 72 foot world was tiny as a pinprick. The slightest deviation of the storm by even a degree or two and it would miss us. What were the odds of being hit head-on?

The barometer began to drop quickly. I sat below at the chart table monitoring the wind as it steadily increased, playing a terrible waiting game. I was completely powerless to do anything about it. I didn't know when to expect the full force of the weather or what that force might be. I felt the first of it in the changing motion. The seas started to increase and *Aviva* began to be thrown around and blindsided by slabs of cresting waves.

FIFTEEN

Sick With Exhaustion

At its peak the tropical storm flayed *Aviva* and me with hurricane force winds that reached 68 knots. As we crashed and hammered through waves I sat below fully dressed in all my foulweather gear and boots, poised to go up on deck and face the storm if there was a problem. I tried to expose myself to the dangers above deck as little as possible, but when I did I was confronted with a scene of nature in utter chaos. The seas were enormous, crests heaped on crests and crushed at their tops by the force of the wind. The whole landscape was grey green and streaked with wild rivers of spume.

I checked on deck periodically but each time I climbed out of the hatch and looked around I was shocked by the violence of the storm. I doubt anyone would get used to a sight like this, no matter how often they had seen it before. It was such a hostile world it seemed impossible anything could withstand it. The waves were so mighty and solid I could imagine them annihilating anything in their path. I was edgy and apprehensive for my own safety and I hung on grimly and moved around as carefully and deliberately as I could. I knew I was the weakest element. In *Aviva*, however, I had absolute confidence. I knew she could take it. She pressed on valiantly and I felt better for her fortitude. Never once did I feel fear, or think that the situation was beyond our control. I firmly believe that if a sailor experiences fear, it means they are in the wrong place in the wrong boat.

Aviva crashed onwards through wave after wave. I was alert and anxious and exhausted all at the same time but there was no way I could sleep: the noise was too distressing. It was impossible to boil water to make a hot meal so I went hungry, though I helped myself regularly to hot drinks using water from the flask.

At last the wind began to subside. The figures on the wind instruments were lower more often now even though there was little perceptible change to *Aviva's* motion. I knew the tropical storm would pass as quickly as it had arrived, leaving us tossing crazily in a wake of confused seas. As the weather system moved away the sense of crisis ebbed and I began to feel overwhelmed by tiredness.

I was thankful that *Aviva* had handled it all perfectly and we had come through together unscathed but it felt as if the storms were coming at me back to back, allowing no time for proper recuperation in between. A new email from Mike Broughton held out some hope that, for the first time, there might be a gap between weather systems that would allow me some time to recover. Even a glimmer of sunshine would lift my spirits.

A day later the wind had eased away and the only evidence of the tropical storm was a jarring sea and some tiny patches of blue breaking through the thick grey sky. Sleep eventually overcame me and for a full hour-and-a-half I was oblivious to everything. When I woke, the sky was bright blue and my black and white world had been suffused with colour again. I shook the final reef out of the mainsail and trimmed the sails for the new weather; then I went for a walk on deck, checking every part of the deck gear thoroughly, examining everything had been reefed or lashed down for preservation. It was great to see that nothing needed serious maintenance.

Below deck, I checked all the bilges and mopped out some water that had been forced in during the storm. *Aviva* was starting to feel shipshape again and that made me feel better. She had done a superb job of looking after me during the last few weeks and now it was my turn to look after her. I cleaned her up, washing, drying and polishing everything inside and out. She looked wonderful again, and as she sailed along in calmer water and sunshine, I sat on deck lapping up every minute of the sailing in flat water, with a constant breeze blowing out of the blue sky. It is amazing how we forget the bad times.

By now I was receiving some very clear synoptic weather charts from New Zealand and it was comforting to compare them with the forecasts that Mike was sending me. There was a sign from all these sources that the wind might go round to the north-east, and this hint of a following wind to speed our progress and smooth *Aviva's* sawing track at last was exciting. In anticipation, I hauled the Code 0 headsail from the depths of the sail locker and hoisted it up on deck to be ready to make the most of the weather that was promised. Slowly, the wind eased and backed and with that a new race began. I busied myself hoisting the sail. Within a few hours I had furled the headsail away and my bright blue Code 0 was set and flying, carrying *Aviva* and me towards the south of New Zealand.

The next two days were wonderful. The wind held and *Aviva* sailed directly for New Zealand, towing a dancing quarter wave in the sea behind us. It was a fabulous break for both of us after our mauling in heavy weather: the boat was quite level, so much easier to move around in, there was no freezing water sluicing down the decks and we were pointing in the right direction. It was dry and warm enough for me to take some clothes and gear from below and bring them up on deck to dry. Even when the wind died away and *Aviva* had to be cajoled across a ridge of variable winds I was able to smile.

On 10 February, we crossed the International Dateline. I had sailed halfway round the world – in geographical terms if not in actual distance to go to the finish. Almost as significant to me was the change in time. Until then I had been sailing away from home; every 15° of longitude I covered put me another hour behind the time in the UK. Now, suddenly, I was 12 hours ahead of GMT and every degree I covered was bringing our days closer together. I was no longer sailing away; I was coming home. This thought made me happy.

I had something else to look forward to as well: the prospect of seeing my first human face in months. The plan I had formed with my shore team in the UK was to have a helicopter rendezvous off South Island, New Zealand so that I could drop off some videotapes and have some photographs taken. It was also a great way of authenticating the voyage, because although I had waved at people at Cape Horn and had spoken on VHF to the radio operator there, I hadn't seen anyone else, and no-one else had seen me, since I left the UK in November.

The arrangements for the rendezvous were uncomfortably reminiscent of John's emergency medevac the previous year, but at least I was closer and we were in the same time zone now. Last year I had been making arrangements covering two different days – our day onboard, and theirs in New Zealand. I didn't want to have to sail too close to New Zealand, as there are always risks involved in approaching a coastline, but when I was some way off the helicopter would come out to me and collect the photos and videotapes from a watertight package.

Everything was carefully planned. On the allotted day, the helicopter flew out from South Island and located me on radar. They called me on their radio and said they would be arriving in about five minutes. I sat on deck and waited, looking anxiously and excitedly at the empty sky. The radio crackled into life again and this time a very familiar voice asked me: 'Dee, why is it that you require helicopter assistance every time you come close to New Zealand?'

I shouted with excitement. It was Rescue Dave, Dave Greenberg, the helicopter winchman who had helped rescue John Masters and gone on to take his position on the leg to Sydney. I laughed as I replied and we chatted for a few minutes, swapping news and gossip. The helicopter came into view and hovered overhead and Dave looked out and waved. It was surreal, probably the strangest human encounter I have ever had. We were a hundred feet apart, maybe less, but although we were close enough to see each other's faces we could only talk to one another on the radio. It was amazing to see someone I knew so close after 85 days of solitude.

I put the videotapes in a container and dropped it overboard. I knew Dave and the other guys on board would find this pick up easy. I had seen at first hand how Dave could cast a throw line to land perfectly on the deck of a bucking yacht 100 feet away in a howling gale, and I figured this would be a doddle. So it was. They plucked the watertight container from the surface of the sea and did a couple of fly-bys before they said farewell, good luck and flew off, waving madly from the door. They must have seen me as a speck out on the ocean, waving manically back at them.

I couldn't quite let go. I dashed down to the VHF radio and called them up. As I thanked the crew and Dave for making all the arrangements my voice cracked with emotion. I could say nothing more, so there was silence. The helicopter crew soberly wished me goodbye and a safe passage, and once more I was completely alone. There was just *Aviva* and me. For another half of the world I would have no more conversation, no more company, no other smiling faces. I was completely bereft. The feeling of isolation was painfully intense. Yesterday, I had been at one with my world; I was enjoying it. Today, all that hard-won contentment had been shattered. What was I doing out here?

For a few hours I was flooded by self-pity and I might have wallowed in that emotion had the weather not had other ideas. Within two hours of saying goodbye to Dave and the crew the wind had risen to gale force and I had more than 40 knots across the deck to deal with. Suddenly, it was wet, wild, windy and miserable. I was too busy getting the mainsail reefed and checking my course to dwell on any sadness. The new wind was from the west, so I now had to try to make the best course to windward, and to get far enough south to make it around the south of Stewart Island. The added stress of being in close proximity to land was unbelievable. I had become so used to the open ocean that I was paranoid about the dangers of getting near land. Nearing land is one of the riskiest parts of any voyage because the smallest miscalculation can end in disaster. A landmass has an effect on the weather, often unpredictable, and the combination of shallow water, strong currents, increased shipping and navigation hazards pose a real threat. I worried more about getting close to land than some of the storms we had faced.

We were hard on the wind, heeled over and tacking in earnest again. Eventually, the wind eased a little. I knew that would be temporary because an active cold front was forecast to pass over me during the night, bringing northerlies of 40 knots or more. The wind is never constant. There is nearly always too much or too little; that is one of the frustrations and challenges of sailing. I suffered most in light winds rather than in gale force conditions because I found it so hard to reconcile myself to *Aviva*'s slow progress, but this was the worst of all worlds: tacking sluggishly in the wrong direction, poised for a battering in 40 knots. I wanted to be content to get round the world safely, not to chafe when our headway was checked, but I couldn't help myself. However hard I tried to talk up my resolve, I felt more and more dejected.

On Valentine's Day, I celebrated rather sadly my fourth anniversary with Harry. I was close to physical exhaustion. I had been sailing in very unpredictable weather that seemed to be changing every five minutes or so, and every time I thought the weather would stay long enough to allow me to rest it forced another sail change. Just when I had finished, the wind would change again, and after hanging on hopefully I would have to relent and set about reefing or making sail all over again. This gruelling cycle continued for 48 hours, during which I reefed the mainsail or made sail 14 times. I was at my wits' end.

Maybe it was the exhaustion or, as I later suspected, something I had eaten, but the day after I was doubled over by the most terrible stomach cramps. The pain was indescribable. I was shocked and afraid. Dr Spike Briggs and I had spoken a lot about illness and injury before I left, but when something is actually happening and you have no idea what is wrong or how serious it might become it's frightening. The pain was acute; it burned into my guts. My head was gripped in a vice so tight that I could only ease it by wedging it firmly in a gap at the chart table and squeezing my eyes shut tight. Light made my head throb. Even my scalp hurt where it was held in place by my hair band.

The symptoms were so widespread I didn't know what to do, and I had no energy to find out. I curled into a tight little ball at the chart table and hoped the wind wouldn't change. I couldn't concentrate and I couldn't get comfortable either. I dressed in some warmer clothes and lolled around feeling extremely sorry for myself. I hadn't felt this level of discomfort for ages. Every movement was painful. I tried to drink lots of fluids. It was all I could manage to do.

The day passed. The wind was constant and *Aviva* kept sailing purposefully, never needing my help. I was sure she was making an effort to look after me so that I could get better. As darkness fell, the stomach pains began to ease slightly and I had some relief so long as I didn't move. I called Harry and told him I felt poorly. He wanted to know if I had contacted Spike. I had to admit that this was the first time I'd had enough strength to get to the satellite phone at the back of the boat.

After I'd talked to Harry, I called Alistair, who in turn updated Spike Briggs. In the next few hours numerous medical questions were sent back and forth between us by email as Spike tried to diagnose the problem. My illness lasted another 24 hours and then was gone, with no lingering discomfort. I was sure it was something I had eaten and I put it down to not rehydrating my food properly. Spike agreed that might be the case but believed it was related to extreme exhaustion.

The next day word had spread that I had been ill and I received lots of messages to cheer me up. I was feeling much better and with that came relief. It had been a scary experience and I realised again how important it was for me to avoid being ill again or injured on this voyage, how easily I could get in very serious trouble out here. I also began to realise how profoundly I might have been affected by the constant tide of adrenaline that had fuelled so much of the voyage. It is incredibly arduous, being responsible for a yacht 24 hours a day, every day. Apart from the continual level of alertness and anxiety, there are all the physical demands of trimming, changing sails, navigating, keeping the mechanical systems going and, more often than not, of fixing something. There is always something to do. You can never, ever, be completely off duty or off guard.

I longed so much for someone else to help, even just to make a cup of tea or keep watch, that sometimes when I was dizzy with fatigue and half-asleep I came to believe there was someone else aboard. It was a perfect example of wishful thinking. I longed to switch off and to leave it to someone else but that was something that could only happen if I carried on to the finish. As soon as I admitted to myself that I was suffering from exhaustion, I began to feel a deep, bone-wearying fatigue. But there was no chance of rest. That night we headed into a huge electrical storm.

Booming peals of thunder rolled out of the sky ahead of us and forks of lightning lit up the sky and came flashing down to meet the sea. I have always been nervous of thunder and lightning. As a child I never wanted to look at the light display and always ran to close the curtains, as if somehow I could keep it at bay. On a boat an electrical storm is even more alarming because there is nowhere to hide; you are totally exposed. I couldn't help fearing the worst and I looked up at the mast hoping we wouldn't be struck. What if we were? I wasn't sure what would happen. I kept watch carefully as the storm passed overhead. At one point I heard a bang and felt a tremor through *Aviva* but there was no indication we had been hit and she carried on without a pause.

The thunderstorm brought with it more wind. Like the thunder, it seemed to have been blasted out of the clouds. We were upwind again and soon there was 35 knots. Being tired made everything feel so much more difficult. It was wet and bumpy on deck, and below the motion made even basic living hard. What could I do? I reefed down and tried to get some rest. My body relented. I was slowly getting better at resting and grabbing 20 minutes' or half an hour of sleep whenever it was possible.

The storm passed but the strangeness of this desolate area under Australia wore on. The area I was sailing in was close enough to the magnetic South Pole to create a large amount of magnetic variation, and the compass became sluggish and inaccurate. I was getting some odd and erratic data from the wind instruments as well, and at first I thought this might be connected. Then I began to wonder if we had been hit by lightning. If so, that explained the intermittent wind data. The more I thought about it, and consulted with the shore team, the more certain we became that *Aviva* had been hit. Andrew and his team had seen this before and it all added up. Our conclusion was that a bolt of lightning had touched *Aviva*'s mast, or got very close, and the huge electrical current had fried a circuit board in the wind instruments at the very top of the mast.

This was going to be a problem for me. I didn't need information about the strength and direction of the wind to sail the boat because I could sense all that by sailing *Aviva* like a dinghy. I knew when she was over-canvassed and I could sail and trim her by feel. It was back to basics sailing and it felt much more raw. It meant being completely in tune with *Aviva* and I enjoyed that feeling of harmony. The problem was that without instruments to pick up on subtle changes in the trend of wind direction, particularly if I was below decks or sleeping, the chances were that I would end up sailing on the wrong tack for longer than I needed to, and consequently would sail far more miles.

Equally importantly, I would not be able to set *Aviva*'s autopilot to steer to a given wind angle. The autopilots could drive from a variety of data sources but I liked to use wind angle. That way *Aviva* would stay on the wind even when big seas were trying to knock her off course. I could use the compass course but this had proven difficult for *Aviva* and it drew more power from the batteries.

As soon as the autopilot stopped doing its job my feeling of confidence collapsed. For months, my life had been governed by alarms. If the autopilot stopped a loud piercing noise sounded that was guaranteed to wake me from a deep sleep if I ever managed to drop into one. If the wind changed direction by a certain number of degrees, the alarm shrieked. If the wind speed dropped or increased by a certain number of knots, the alarm went off. At first, the noise had been wearing but in time it became a safety net for me. Silence meant everything was OK. The alarms gave me confidence to close my eyes. Now it was gone I could never relax.

There was nothing for it but to climb the mast when conditions allowed and replace the circuit board, a tiny component the size of a matchbox worth about £200. Anywhere else on board, this would have been a small job that could be accomplished in minutes, but the unit was at the masthead, 96 feet up in the air, where every movement I could feel on deck was exaggerated hugely. I began to visualise what I needed to do.

Better weather arrived. We were able to head north of west again and as *Aviva*'s motion steadied I took a hot shower, changed into clean clothes and felt miles better. Another low pressure system was on its way, and while I tried to make some northing to pass around it I also needed to use this lull to work through the jobs list and fix the wind instruments.

Getting ready to go aloft was like getting ready to do battle. First, I had to dress in layers of thermals and foulweather clothing. When you climb the mast at sea you have no idea how long you might need to be up there, and it's important not to get cold. After the strenuous activity of getting to the top you cool down pretty fast and life gets miserable very quickly up there if you are cold.

I put on my boots for protection. It would be easy to slip up or down the mast or to get a foot or a leg caught, jammed or scratched. The last thing I needed to be dealing with was an injury. To protect my body from the hammering it might get if I swung around up there, I attached body armour. It had been recommended to me by Steve Gush, one of my adventurous Global Challenge crew who seems to spend a lot of time falling off mountain bikes. The mesh jacket had protection round the chest and rib area as well as the shoulders and elbows, all the areas most vulnerable to injury on impact.

To climb the mast, I used a Spinlock deck harness and mast harness. The mast harness is basically a climbing harness that has been adapted for marine use, with stainless steel buckles and wider leg straps that are a little more comfortable to sit in for long periods of time. I fitted the harness around my waist and upper thighs and started up. To get up alone I was using rock climbing gear: a Petzl Ascension ascender and loop strap for going up and a Petzl Grigri for descending the mast. I also carried a Petzl shunt as a safety measure, attached on a long line, which pulled up the climbing rope with me but would not go down. If anything went wrong and I lost my grip or the climbing gear failed in some way, I would only fall as far as the shunt. This was essential for my peace of mind, as I was never comfortable going aloft.

The deck harness was a basic boat safety harness and to this I attached a Petzl Croll ascender that can slide up a rope but will not slide down. That would take the strain if I wanted to take a break part of the way up the mast and rest my hands and feet. All this gear gave me confidence I would not fall, but to get back down again I would have to change over from the ascending gear to the descending gear, removing the Petzl Croll and changing over to the Grigri self-braking device to abseil down from the top of the mast. If I had a problem at any point, the shunt would stop me from falling.

Finally, I put on my Gecko helmet, tied a bag of tools on to my harness and took a deep breath. The wind had eased and I only had one reef in the mainsail now. It was the afternoon and I had about four hours of daylight left. There was a slightly menacing band of cloud ahead on the horizon but I was sure I wouldn't be long up there.

I hate heights. Fear is something I have to overcome each time I go up a mast. This time was much, much worse. It is a very different sensation looking down from nearly 100 feet up and seeing a crew sailing the boat and looking after you compared with the sight of a deserted boat sailing heedlessly onwards on its own. I was carrying a small wireless remote control for the autopilot but it took some serious mental strength to put all my faith in this device and continue climbing away from the deck.

The climb was slow and I was buffeted against the rig repeatedly. I had become so used to heavy weather that 20 knots of wind had felt quite calm on deck. Once I was aloft where *Aviva*'s movements were amplified, I realised just how much we were bouncing around. My hands were sore from gripping the rope and hauling myself upwards. When the boat pitched I clung on to the mast like a koala but sometimes I couldn't hold tightly enough and I swung wildly away from the mast and returned with a huge thump. The swaying motion became greater and greater every metre further up I climbed. I was being swung around like a rag doll. Each time I was flung from the mast and clattered back into it the breath was forced from my chest.

After half an hour, when I had climbed about 70ft and was just above the second spreaders, I finally admitted to myself that this hadn't been a safe or wise idea. I should head back down and try again on a better day. As soon as I made the decision to stop I felt a great sense of relief, and I knew I was doing the right thing. I fumbled to change over the climbing mechanism on my harness and switch to the descending gear but the ascender was jammed. My hands were numb with cold and unco-operative. I tried and tried until the muscles in my forearms were burning with the effort. I just could not manage it. I looked below at the deserted deck and ahead at the darkening horizon, hemmed with a new band of squally clouds, and felt very afraid.

I told myself not to panic or cry. I was the only one who could get me out of trouble and this was no time for emotion. I struggled with two hands to release the seized jammer but I was swinging around the rig so violently I had to let go and cling on to the mast. Now what? I forced one foot between the mast and the mainsail in a vain attempt to keep me tight in to the rig. It was proving futile. To release the ascender I needed to get my body weight off the harness, but I no longer had the strength to heave myself up and I was too far above the second spreader to sit or stand on that. But I could not give up; there was no-one to help.

I kept trying for the next hour-and-a-half, heaving and fumbling as I swung helplessly around the rig. An albatross flew around *Aviva* a few times, looking at me comically. The afternoon light was fading. My grip was getting weaker but my instinct for self-preservation was as strong as ever and I told myself to give it one more effort. Wedging my feet and hands into the mast track and mainsail slides I lifted my body up to take the weight completely off the Croll ascender so that I could disconnect it from the line and change over the Grigri. As I did, I was sent flying out over the sea again and was swung back face first into the mainsail.

I didn't care. The Grigri was attached now and my entire focus was on keeping hold of that line. I clung on to it for dear life and began sliding back down the mast.

The moment my feet hit the deck my legs went weak. Trembling, I shuffled back to the cockpit and removed all my climbing gear. I trimmed *Aviva* for her course and the new wind coming in and went below into the saloon where I burst into tears of relief. My left arm was throbbing painfully and when I took off my jacket I was shocked at the purple-black contusion that had spread across the whole of the inside of my arm from my shoulder to my elbow. My body ached all over. I had made a bad mistake. The wind instruments were still not fixed and I taken myself as close as I had ever been to a really serious catastrophe.

SIXTEEN

The Epiphany

My ego was as bruised as my arm from the mast climb but I had learnt my lesson. Going aloft was not worth the risk. It could wait – it would have to. Less than an hour after I got back down from the mast, the clouds I had seen on the horizon closed in overhead and the wind increased to 30 knots. Daylight faded and *Aviva* shouldered on through the waves in thick darkness.

Gradually, I cleared Tasmania and continued south of Australia. My route was punctuated by three 'Great Capes' – Cape Horn, Cape Leeuwin, on the south-west corner of Australia, and the Cape of Good Hope – and getting past Cape Leeuwin was the next milestone for me. You realise what a huge continent Australia is when you are trying to sail past it. Day by day, *Aviva* and I nibbled a bit more off the distance to the Southern Indian Ocean. At the back of my mind, I knew that the Indian Ocean might be the worst part of the voyage. I remembered it as being greyer and stormier than the Pacific, somehow even less forgiving, but I preferred to think of it as the beginning of the end of our time down here. Unlike the Pacific Ocean I could break the crossing into stages: from Cape Leeuwin to the Kerguelen Islands; then to the Isles des Crozet; and finally to the warmer waters of the Aghulas Current. All of these steps made the 6,000 miles easier to stomach, and our new course to the Cape of Good Hope was north of west, a slight turn for home if you thought of it that way.

I passed my 100th day at sea contentedly, feeling that I had managed to settle back into a good routine. My own little world was miles apart from the real one, but it was sustainable and I was living quite happily. Every now and again the weather worried me and made life on deck and below unpleasant, but *Aviva* and I managed and we were able to carry on.

My body still hurt from the failed mast climb and I wasn't feeling very strong, so when I read a weather update from Mike warning me to expect a tough week ahead my heart sank. There was a depression in my track with a secondary low pressure developing behind it that would have a much nastier sting. The north-west quadrant of the main system contained approximately 60 knots of wind and the secondary low was deepening all the time and looked as if it might be worse than the mother system. I thought to myself: here we go again. Already the ocean swell was large and overlaid with a cross sea that was making life pretty uncomfortable, but this was only a taste of what was to come.

Mike and I emailed each other back and forth about the frightening weather ahead. We both agreed that there was no way I could get far enough north in time to clear the uncertain and treacherous north-west quadrant of the secondary low, where satellite observations were now showing winds of 70 knots. We needed another plan. So we decided I'd sail south of west and use the following winds of the main depression to slingshot us as far away as possible from the secondary low.

I had very mixed feelings about this. On the one hand I wanted to avoid an unnecessary thrashing, but on the other I was quite upset that we were going to lose miles by sailing away from our proper course. Worse, this diversion would plunge us deep into the Southern Ocean. Although I had tried to stash it away at the back of my mind, everything negative came bubbling up. I was heading squarely into a 6,000-mile expanse of godless ocean that is historically far more dangerous than the Southern Pacific. Ask any round the world sailor where he or she fears the most and most will say down here. The Southern Indian Ocean is where nature seems to let loose the worst weather in the world.

Heading south again to avoid the storm was the only sensible tactic but as I freed off I felt extremely uneasy. My gut instinct told me that there was going to be trouble at some point down there. If I kept putting *Aviva* under pressure in these conditions she would eventually get tired. The risk of damage to essential equipment was increasing enormously. One of the hardest lessons of sailing is that when something goes wrong it so easily knocks on until you are dealing with a succession of problems that amount to a major crisis. I had never felt this wary or uncomfortable before, and although I couldn't put a finger on the cause I sensed that somewhere on *Aviva* the ceaseless thrashing to windward was taking its toll.

I carried on as before with my round of checks: a daily inspection around the deck before sunset, no matter what the weather or how horrid the conditions, and an examination below deck. Every week I checked all the key electronics and hydraulics. I had serviced the winches before Cape Horn and planned to strip and overhaul them again before I reached the South Atlantic. I greased the steering gear and carried out my generator checks. I made a careful note of all these in the ship's log and I hoped that by being organised I would catch any problems before they became serious. So far, I had been fortunate. I hoped my luck would continue.

The first depression thundered over us. On the occasions when the wind instruments stirred into life they registered a top mean wind speed of 57 knots. I had seen these storm conditions so often that the sea state felt normal. Only when I went up on deck did the sight of the mountainous cresting seas around us remind me how severe this weather really was. On a foul night, pitch dark and full of spume and spray, the waves looming towards us were all the more intimidating.

From my crouched position in the cockpit I shone my torch around it, checking everything. I could see that the runner tail was streaming out from the winch into the water behind us, so I crawled gingerly to the back of the boat to haul it in. I clipped on carefully and moved away from the shelter of the cuddy, just as a huge wave broke over *Aviva*'s bow and came coursing down the side deck in a curling mass of white water. It washed over me, taking my feet from beneath and hurled me to the end of my lifeline. I fetched up at the quarter of the boat, suspended above the sea with my nose pressed hard up against a stanchion and the lower lifeline taut as a cheese cutter across my face.

I took stock and wedged myself back into the cockpit. I pulled the line back onboard and shone my torch at the other winches, then checked the sails and the mast. Everything else was fine. I crouched low and crawled back to the companionway where I slipped back down to the relative peace of the chart table. There was a new message from Mike regarding the weather. Looking at *Aviva*'s latest position and my current course I was not going to clear the path of the secondary low behind this depression. Mike suggested that I crack the sheets a little more and head further south. Sailing faster was my only hope of skirting the worst of the oncoming weather.

I wasn't sure about *Aviva* but I was certain I couldn't cope with any worse weather so I worked out a new course and returned to the deck to ease the sheets. Cracking sheets was the right description. In 55 knots of wind the headsail sheets were as rigid as wire and when I took them from their self-tailers and eased them round the winch drum the load released with a sound like gunshot. *Aviva* sprinted off on this faster angle, picking up speed and crashing faster across the troughs.

Less than 12 hours later we had run straight out of the back door of this system and were becalmed. From surviving in 50 knots we were now slatting around in the waves, pitching up and down so hard that the little wind we had was flicked straight back out of the sails again as we rolled. It was weird. However, I had learned enough by now that rather than celebrating and rushing to make sail, I went below to check the latest weather chart. The barometer was steady and the wind direction was constantly changing. I plotted my position on the weather chart. I rechecked it. It was incredible – I hadn't made it through a back door or dropped down some sort of escape hatch out of the storm; I was directly in the eye of the secondary low.

It was a strange sensation knowing that I was in a bubble of calm while around me in every direction was wild weather. There was no way out of the centre without going back into a howling gale, but the fact that I was here at all meant that I had missed the winds in the northern sector by the skin of my teeth. I smiled because in theory all I needed to do was wait, and as the wind filled in again it would change direction allowing me to tack and push through the back of this depression.

Soon we were sailing again and the wind was rising. *Aviva* was well reefed down and soldiered on, as she always did. Just as Mike had forecast, the wind backed and I was able to tack carefully and laboriously. As we headed west again the wind started to ease progressively and the barometer crept up. So often I had followed all the rules yet things had turned out wrong. The sea has a nasty habit of resisting predictions. Thankfully this time everything had gone according to plan.

Sometime around this point I began to think about ice. I can't say exactly if I was worrying about it but the idea was there in my head, the thought rolling around insistently like a ball bearing. I had a vision of seeing ice on the horizon but I wasn't sure if I had dreamed it, or hallucinated it or just imagined it from the book I was reading. I was part of the way through *Sir Peter Blake: An Amazing Life* by Alan Sefton and had been reading the part where he was sailing through the Southern Ocean in the Whitbread Round the World Race. It was a tough race back then, sailed through the deep south without waypoints to hitch the route north away from dangers of ice, and Sir Peter describing with a mixture of fear and awe how these big maxis sometimes careered downwind with icebergs visible on both sides.

The thought that I could find myself in this situation became more and more insistent. Although the radar guard zone was set at five miles and ten miles and nothing was showing up, I had a strong feeling something was wrong. *Aviva* was sailing on without complaint, but I had a sixth sense that made me scramble into my foulweather gear one day and climb up on deck with a real sense of urgency. When I got there and looked out there was an iceberg right next to us. I gasped with a mixture of delight and horror. It was magical seeing an iceberg so close and yet terrifying at the same time. It was freaky and I was aghast at how accurate my hunch had been. It was as if I could think about it, take a look and make my fear a reality.

I checked the sea temperature on the depth sounder instrument and it read 6.4°C. Up until now I hadn't thought it was worth worrying about the risk of ice until we were close to the Antarctic Convergence Zone, and I considered the warning signal would be when the sea temperature dropped to 5°C. It just goes to show how wrong you can be. At least I was on port tack and heading north of west so I should be travelling into warmer conditions. As daylight faded, however, I began to feel very nervous. I peered out into the twilight and strained my eyes over the line of the horizon. I realised that where there was one berg the chances were there were more lurking out here somewhere.

The next day, 3 March, I came on deck and counted six icebergs around *Aviva*. Two of them were bang on our course and the others were abeam on each side. When I checked the radar I was relieved to find that all of the icebergs visible to the naked eye were being painted clearly on the radar display. This is not always the case with icebergs and it's one of the reasons why they are so dangerous, especially at night.

It is absolutely true what everyone says about bergs: they are a wonder to behold, pure white and seemingly immovable. The sight of one in the open ocean is majestic and terrifying, as eerie as a mirage and yet all too solid. If you run into an iceberg it can rip open even a steel yacht as easily as a can opener. In 1921 some of the world's greatest engineers thought they had produced a ship that was unsinkable. The fate of the *Titanic* disproved this theory for ever.

Typically, the part of an iceberg that you see above the water is only one ninth of its total volume, so even a large berg can be quite difficult to detect. They really are a hidden danger. To try to keep track of them I set up a guard zone on the radar which would trigger an audible alarm if any came into range. I took photos of the icebergs I could see and sent them back to the shore team. In the UK, Andrew began trying to find out if anything was known about the distribution of ice in this area, why it was here, and how widespread it might be. Information on ice in the Southern Ocean is extremely scarce compared with the North Atlantic, as there are very few ships down here and no commercial requirements for satellite observations. As far as we knew, there were no accurate predictions or detailed observations for the area *Aviva* was sailing in.

We felt reasonably confident that the radar would pick up bergs with a waterline length of 10 metres or more. The biggest danger, however, was from so-called 'growlers', smaller bergs that barely broke the surface and were invisible to radar. They might be small but if I hit one the result would be the same as if I ran *Aviva* up on the rocks.

I began to prepare for the worst, just in case. First, I went round *Aviva* shutting the heavy steel watertight doors and pulling the lever down so that it locked to form a seal. If we were holed, only the compartment between the doors would flood and *Aviva*, although disabled, would still float. Then I prepared grab bags of emergency equipment that I could snatch up in an instant if I needed to. I put in a VHF handheld radio and spare batteries, some food, water, a first aid kit, signalling heliographs, a handheld GPS and other basic survival items. These precautions felt a little extreme, but I knew that if something were to go badly wrong down here I might be forced to leave *Aviva* and have to risk survival in a liferaft. This was such a remote area and the weather here was so extreme that leaving *Aviva* could only be considered as a last, desperate measure, but if ever I had to abandon ship, my life could depend on the preparations I had made. There was so little shipping at these latitudes that it would take a rescue operation a week to reach me. This was about self-preservation.

Seeing the grab bags sitting in *Aviva*'s saloon was sobering. It seemed to bring a disaster closer somehow, and afterwards I continued a lookout on deck fearfully. I kept thinking I could see icebergs in the distance and hopped up and down to the chart table continuously to double check with the radar. As the day wore on I became tired and unhappy. Andrew was still working away trying to find out more about ice and he sent me an email saying that, according to the round the world sailor and Antarctic explorer Skip Novak, icebergs are visible at night by a halo of brightness. It was as if, he said, they glow in the dark. When I read that, in my overwrought state, I scoffed. What a stupid thing to say. A theory was all very interesting if you were on land, but how exactly was an old wives' tale going to help me deal with a real threat?

Darkness engulfed *Aviva* and I had an overpowering sense of danger all around me. As my eyes adjusted I carried on restlessly keeping watch on deck. Before long I saw something unusual. On the horizon I could make out a strange, faint blue loom, a light as delicate as mist, and when

I put the binoculars on it I could see it was an iceberg. I was stunned. So it was true: icebergs really did glow in the dark. I was spellbound. The milky outline in the blackness was like an apparition, so oddly spiritual that when I went below to get the video camera and start shooting I found myself whispering the commentary in a hushed, reverential voice. I am not sure who I was being careful not to disturb; it just felt wrong to be too loud.

I wasn't surprised, however, to discover later that when the moon sank and there was no ambient light whatsoever the ghostly auras vanished, and no matter how hard I strained my eyes I could see no sign of the icebergs. I swapped my position on deck for the seat at the chart table where it was warmer and I could watch the radar tracking 360° around us. My eyes followed the radar beam and every now and then I would see an additional blip on the scanner and would have to wait nervously for another full sweep to confirm what I thought I had seen. I was worried about my own judgement because I felt so frayed. When I thought back to the mast climb and the storms that followed it I realised that I had slept for only eight hours in the last nine days.

There was no hope of sleeping now. The situation was far too dangerous and stressful. I sat at the chart table, distracted with exhaustion, counting every minute until it was daylight. The weather was easing but I was loath to shake out any reefs and increase our speed until I was confident that my course ahead was clear. I needed to see it with my own eyes.

When dawn broke the wind had died away and we were drifting listlessly in an ice field. I broke down in tears of desperation. I was frantic to clear this area but *Aviva* was moving so slowly that we barely had steerage way. This was a complete disaster. I was going nowhere, and when I checked the sea temperature it wasn't changing. There was no sign at all that we were moving away from the ice. My big worry was that we were inadvertently heading deeper into it.

Whichever way I tacked, it was away from the shortest course. One tack would take me slightly east of north; on the other I was being sent south-west. It was a stalemate. I was trapped. As the day wore on I passed one iceberg only to see another appear ahead or to the side of *Aviva*. We inched along so slowly that at times I could swear the bergs were gravitating towards us. It was extremely disconcerting. Throughout the afternoon, my fears grew. I faced another night of iceberg dodging and there wasn't a single thing anyone could do for me.

At dusk, a little breeze filled in and I had an email from Andrew.

He had been busy that weekend tracking down someone who might have information on the ice field, and had talked to the Commonwealth Scientific and Industrial Research Organisation in Hobart. They had access to some satellite images that showed a large chunk of Antarctic ice shelf measuring 20 by 15 kilometres that had broken off and was drifting north into warmer waters, where the pieces were dividing into smaller icebergs. The fragments were spread over 90 square nautical miles of the area I was sailing in now. Low cloud cover at the time of the satellite observation made it difficult to determine the exact perimeter of the ice field, but their advice was to head north-west to thread my way out of danger. North-west was the direction in which I was trying my hardest to go but couldn't.

I was amazed to hear of such a large amount of ice calving from the Antarctic continent. It seemed likely that I was being directly threatened by global warming. Strange as it might sound, though, I felt a sense of relief at knowing why the icebergs were there and that there was an outer limit somewhere ahead of me.

The relief was short-lived. In the afternoon, I checked the sea temperature and found it unchanged so I went through the same procedure: grab bags at the ready, watertight bulkhead doors shut and a constant check on the radar. The beam swept round and painted new blips on the screen. There was still more ice ahead. Another 24 hours had passed without any sleep and I was dazed with weariness. I had no feelings about my situation any more; I was numb. I had run out of emotions. I sat on deck or at the chart table with a sense of complete detachment. I didn't care what happened to me. Nothing mattered any more. I had never felt this way before and I sat down to write to the shore team to tell them it was over. I couldn't keep this up.

It was the early hours in the UK when I sent an email explaining my despair.

Date: Saturday 4th March 2006
Title: Suicidal!
I need to say something because I am just about as frustrated as I could possibly be; but you are all sleeping and so I couldn't phone Harry and cry at him as usual. So I am hoping that writing how I feel will have the same effect.

Today is the first time I have heard myself say that I can't do this. After all I have been through I could have given up today. I wouldn't have but it is how I feel. I am surrounded by bloody icebergs, I can count six that I can see. I have a maximum of 4 knots of breeze for the last 12 hours so I am going nowhere and will spend another night dodging them. I can go SSW and head back towards the ice or head east of north, which is basically backwards.

I haven't slept more than a couple of hours all week due to the conditions I had at the beginning of the week and now I am playing Titanic.

I am so tired. I don't know how long I can keep this up for.

Can you believe two days ago I thought I had taken on the world and won? I knew I had 11 000 miles to go and felt good for the first time in ages and now I have reverted into a paranoid mess.
Dee

I guess I knew this email would freak out the shore team but it was an impulsive and selfish need to get the terrible deadweight of these feelings off my chest. I hadn't told anyone how wretched and hopeless I was feeling and how panic-stricken that, for the first time, I could find no way of snapping out of it. I needed to admit this to someone. So I laid it all bare in the email and as soon as I had clicked on the send button the weight began to lift. It was really strange. It was as if I had to admit that I was beaten before I could be reprieved. My email was a sort of confession and as soon as I had made it I felt a flicker of new resolve.

Harry awoke early that morning. He had got into a habit of waking at 2am to check for an update on my progress so he was the first to read it. When he read 'Suicidal' it was as if someone had punched the air out of him. Like most sailors, Harry had experienced storms and severe weather but had never sailed amid ice. For the first time he was unable to comprehend my situation or imagine how I might feel. His first reaction was to send an email offering a friendly ear, but when he heard nothing back he couldn't bear it any longer and called me up, dialling *Aviva's* satellite phone number with deep trepidation. He didn't know what state he would find me in but he knew this was the biggest crisis of the entire voyage.

When I answered, his voice was cautious. 'How are you?' he said.

'Fantastic,' I replied. 'Everything is great. I'm doing what I've always dreamed of doing.'

Harry was stunned. The voyage had been a rollercoaster of emotions but it had never been as wild a ride as this before. I think he wondered if I had finally flipped and gone insane. Amazingly, in the hours that had passed since sending that despairing email my outlook had changed radically. After sending the message I went back on deck.

Later in the afternoon the wind increased slightly and *Aviva* picked up speed. The sails drew beautifully and her bow wave sparkled in the weak sunlight. She was doing what she was made to do and she was at one with the wind.

The sun sank lower until the sky was lit up with the most amazing colours. We were heading west, straight into a crucible of fire tinged by orange, red, purple and blue. The streaked sky was reflected in the sea ahead of us and it lit *Aviva* in a rich glow. We were rushing towards a rim of colour and the future that lay ahead. *'Treasure all the yesterdays then stretch out your arms and grasp with both hands all your tomorrows. You are doing fine . . .'*

It was truly a magical moment. *Aviva* surged effortlessly onwards as if she knew something special was happening. When I looked astern I saw the most recent icebergs slip beyond the horizon. There was nothing more ahead. I sat and watched, smiling euphorically as the burning shape of the sun slid down to meet the sea. I knew that I would get some sleep and food this evening at last, and that while I did *Aviva* would eat up some of the miles that stood between us and clear ocean.

Harry was as amazed as I was by this turnaround. I tried to explain what it felt like. A spiritual side of me believed I had been tested. I had gone through as much I could take and when I finally admitted I had reached my limits I was granted a sign and a way out. That may or may not have been the case, but we were now heading west under full sail and the sea temperature was rising just a little. The sunset was a moment of epiphany. *Aviva* and I had come out the other side of our ordeal. I believed that we could handle anything else that happened. We were going to complete this adventure. However hard it was at times, I reminded myself that I was out here doing something I had dreamt of all my life.

SEVENTEEN

Goodbye to the South

I had some icebergs around me again the following day but fewer were appearing on the horizon and I was encouraged by a rise in sea temperature to 7°C. Finally I could see an end to this misery. The wind was also changing as if it was encouraging me to steer a particular course, one that would take me beyond the ice field. In the meantime I had to stay south of west to track round the next weather system. The nights were cold when the sun set. I kept the radar on permanently and prepared myself for restless nights.

As I reached the next stormy weather front I broke through the 10,000 miles to go barrier. I was excited and more than ready to trade icebergs for flying fish, but the days passed in slow motion. Time had become irrelevant to *Aviva*. I calculated that the Cape of Good Hope was only about three weeks away at this rate but it meant very little. Our world was measured wave by wave, reef by reef, log entry by log entry. A week meant nothing to me any more.

As the front passed I was able to tack at last to the north-west and head in a better direction – but the change came with a counterpunch. In a matter of hours there was 55 knots of wind accompanied by a confused and icy sea. The waves that broke over the foredeck in the dark and washed down to the cockpit drenched me with freezing water within seconds of coming on deck. The force of the water pressed my foul weather suit close against my skin and forced out the insulation of warm air between my layers of clothing. I set up to tack. I winched both running backstays and centred the mainsheet, then I untangled the lazy staysail sheet and yankee sheet. Once they were sorted out I loaded the new staysail sheet round the drum connected to the central pedestal winch, and when I was happy I pressed the autopilot button to tack.

The bow of *Aviva* began to swing through the wind, and as it did I released the yankee sheet and starting grinding it in on the other side.

In this weight of wind it was going to be a long winch. The sail flogged in the dark and I put my head down and wound the handles as fast as I could. As I began to get short of breath I hesitated. Something felt wrong. Despite the sheet I had wound in, the yankee was still flogging hard. I picked up the high powered spotlight I kept stowed on deck and shone it forward. *Aviva* had been caught broadside by a wave as she went through the wind and had been pushed back again. The clew of the yankee was whipping furiously and the 18mm sheet attached to it was flaying about and threatening to wipe out anything in its path. I worked the beam of the spotlight along the length of sheet from the winch to the turning block aft and back up to the sheet track. There was the problem. A huge knot had wedged the sheet into the car on the sheet track. All my winching had done was tighten the part between the winch and the car.

Inches from the knot the sheet ended in a frayed tail where it had snapped. I shone the light again at the clew and there, hanging from the corner, was the rest of the rope and another frayed end. The lazy sheet had looped itself around the working sheet until it was so knotted and under strain that it had parted. I shone the torch around the side deck and was aghast at the damage it had done. The bitter end of the flailing rope had wrapped itself round the top guardwire and flogged so hard it had snapped the wire and bent four stanchions. I was appalled by the damage. *Aviva* and I had been through so much together and looked after each other so carefully. Now she had been scarred all along one sidedeck in the course of a single tack.

I apologised to her and quickly tried to work out what to do before the yankee shook itself to shreds. I still needed to tack and yet I had only one sheet on the headsail. I had a major problem on my hands. All I could do was furl away the yankee, try to tack *Aviva* through, using only the staysail to push us over and sort out the mess in daylight. *Aviva* was reluctant to fall over on to the other hand in the wind but eventually she came round and I was able to set the mainsail and staysail and go below deck to warm up. I wanted to put poor *Aviva* right as soon as I could, so I wrote down a damage report and started to look out the spare stanchions, a replacement sheet and something to fix in place of the top guardwire.

When dawn came, the destruction was all too clear. I was still shocked at how easily an 18mm diameter rope had been able to snap. Equally impressive was how it had severed a length of 19-strand stainless steel wire. These are not average strengths for a yacht of this size and I had never seen this kind of damage before. When I had sailed with a full crew we had bent and snapped stanchions but we had never snapped a sheet or a wire.

The wind had eased to 35 knots, still too much to unfurl the yankee and bend on a new sheet but I set about trying to fix the guardwires. This was a treacherous job. The damage was on the leeward side of the boat and with the stanchions bent and the top wire gone there was very little to protect me from falling into the water streaming past. The lower guardwire was still in place, but if anything it was a hazard because it was at mid-calf height, the perfect height to trip me up. I was too nervous to stand and walk along the sidedeck so I shuffled along on my bottom. I inspected what needed to be done and shook my head. No, it was still too windy.

The following day the wind moderated and I tried again. Replacing the bent stanchions was the easy part. First I took away both guardwires and then removed the stanchions from their fixed bases, being careful not to drop the tiny 8mm nuts that held them in place. In their place I put the spare stanchions I had been carrying on board. Once I had them all fixed into the bases and lined up I fed in the lower guardwire and tensioned it up. Now moving around felt safer. I didn't have spare guard-wire so instead I used a length of very strong Spectra line. The top guardwire is your handhold as you walk round the deck and it would have to take my full weight – more if I was swept against it by a wave. I was aware that knots weaken a rope so I fed the line all the way through and decided to splice rather than knot the end on to the pulpit at the bow.

When I finished feeding the Spectra rope through the line of stan-chions, I collected the tools I needed for splicing and sat on the foredeck to start work. The wind was less strong than it had been but we were still jolting through rough conditions, and as *Aviva* crashed through the waves I was submerged underwater. My hands were frozen and it made the work awkward, but I had to get it done. When the splice was complete I went back aft and began to tension the new line. It wasn't as good as new but it was a fair job and I was pleased. Now I needed to wait for conditions to improve so that I could unfurl the yankee, drop it to the deck, replace the snapped sheet and rehoist it.

The next day in sunshine I did exactly that. I had already run the new sheet ready to be bent on to the sail but I hadn't considered how difficult it would be to remove the snapped sheet. The bowline attaching it to the clew ring had been in place the whole way across the Southern Ocean and was tightened by unimaginable loads and hardened solid by salt. I tried a marlin spike, pliers, both hands, but there was no way I could budge it. I went to the toolbox and grabbed a hacksaw and sawed it off. While the yankee was on deck I took off the other sheet and swapped it over end for end so that it would have a chance to wear in different places. When everything was done I raised the sail again, trimmed it and *Aviva* leapt forwards. My sense of satisfaction at putting her to rights again was immense. When you are alone, completing jobs like these lifts your spirits tremendously.

It was many thousands of miles since I had hoisted a sail completely by grinding up the whole length of a halyard, and I was surprised I wasn't out of breath. Despite having been ill and exhausted I was actually fitter and stronger than when I left Plymouth. My shoulders had bulked up with muscle. I hadn't lost any weight as far as I could tell. I was eating well, and although I craved a crunchy apple or the taste of a juicy orange I was getting all the nutrients I needed. I felt like I needed a treat now and I hunted through the cupboards and found a large packet of Rice Krispies. It was there as a back up if I ran short on cereal but I was so excited to find something tasty and crisp that I rushed off to the galley, mixed up some powdered milk and scoffed a huge bowl. Over the next few days I substituted Rice Krispies for quite a few rehydrated meals. I didn't care if I ran out later; I needed them now. You wouldn't believe what an uplifting effect a bowl of cereal had on my mood during those final three weeks in the Southern Ocean. With every bowl I munched I was getting closer to the exit.

The sea temperature rose and it felt warmer on deck so I spent more time checking and examining the deck gear. We had been in the Southern Ocean for 74 days and I could count on two hands the number of days without waves breaking over the deck. The wind instruments were still intermittent but it was clear from the average wind speed in our time down south that it had never dropped below a gale. What was amazing was how accustomed I had become to these conditions. It is incredible how the mind and body adapts. In normal life you would never choose to go out in a gale, yet now I found it a comfort when the wind dropped back to 35 knots of wind. In 30 knots it felt tame.

I crawled all round the deck on my hands and knees so I could check everything at close hand. Up at the bow I was astounded to find that the non-slip paint had turned green. It had been submerged for so long that it was covered with a fur of green algae. Areas less exposed had a thinner layer of green growth, but it was all over the front of the boat. Every inch forward of the mast was coated in slime, like a lock wall at low water. I took a photograph and sent it to the shore team for their comments. Considering that *Aviva* was the 50th yacht Andrew and his team had sent round the world against the winds and currents I was amused to hear they had never seen anything like it either. It was a graphic illustration of how much time and heavy weather we had ploughed through in the Southern Ocean.

The primordial slime was surprisingly hard to shift. A simple rinse with fresh water had no effect. Scrubbing with a brush was going to be a painfully slow process and I found the most effective algae remover was Milton sterilising fluid and lots of elbow grease, and I brushed at it until the green carpet was gone. I had kept my part of the bargain with *Aviva* and when I was done I complimented her. 'There, you look lovely again,' I said.

There were more signs that we were slowly but surely leaving this icy, hostile world. As the sea warmed up more birds appeared overhead and I saw strands of seaweed that had strayed from warmer parts of the ocean. The strong southgoing Agulhas Current runs down the east coast of Africa and meets the cold water of the Southern Ocean off South Africa, and in the temperature differential between these two mighty bodies of water the ocean teems with an abundance of life above and below the surface.

My impression that things were changing was reinforced by an email from Mike saying that I was about to have a break in the weather, and I decided to use it to prepare for the Atlantic. I was approaching the final run home and it was time to get ready. I would need the larger headsail as I headed north, and although there were almost certainly more gales to come before the Cape of Good Hope this was a great time to get the sail change over with. I managed to swap the yankee for the larger headsail with ease and reflected on how much I had learned since the last time I was in the Atlantic. Each time I used a sail now I had it under my control. I flaked and folded the yankee into its bag, lowered it into the sail locker and rearranged the space so that the asymmetric spinnaker and Code 0 headsail we would need when we reached following winds were near the top. Once hoisted, the larger, yellow headsail looked strange and it took me some time to get used to it. I had trouble remembering the wind speed at which I needed to start furling and, without wind instruments to back me up, I resorted to feel and let *Aviva* tell me when we wanted more sail area or less. It felt good to take another step towards leaving the Southern Ocean.

I started to reflect more on life, not just my time on *Aviva* but life beforehand and afterwards. I had spent so many years going where events led that I had rarely thought hard about the pattern of it all. Now with time on my hands I became introspective. What direction did I want my life to take? Was I happy with the person I was perceived to be? What things did I want to change and what aspects of life were beyond my control? These were all the fundamental, searching questions that the pace of modern life makes it so hard for us to ask, let alone answer. The time on *Aviva* revolved around me, and it made sense to use it to evaluate things and listen to myself properly. Slowly, I began to separate the peaks and troughs of my emotions on this voyage, which were intrinsically connected to sleep deprivation, from my real and true feelings.

This was a big step for me. The world of the single-handed sailor is raw and urgent but it is often tinged with unreality. When I was nursing *Aviva* through storms and ice, I had managed nine hours sleep in nine days, captured in tiny catnaps here and there. You lead a life under such duress and extreme sleep deprivation that in any other situation it would amount to torture. Like most other solo sailors, it made me highly emotional and tearful. I often found myself wanting to cry so as to feel better, not necessarily because something was wrong. I don't believe this is a female thing; it's just a natural human reaction when you are subjected to this degree of intense stress.

Now I was leaving it, however, the Southern Ocean started to tug at me again. At its worst, it is a godless grey place without mercy, but it is also the purest force in nature that you will ever come across and no-one who has sailed there can ever forget it. Its might is a mark that you never lose. There is a magic about the Southern Ocean that cannot be described, it can only be experienced, and so that I could recall it in years to come I sat down at the chart table, took up a pen and began to write in my diary:

Reflection of the Southern Ocean:

It seems an absolute eternity since I rounded Cape Horn and entered the Southern Ocean. Since 4th January I have encountered all types of weather. I have been becalmed and have been in severe storm force winds. I have experienced more of the latter. The weather has seemed at times relentless in its attack on Aviva and myself. Every day I grow more impressed with Aviva and the way she has withstood the punishment delivered by the forces of nature.

It has been a testing 12 weeks in the most remote part of the planet. I have had to find an inner strength to keep rebounding from each storm and each setback I have encountered. As time has worn on this has become more and more difficult. I have been physically and emotionally drained at times but have also had unique opportunities to experience what a wonderful environment this is. I feel privileged to have sailed across this vast wilderness for the second time. Every sailor has utmost respect for the Southern Ocean and we thank you, Neptune, for allowing us a safe passage yet again.

Where does the Southern Ocean really end? That is a difficult one. There is no precise boundary, although it is generally thought that it begins and ends at 40°S, the Roaring Forties. It was Sunday 26 March, Mother's Day, when I passed this latitude. It was the furthest north I had been since Christmas. The weather was warm enough for the first time to change into shorts, which felt unbelievably good, and I called Mum on the satellite phone to wish her a happy day. I knew she would be relieved to hear that I was getting closer to the Cape of Good Hope where the risks of the voyage would reduce dramatically and a safe port and the possibility of rescue were that much nearer.

All of these things made me feel I was rejoining humanity and life was returning to normal. With that, I began to get impatient and irritated by the monotony of sailing *Aviva*. Every day and every week was the same: fill the day tank, run the generator, run the watermaker, carry out generator checks, sail the boat, check the weather, do some navigation, fill in the logbook. I was always busy but it was with routine duties. I was a slave to the machine. Now that I was no longer scared or exhausted, what I was most of all was bored.

I played some music really loudly. I checked my emails and saw that I hadn't received any from the shore team. This put me in a black mood and I stomped around the boat and sulked. Then I curled up and slept well for some time and when I woke I went on deck, sat in the sun and let the rays warm my skin. I was ready for the voyage to end.

EIGHTEEN

Hot and Bothered

After 86 days of silence, the VHF radio crackled into life. The sound of other human voices invaded *Aviva*, interrupting my thoughts. It was Cape Town Radio answering routine traffic calls. The Sea-Me active radar transponder beeped to alert me that we had been swept by someone else's radar. I hadn't heard it make a sound since Cape Horn, and here we were 169 miles from the Cape of Good Hope. I fired up the radar and saw a couple of vessels, probably fishing boats. So there was life out here on the ocean after all.

It felt very strange and not entirely pleasant knowing that I was close to other boats again. Now I had to be especially vigilant. I was heading towards the Cape at 9 knots, surfing occasionally on a large following sea. In such heavy reaching conditions, I would need time to gybe out of someone's way, so I spoke to every vessel that looked even vaguely as if it might cross my path. Most of these were a long way off but I was so unused to seeing shipping that I had lost confidence in my ability to judge speed and distance. It was better to be safe than sorry. Anyway, it was good to talk to other people.

Another rendezvous had been arranged off Cape Town, but I was very anxious about getting too close to land in case the wind failed. I bitterly remembered how we had run out of wind last year in the Global Challenge and I had a superstitious sense that I would get caught again if we went in too close. I was impatient, too. I badly wanted to get the rendezvous out of the way and get round the corner so that I could start the long journey home.

At 1600hrs GMT on Monday 3 April 2006 I rounded the Cape of Good Hope, overjoyed at closing this chapter of the voyage and finally leaving the Southern Ocean behind after 88 hard days. A helicopter came out and lifted some videotapes from the boat before buzzing round *Aviva* and taking photographs. Once again it was great to have contact with people, but they were not around for long and I didn't know anyone aboard, so when they flew off and left me alone I did not have the same sense of loss and sadness I'd had when I saw Dave Greenberg's face disappear in the helicopter off New Zealand. I just wanted to get on with it.

During the last three months, the Cape of Good Hope had taken on huge proportions in my mind. Psychologically, it became the fulcrum of the voyage. If I could make it to this point, I was safe on the home straight. The temperature would improve, land would be closer and I could finally make a turn north and point *Aviva*'s head towards home. Now that I was here and the next stage of the voyage came into sharper focus, it looked slightly different. Home was still 7,000 miles away. I had a third of the entire distance still to sail and I had no illusions: anything could happen. At times, the Atlantic can be as treacherous as the Southern Ocean. Nevertheless, I had cleared a hurdle and I felt a lightness of spirit again, as if a great burden had been lifted.

The Atlantic welcomed *Aviva* and me back with open arms. We sailed on in flat seas despite the strong wind, creaming along through blue water with the sun warming our backs. I was on top of the world. For the first time in my voyage, the sun set to port and rose again on starboard. My world had shifted. These small things were hugely significant to me as signs of our progress. So were the frequent visits by dolphins that came and danced in *Aviva*'s bow wave and the flying fish that skimmed inches above the surface of the water. I returned quite happily to the morning routine of scooping dead fish off the decks with my dustpan. During the day, I could peel off layers of clothing and thermals, and as I warmed in the sun and air, skin peeled off me like an onion. That, too, was significant. It felt as if I were sloughing off months of hardship.

Now that we were back in the Atlantic I wanted to push *Aviva* harder and try to make up time. I also needed to work through a long jobs list. If I took it too easy or got complacent, I could have trouble. There was still a long way to go. Some of these jobs were preventative; basic servicing that was fiddly and needed better weather. One task was to overhaul *Aviva*'s hardworking winches, all 15 of them. Inside their drums I found the winches caked in salt, and for several days I sat on deck carefully dismantling the cogs and greasing them, then oiling the springs and replacing any that were broken.

This was a messy job, so when I had finished I went to start the watermaker and take a shower. I fired up the generator and pressed the watermaker start button. It began making water for about three minutes and then everything stopped. There had to be something! I had a feeling everything was going too smoothly.

When I checked what was left in each of the water tanks I got a shock. Because the watermaker had been working fine for months I had not been keeping proper tabs on the level of fresh water. What was left might just give me enough to drink and rehydrate food until the finish if I was careful, but if we were becalmed and had to be at sea for longer than we had anticipated I would be in big trouble. I could perhaps collect rainwater to give me a little more but what if it didn't rain? I couldn't believe I had let this happen. After all we had been through, the whole voyage would fail if I ran out of water.

I emailed the shore team and began to check over the watermaker. How ironic to be back in the Atlantic facing the same problems I'd had on the way out. Here I was again in the cramped oilskin room surrounded by tools, sweating in the heat over parts of the high pressure pump. I bled the system, changed the filters and even changed the fuses, which promptly blew again. The problem, as far as I could make out, was electrical but I also found a leak in the high pressure side. Taking the pump apart was something I'd had plenty of practice at last time I was in the Atlantic and I was happy doing that until it came to replacing the seals – then I got completely stuck.

In an effort to help me the shore team took an identical watermaker pump and stripped it to exactly the same state as mine. Once that was done they called me up, helped me identify the seals, and gave me a few tips for changing them. I put the phone down and launched into what I thought would be a five-minute job. Three hours later I was no further on. I tried everything I could to fit the pistons back together and get the washers in place but it just was not working. I got up and walked around the deck shouting at the ocean. When I'd finished ranting I went back down and got on with it again. I was not going to be beaten.

Eventually, I did give up and called Plymouth again. I spoke to Peter Pearce and ran over the whole procedure. Something was not right, and as we talked it dawned on Peter what that might be. Was there any chance I could have been trying to fit the seals the wrong way round? I lifted one of the black plastic seals and turned it over. Both sides looked pretty similar to me. Well, it was worth a go. I put the phone down again and went back to the high pressure pump. Within minutes I had fitted the seals in place the other way round. They fitted, and I laughed. Like trying to put a square peg in a round hole, the seals were never going to fit the other way round. Why hadn't I seen that?

Pleased with myself, I screwed it all back together and started up the watermaker. It worked! The pump whined into action and ran for two minutes. Then it all stopped again and there was complete silence. Maybe another fuse had blown. I didn't know what the reason was, but I'd had more than enough of it all for another day. I sat down and wrote a long email to the shore team describing everything I had done in the hope they could work it out.

The next day Keith Baxter, the electrician, sent me some instructions for rewiring the watermaker. This was an area totally beyond me. The Challenge team knew these boats inside out, they knew every inch of them, and I was sure there wasn't any problem they couldn't solve. The question was: could we do it together? That was going to take a new level of understanding, patience and trust.

When I opened up the watermaker's electrical control panel my heart sank. Inside was a mass of wiring as complicated as a map of the London Underground. Keith's instructions detailed the fuses I had to bypass and relays that needed to be made redundant. The technical terms went over my head but I got the general idea. I followed the advice step by step, screwed the cover back on and hoped for the best. If it worked I was under strict instructions to fill two of *Aviva's* four water tanks right away to make sure I had enough water to keep me going until the finish.

I flicked the switch. The watermaker pump started up again with a loud whine and I held my breath. Water began to pump through and when I tasted it, it was fresh. So the pressure was holding OK. I sat beside it like an anxious parent for the next hour and watched the levels in the water tanks gradually rise until I was confident enough to leave it going and check things on deck. With every faint change of noise or pitch I dashed down again expecting the worst, but the pump carried on and the tanks kept filling. When two of them were completely full I emailed Plymouth to tell them their magic had worked again. After that, I treated myself. Five days after the watermaker problems had started I went forward for a shower and washed my hair. I can't say how good that felt.

Although it was 1,500 miles away the Equator felt close. Emails from Mike contained weather files showing that the Doldrums lying on the far side were extensive and I tried to resign myself to a slow crawl northwards. I was being torn in two different directions. Part of me was desperate to get home. I couldn't wait to taste fresh food, to stop spending my life fixing machinery and waiting for the next thing to break, and to see and talk to other people. Yet I had regrets about finishing and a powerful anxiety about the way my world was going to change. The very thing I looked forward to most – being with other people – also made me nervous. I dreaded others coming aboard *Aviva* after I crossed the finish line and having to share her with them. They would be a great help but the flip side was that I would no longer be in control of everything. I would have to get used to other people being in charge and maybe taking decisions I didn't like. That would be hard. Life will be all about small adjustments, I told myself. Right now you have to get used to the sailing slowing down.

Everything seemed to irritate. The sun burnt part of my back that I couldn't reach with sun cream and when the itch of the healing skin tormented me I couldn't scratch it. *Aviva* floundered in patches of light wind. A new sense of frustration took hold of me. The sea temperature rose, and where I had been suffering from the cold only weeks earlier, now it was 36°C and I was stifling. *Aviva*'s steel hull heated up during the day. When the wind went light no air came down through the hatches and it was as hot as a sauna down below. It was too hot to sleep. I was tired and dehydrated and extremely restless. I gave up trying to nap at the chart table and tried my bunk in the saloon for one of the first times in the whole voyage. Until then, my preference had been to curl up where all the instrument controls were within reach of an outstretched arm, even though that seat did not allow me to lay out at full stretch. Now I went to the full-length bunk, which was just below a deck hatch and was one of the only places I could lie in a draught of cooler air and I slept fitfully.

Easter passed uneventfully and I spent a lot of time thinking. It coincided with the anniversary of my father's death and I talked to him about what I had achieved so far and my hopes and ambitions for the future. Since I was getting close to the Equator and, like most sailors, am superstitious about observing the crossing ceremony, I planned a special tribute to Neptune. On the way south, I had toasted him with champagne and chocolate and asked for a safe passage in the southern hemisphere. It had been difficult, so I owed Neptune an extra special gift this time as a mark of gratitude for being allowed to pass north. This would be my fourth Equator crossing in two years.

The summer after Dad died, we had scattered his ashes at sea. Dad had always dreamed of 'sailing south until the butter melts' and he'd joked about retiring to live on a yacht. At sea I felt closer to him than anywhere else and when times were hard, when *Aviva* was adrift on a glassy ocean or buffeted by wind and waves I wished would subside, I often asked for his guidance and his help in making life easier. I felt he could see and was watching over everything I did and, like Mum, he was still there caring for my safety. So when we crossed the Equator I wanted to mark that and show him how well our family was doing.

I asked Mum if she minded me dropping a photograph of us all into the sea on the anniversary of Dad's death. The photograph I wanted to give up was the one of us all together at the pizza restaurant the night before I left Portsmouth, the one which had looked down at me from above the chart table all the way round the world. Mum said she couldn't think of a more lovely tribute. So on 26 April when I finally passed into the northern hemisphere once again I gave Neptune some more champagne and chocolate and quietly dropped the photograph into the sea. *Aviva* sailed on and I watched it bob in the waves behind and finally disappear. I cried but the tears felt good.

A day later my morale dropped like a stone when I read an email from the shore team stating that my arrival day had been put back by a week. I didn't get this at all and I was furious. What were they thinking? I was going to get to the finish as soon as I could and when I did I was going to sail straight over the line. Did they want me to stay out here and have a bit of holiday while they got themselves ready? Ever since I had turned the corner at the Cape of Good Hope there had been talk of arrangements for the finish. It annoyed me because it was as if the 7,000 intervening miles were nothing, my success a given. There was still the equivalent of two transatlantic voyages to go. Things could easily go wrong. I could not believe that people ashore were taking all the hard work I was going to have to do so lightly. Agreeing an arrival date and sticking to it was not possible. No matter how good the weather forecasting, no-one could predict an exact date of arrival a month away. No, I wasn't going to have that at all.

After a few phone calls I found that we'd had crossed lines again. This was another repeat episode of our Atlantic problems. When I calmed down I realised that the shore team wanted me to cross the finish line at The Lizard just as soon as I got there but then to stage manage a weekend arrival ceremony in Southampton. The planning of all this took time and they needed to start now. As soon as I crossed the line a crew would come aboard *Aviva* to ensure our safety as we sailed up the English Channel and allow me some rest and recuperation before I came ashore.

The misunderstanding was another reminder of how radically my solitary life was about to change. For five months I had been entirely responsible for my own destiny and life had not been ruled by anyone else. The only forces I had to reckon with were the wind and the sea. My contact with other people was by phone or email, and although it helped connect me with the world it was not like being in the same room as other people, seeing from their expressions the true meaning and intent of their words.

One thing this voyage taught me was how problematic emails can be. I had time, too much time, to read and re-read messages in an effort to savour words of encouragement or work out what was being said between the lines. On several occasions I got upset, usually because I had misread the meaning. Once or twice I was confused or annoyed by jocular or funny emails that were only intended to cheer me up, and I quickly learned how easily irony and humour can be misinterpreted when they are in writing. In my tired and sleep-deprived state I was more sensitive than normal, but it was a simple mistake and one that is common in the workplace. Technology has made it so simple and quick to send an email that would be better read, reread and reflected on before sending. By far the best thing is to get up and go and see the person face to face. On *Aviva* I didn't have that luxury, but it would have made all the difference if I'd been able to see people's faces. Without real interaction with others it is very hard to see things in a balanced way. I decided it was better not to know all the details about the finish and I asked to be left alone so I could focus on sailing.

By then I was almost totally becalmed. The Doldrums had captured me and we were stuck. *Aviva* and I were floating nowhere slowly. The oppressive heat was unbearable and it made me grumpy and frustrated. When you are in a storm you have something to deal with but now I was lost. Everything I tried was in vain. Once a 46-tonne yacht stops moving it is the devil's job to get it moving again. The autopilot cannot steer well when there is no movement of water over the rudder surface. I hand steered to try to keep *Aviva* creeping along. At times I lashed the wheel in position and trimmed the sails minutely in an effort to maintain some forward momentum but she sat there with her sails empty and lifeless. The hot sea which, only a week ago, had been so full of life, was blank and the white hot sun reflected on an oily calm so smooth it looked as if the surface had been wrapped in clingfilm.

Frequently an electrical storm passed overhead and we were blasted by fierce and short-lived squally winds. I could see them coming by the dark line of cloud on the horizon, but it was invariably a scramble to prepare. They always came at a bad time and I had to be very careful not to get caught out with the spinnaker up, as the wind could easily top

45 knots. When the first gusts came I would dash around the deck reefing and furling as quickly as I could, knowing only too well that 20 minutes later I would be making sail again and grinding in all the line I had let out. The only consolation was that it was action each time and something to keep me on my toes, and that when everything was snugged down I could go on deck with some shower gel and have a tropical fresh water shower for free. Then I was able to forget the frustrations and everything was worthwhile again, at least until the next time.

NINETEEN

Stop and Go

Why did I feel so frustrated? However slow our progress, every day was bringing me closer to success. Yet I struggled to speak to the shore team on the phone and had great trouble concentrating. My attention span was worryingly short and I was irritable and impatient. Harry and I talked on the phone and our moods clashed. I was miserable; he sounded flat and negative. We stumbled through a conversation marred by delays in the satellite transmission and long silences and my temper rose until, fuming, I put down the phone. Immediately I regretted this. I was tired of it all.

The first clues appeared that we were edging out of the Doldrums. Fluffy cumulus cloud bubbled up by day across the clear blue sky. A breeze, sporadic at first, started to fill in from the north-east and ease the sweltering temperatures. *Aviva's* sails filled again and she bent to the task. The transition was perfectly timed. I was weary from sleeplessness and the continual round of reefing and making sail, and I longed for the steady and consistent weather of the tradewinds. So I took this chance to escape beyond the fluctuating belt of the Doldrums and headed north as fast as the wind would allow us. I was so relieved at moving again that I called Mum to tell her. When she heard that I was finally moving again, she was excited. That brief contact was enough to make me feel that I had enough strength left to race for the finish.

May came round. Surely whatever happened this was the last month I would have to spend alone at sea. My time from now on would be counted in days, and that felt wonderful. As the tradewinds became established and the sea temperature cooled by a few degrees the sailing was far more pleasant. *Aviva* surged effortlessly over the long swell and it was dry enough on deck to open some deck hatches and let the breeze fill the boat. Our progress speeded up and I crept closer to the point where our course would pass over my outgoing track. Then, technically,

I would have completed another circumnavigation of the world. So that was something to look forward to.

When I got near the Cape Verde Islands the radar showed a marked increase in the amount of shipping. In the early hours of one morning the first ship I had seen in two weeks crossed my track and I could clearly see its lights. It was a reminder of how much more careful I would have to be as I got nearer the Bay of Biscay. Another signal that things were nearing the end was my depleted food stores. My choices were extremely limited now. The Rice Krispies and all the other cereals I loved so much were long gone. The only thing I had plenty of was a food I hated: mashed potato. I looked forward to sitting down in front of a plate and using a knife and fork; I was sick of using a spoon to shovel down gloop the consistency of babyfood straight from a bowl. I fantasised about the things I'd be able to eat when I got ashore and these were always the same: Diet Coke, fresh fruit, toast with Marmite and chocolate.

The snacks were all gone, too, and I wondered if my gnawing weariness and irritability was partly down to diet. I was eating two main meals every day, both served with the dreaded mash. There was no variety and the only food I looked forward to even vaguely was boil in the bag chicken casserole. I counted how many were left and worked out that if the weather was favourable and I pushed Aviva hard I might be able to have one every other day until the finish. I was obsessive about reserving the last one as a treat for my final day at sea.

My emotions continued to see-saw. Most of the time I was happy. Aviva was in good shape, the sailing was great and every few days I was sent messages of encouragement that kept me motivated and focussed on the finish. I made a big effort to stay positive and took some pleasure in the feeling of inner strength that this fostered. It made me appreciate that this was truly a once-in-a-lifetime adventure and I should make the most of every single moment. Some days I was euphoric, yet on others I felt an ache of despair I just couldn't put my finger on. At times I felt dislocated. Maybe because I was close to the end I found myself wondering what the voyage signified. I felt as if I were on a delivery trip back home, not much different from so many others I had made. When I arrived there would be no outward sign at all of what Aviva and I had done and where we had been. When I read my diary it was as if I was reading a book about someone else, a girl who had sailed round the world. The story was exciting but somehow I didn't feel it was about me.

On 6 May I passed the Cape Verde Islands and at exactly 0217 GMT

I crossed my outgoing track. I had completed two circumnavigations in two consecutive years on the same boat. That is quite an achievement, and early the next morning I received some great email messages from the shore team congratulating *Aviva* and me. It was the first time a Challenge 72 yacht had circumnavigated non-stop. That was a tribute to all of us, and I emailed back to congratulate all the guys on the special feat we had achieved. I never forgot that although I was alone on *Aviva* the shore team was always behind me. There was no way I could have done this without their constant support and back-up, or their belief in me. I took a little time to reflect on the 60,000 miles I had added to my logbook in two years. When I had started out in the marine industry six years ago I never dreamt that I would be doing this many miles, let alone sailing in such extremes. What we had done was way beyond any expectations I had when I left teaching. I was pleased and excited and faintly sad. It was a real conundrum.

We ran out of the tradewinds as we climbed north, and before long I was picking up weather from the edge of the low pressure systems that march across the UK and Northern Europe. I altered course, heading east of north for the first time since I had left, and it felt as if I was taking *Aviva* on to a landing path. The wind increased and we were back to heavy reaching, with *Aviva* crashing across the waves and shouldering aside water in cascades from her bow. In these conditions the pitching movement was greater and the autopilot alarms started to go off again every few minutes with a piercing screech.

On the advice of the shore team I replaced the solenoid that controlled the flow of hydraulic oil and operated the drive ram that turned *Aviva* to port and starboard. Everything went well and I assumed that I had fixed the problem. A day later, however, as we thundered along, *Aviva* abruptly put her helm over and turned a full 360°. The headsails backed against the rigging and she heeled violently. I ran back to the wheel and switched off the autopilot but I couldn't get her to stop. She was out of control, turning round and round until we lost momentum.

When I peered down through the grating above the quadrant I could see that the autopilot ram driving the rudder head was stuck hard over to port, sending us off to starboard. The only way I could stop us turning in circles was to disconnect it. I emailed the shore team. They suggested that the cause might be air in the system from when I had changed the solenoid. I was going to have to deal with this and change the solenoid on the back-up autopilot, but now wasn't the time. Once I'd got back on course *Aviva* was storming along in 30 knots of wind, corkscrewing down the faces of the following waves at 10 knots. There was no hope of doing any kind of delicate repairs right at the back of the boat in these conditions. Neither autopilot could be trusted to steer the boat. One error in these winds and we could have serious damage that might put the rig at risk. All I could do was stand there and steer her myself.

I was going to have to stay behind the wheel until conditions improved or I reached the finish line. I wasn't sure which would come quickest. I could use the autopilot system for a maximum of 15 minutes before an alarm sounded and I had to reset the system or take over the steering. It gave me just enough time to dash below deck and send a two or three line email to the shore team and hurry back up on deck. While I was down below I tried to grab a hot drink and stuff my pockets full of things to eat. I had to plan my visits to the heads carefully, making sure I was back up and at the wheel again as soon as I could. As for sleeping, there was no hope.

This posed another problem. The approach to the English Channel has some of the heaviest shipping in the world and I could ill afford to make a mistake through exhaustion or poor judgement. My options, however, were limited. I tried telling myself we had been through worse and the important thing was to get to the end. I could sleep as much as I liked when I finished. So I plugged in my iPod, turned it right up so that it competed with the sound of the wind and the rain, and sang along to keep myself awake and alert.

Ironically, the sailing was some of the best we'd had, fast and furious, and *Aviva* tore along as if she was unstoppable. It was wearing physically and mentally, and being exposed behind the wheel made it hard to keep warm. I sent a quick email to the shore team:

'Not only is it lonely, dark and windy but it is rough and raining! Still I am singing louder than the rain to Robbie Williams.'

Every time I tried to take a break the alarm went off. The piercing sound every few minutes was driving me insane. After 4,000 hours of hard work maybe the components had been tested to their limits. No other equipment had been asked to steer such a heavy displacement boat continuously against the prevailing winds and currents. I was about to give up hope of a solution when an email came in from Keith Baxter reassuring me that the autopilot could be repaired, so I wasn't to give up. A series of manual valves had been fitted that might help. I was to concentrate on repairing autopilot one and forget autopilot two. The repair came with this health warning: it was an all or nothing solution. But if it worked I could look forward to a functioning autopilot and life without sirens.

I followed Keith's advice and replumbed autopilot one so that it operated permanently. However, I could no longer just press the standby button if I wanted to take over the helm; I had to remember to stop the pilot and physically disconnect the ram. This would take some time so I had to try to make sure things on deck didn't get out of hand all of a sudden. When it was done autopilot one took up the steering with a consoling drone. I could have hugged Keith at that moment.

We sailed on and I marked off our track on a chart that showed the Western Approaches at last. It looked like we might arrive quicker than I'd thought, but my celebrations were shortlived. As Mike had forecast, the wind died away and *Aviva*'s speed dropped until we were wallowing along at a pathetic three knots. The sluggish progress was painful. The nearer we got to home the more our speed affected the ETA because it was time we could never make up. We were constantly losing hours. I couldn't bear to watch it ebb away in every lazy bubble that idled past in *Aviva*'s wake so I got out the cleaning gear and began to spring clean. I wanted *Aviva* to look her very best for her big public appearance and I polished and scrubbed until she shone.

As if in reward, when I'd finished the sun sank in a blaze of colour and once more I sat on deck and marvelled at the glories of nature. The spectrum of colours washed across the sea was incredible and each band of brilliant orange or red or purple was reflected in dazzling shapes on the dark sea like the patterns in a kaleidoscope. The sight of the sun rising and setting was among the most amazing sights of my voyage. This time an extremely playful and energetic pod of dolphins came alongside to add to the experience. I'd always thought of dolphins as a good omen, and I took them as a sign that everything would be okay and things would improve. They stayed beside us, darting under the boat, leaping up and spinning in the air and swimming alongside us for hours, until long after it got dark. I think they knew they had an appreciative audience and I told them so as I watched and laughed. Their grace was mesmerising. After dark they continued to swim along beside us, making sparkling trails of bioluminescence in the inky water. It was magical.

Sure enough, not long after the dolphins departed the first wisps of wind began to fill in and to build. *Aviva* seemed to shake herself awake and soon we were off again. There was only a week to go now but I had my suspicions it would be a particularly tough one. I was right. The next morning started with a bang. I was down below when I heard the sharp crack and my first thought was: 'Oh, God, the mast!' I scrambled up the companionway ladder as fast as I could and leapt out on deck. The first thing I did was look aloft to check the rig. It was all still in place. I looked at the mainsail. That was fine, too. Slowly I walked round the boat checking everything to see where the noise had come from. It was not immediately obvious, but as I reached amidships I saw the boom bouncing uncharacteristically. I examined the vang. It had a two-to-one purchase system using 18mm diameter rope and that had snapped with an enormous crack. The sense of relief was huge at discovering what was quite a simple job to fix. I secured the boom, fetched a replacement vang line and prised the broken rope off using a spike and pliers to tease out a bowline fossilised in salt and compressed by tens of thousands of miles of hard loading. As I reeved the replacement I thought about how quickly things go wrong at sea. For now, this was another problem solved.

The days and nights got colder again. I had been through every season in less than two months. I didn't mind the cold since it was proof of how much closer to home I was getting. I dug out my fleece and thermals and bulked up the layers. I had asked the shore team not to send me all the details for my arrival, but now it was essential to co-ordinate all our efforts. One of the arrangements was for a rendezvous with the frigate *HMS Chatham*. She was leaving the UK on deployment to the South Atlantic. Everyone on board had left loved ones for six months at sea; I was coming home after the same time alone. When we were close, they dispatched a Lynx helicopter to locate *Aviva* and it flew around us. I talked to the pilot, Russ, and discovered he was an old friend of my weather forecaster, Mike Broughton, and that we had actually sailed together one year during Cowes Week. I couldn't believe it. It was incredibly strange after spending such a long time on a vast and indifferent ocean to rediscover the truth of the cliché that the world is a very small place. It was shrinking by the second.

The Lynx helicopter passed on my exact location to *HMS Chatham* and soon afterwards they steamed into view and came ahead of me. The sailors had lined up on deck to wave at me and I waved back. I was ecstatic to see so many faces. It was only natural for a girl to get excited at the sight of 200 sailors after so long at sea alone. I discussed this on the radio with the navigation officer, Lt Jim Edmunston, as *HMS Chatham* was manoeuvred off my port quarter for some photographs. Lt Edmunston was quick to tell me that there was a mixture of male and female sailors on *HMS Chatham* and I laughed. It was great to see them all.

They offered to send over some fresh, hot bacon butties and a few beers. My mouth watered at the thought. I thanked the Royal Navy for their kind offer but replied that sadly the record rules were strict and prohibited me from taking anything onboard. I waved again and *HMS Chatham* turned to head south once more and sail for the South Atlantic. I assured them the time would pass quickly and told them they were fortunate at least to have each other to talk to and hopefully they would not have to resort to conversation with inanimate objects.

When the frigate disappeared I sailed on happily. It was the first time I'd had a human encounter that had not left me sad or restless. I realised that I was finally enjoying every minute of my time on *Aviva*. This time was precious and would soon be over. The remaining few days were ours alone and we were going to take pleasure in each other's company while we could.

TWENTY

Coming Home

Rain lashed *Aviva*, blowing sideways across the deck. The sky was darkened by thick, heavy clouds that scudded over us on the wind. We careered downwind under reefed sails. Wrapped up tightly in my foulweather gear I dodged the waves that broke over us and tried to keep dry. I had just had a shower and changed all my clothes and I didn't want to spoil it now.

This was my last night at sea on *Aviva*. We had rounded the corner of Ushant in France and were nearing the Western Approaches to the English Channel. In some ways this was one of the most dangerous parts of the voyage and I needed to stay awake and be on my guard. I was checking things when I heard the satellite phone at the back of the boat ringing. I hurried back down the corridor, holding on tightly as the boat bucked, and picked up the receiver. I assumed it would be someone from the shore team, but when I answered a stranger spoke and introduced himself as Mike Sanderson. We had never met but I knew all about Mike. The New Zealand sailor was skippering *ABN AMRO One*, the yacht leading the Volvo Ocean Race round the world. They were not far from me, leading the fleet on the leg from New York to Portsmouth.

Mike congratulated me on what I had achieved and we talked. By scoring a first on this leg Mike was about to win the race overall on points, and I congratulated him, too, on a fantastic job. He told me they'd had a very tough leg and a horrible time pounding upwind the week after leaving the east coast of the US. He guessed I knew all about that. 'Yes,' I agreed, 'I've spent 70 per cent of the last 177 days beating to windward!'

There was a short silence on the line and then Mike laughed. I was mad but I had done an amazing thing, he said, and he sent congratulations from all his crew. I was thrilled at the praise from such an accomplished team of sailors. Our challenges were very different yet here we were in the same piece of ocean with the same problems: a wet and very windy night and all the stresses involved in making landfall.

When we finished the call I went back on deck and checked and adjusted things carefully. Shortly afterwards I was joined by a tiny bird that came and perched on the pushpit rail at the back of the boat. When I went over he made no attempt to move and simply ducked his head down. I looked at this shivering ball of feathers and saw how weak and exhausted he was. We were still 140 miles from land and I could see that the little bird had run out of strength and was no longer able to fly against the wind. I leant across, picked him up very gently and bought him over in my cupped hands to the cuddy at the top of the companionway where I put him down so he would be sheltered from the wind and waves. Then I went below and took a Tupperware box out of a locker, lined it with tissues, carried it up and popped the bird inside to rest.

I checked on him regularly throughout the night. I knew in my heart of hearts that this was probably his last night. I had seen tired birds hitch a lift before on transatlantic crossings, so I knew that if they don't fly away from human contact it is usually because they are at the end of their lives. My visitor seemed to rest peacefully during the night but as dawn broke I checked him again and saw he was dead. I was grief-stricken. As if to make up for this, I had a visit an hour later from three pigeons, which flew around *Aviva* before perching well apart at the back of the boat. It was a reminder of how close to land I was getting. I was glad of the company but I had worked hard at getting *Aviva* spick and span and I didn't appreciate having to clean up bird droppings in this rough weather.

The depth sounder registered the bottom for the first time and began giving me soundings. There were fishing vessels and container ships around. Everything was busier and I kept track of the traffic on radar. This was not a time to relax or be complacent. My plan was to sail across the entrance to the English Channel as far as Wolf Rock lighthouse off Land's End, where I would gybe and head along the coast inside the westbound traffic separation scheme until I reached The Lizard. There, I would meet *HMS Cumberland*, which was leaving Plymouth to escort me across the finish line. The weather was cold and foul. It would have been a nasty day for anyone who was setting out from land but for me, used to worse weather, it was tolerable and I savoured every minute of sailing *Aviva*.

The pace of everything seemed to be speeding up. The phone rang six times in the space of three hours as the shore team passed on information about the finish. Their wound-up energy made me laugh. I kept saying that I would not be at the line until about 1700 but no-one seemed to be listening to what I was saying, they just wanted to pass on information. The calls didn't let up. Journalists wanted to ask me questions. People wanted to confirm arrangements. A part of me longed to be back in the open ocean and at peace with *Aviva*. When the GPS was showing 88 miles to go I spoke to Harry and told him my predicted ETA. I was storming along; even under reduced canvas *Aviva* was making 10 knots. As I talked to Harry I felt really excited. 'See you soon,' he said finally, and this time soon really meant something. My stomach flipped.

It seemed to take ages to clear the shipping lanes near Wolf Rock, but eventually I was close enough to the right position to make my final gybe. Emails were still coming in and I made one last check before going up on deck. One caught my attention right away. It was the news that during the night *ABN AMRO Two*, Mike Sanderson's sistership in the Volvo Ocean Race, had lost a crewmember overboard. Hans Horrevoets had been washed over the side, and although his crewmates had performed a skilful recovery it was too late. Tragically, Hans lost his life. The news chilled me, as it would anyone out on the sea. I had been fortunate to face hostile conditions and survive them but I could never kid myself I had conquered them. No-one conquers the sea.

The wind was now over 35 knots and was forecast to build throughout the day to perhaps as much as 50 knots. This was getting serious again. The news of Hans Horrevoets made me reconsider how easily and quickly an accident could happen. I clipped on and set *Aviva* up for the gybe with great care. It was a long grind to winch in the mainsheet and centre the boom and I was exhausted when I had finished. I brought the boat round cautiously. The boom thumped over on the new side and I sheeted in the staysail. I was absolutely buzzing now. I had completed my final manoeuvre and we were on course for the finish line.

I heard *Aviva*'s name being called out on VHF radio. It was *HMS Cumberland* wanting to check my position, current course and speed. They estimated that they would be with me within the next hour and informed me that when they arrived they would turn around and remain off my starboard quarter until the finish line came into view, when they would steam ahead and take up station on the line to signal my crossing. The swell was increasing all the time and the ride was very uncomfortable.

As we sailed into shallower water the sea state got even worse.

Before long I had an 8 metre swell and big, cresting waves were towering above the transom of *Aviva*, shoving us roughly from astern and occasionally swiping our quarter. The wind was touching 40 knots. I sat on deck and looked out. Somewhere out there I was leaving the fringes of the Atlantic where they met the enclosed waters of the Channel but I could not see land; the visibility was too poor. The wave pattern was still changing as it was funnelled, and as I looked around and took in the angry seas charging eastwards with me I realised with a start that I had not seen waves this big since the Southern Ocean. These were frightening conditions.

HMS *Cumberland* came into view and, as her commanding officer, Captain Simon Ancona, had promised, she took up position astern of *Aviva* and continued with us towards the end of our incredible journey. *Aviva* surfed on the steep waves and we rolled from side to side, dipping the boom into the sea until the boat rolled back and lifted it out. The deck was slick with water, and as waves broke over us water sluiced out through the gunwales and poured into the cockpit. I swept my eyes across the horizon ahead looking for the lighthouse on Lizard Point, the most southerly point of Britain, but I could see nothing.

At 1430 I felt a vibration in my pocket. I had come back into mobile phone range. Although I had put the phone in my foulweather jacket in anticipation, it felt odd to be using it again after 178 days. I answered and it was Andrew Roberts asking for an update on my position. I had over 20 miles left to run. Dark, squally clouds rushed up from astern and closed in behind us. HMS *Cumberland* said she was increasing speed and leaving me to take up position on the finish line. As she steamed ahead, heavy rain lashed down and the visibility reduced so much that she was totally obscured.

A helicopter came out to film us and I stood on deck and waved. The phone rang again and I was asked to check in with timekeepers from the World Speed Sailing Record Council in place on The Lizard to record my time. Everything was happening at once. I felt burdened by requests. *Aviva* raced on regardless, rolling down the steep seas. Another squall bore down and enveloped us in rain just as I approached the finish line. I could see nothing of the land except a grey smear to port, but there was HMS *Cumberland* marking the end of my lonely journey.

I went below to take my time and position, as instructed, so that when *Aviva* crossed in front of *Cumberland* and she fired her gun I did not see it. On the VHF radio the crew of the frigate and the man from the Speed Record Council called in to confirm that I crossed the line on Thursday 18 May at exactly 1755 GMT, an elapsed time of 178 days, 3 hours, 5 minutes and 36 seconds. I noted this down in the log without much emotion. The wind and the proximity to land worried me too much. These were bad conditions and it was a dangerous place to be. Although I had crossed the line I was far from finished.

I ran up on deck again. Another line of black squalls was forging up behind me and before they arrived I had to furl the headsails away. First I rolled away the yankee, then the staysail. *Aviva* slowed. It was a relief to feel a little more under control. We ran on until, ten minutes later, a rigid inflatable boat appeared. It was so rough it was disappearing completely in the troughs, but as it got closer I could make out some of the shore team onboard, weather beaten and completely soaked. They were grinning from ear to ear. I waved frantically but it was too rough for anyone to get close. The squalls behind were close now and ahead of the rain the wind increased sharply.

Steadily I was closing in on the land on port gybe, doing more than 10 knots under reefed mainsail alone. Visibility was poor and the rain now pelting down was only going to make it worse. It was unsafe to continue on this course so I set up for one more gybe. The wind was so strong that I struggled to centre the mainsail, but eventually I was ready and brought *Aviva* round on the new gybe. The guys from the shore team had gone again to find shelter ahead of the squall. *HMS Cumberland* was waiting for calmer conditions before launching a boat to bring me over some fresh food. Help was near at hand but in the meantime I was all on my own again.

I used this time to make some phone calls. I stood on deck in the pouring rain with 50 knots registering on the instruments and my mobile phone tucked into the hood of my jacket to keep the wind off. My first call was to Sir Chay Blyth. He had already heard the news and had opened a bottle of champagne to toast my success. He sounded really proud and my eyes filled with tears of delight. My second phone call was to Patrick Snowball at Aviva. I wanted to tell him before anyone else. He, too, sounded proud. Then I called Mum. We both cried and said very little. When I called Jane she burst into tears.

I was ready, finally, to share responsibility for *Aviva*. The conditions were awful and I needed help now. The satellite phone kept ringing but I couldn't leave the deck to answer it. I called the shore team on my handheld VHF. Where were they and when were they coming out to me? I was only a few miles offshore and the coast of Cornwall was plainly visible abeam. The autopilot ram was working hard and disconnecting it to steer manually would take some time. I was starting to break into a panic when I saw the rigid inflatable boat reappear with the grinning boys aboard.

It was so rough that it took the driver several attempts to manoeuvre alongside. To transfer onboard, each of the shore team had to make a leap across. Harry was the first and was pushed up so firmly that he arrived on *Aviva*'s deck in a heap. After all the imaginings of a loving reunion that had sustained me through hard times in the Southern Ocean there was no time for any of that. We looked at each other and I asked him to take the mainsheet and slow *Aviva* down. Alistair Hackett and Neil Gledhill clambered onboard and only then did it sink in properly that I had help, that finally I was no longer alone. We all threw our arms round each other.

Harry, Alistair and Neil set to work with few words and took control of *Aviva*. I sat down on deck, overwhelmed but unable to stop smiling. The last of the photo boats was nearby, ready to return to Falmouth. They shouted over at me and I reached down, took a flare and walked up to the foredeck.

Standing alone at the bow, I pulled the cap off the flare and fired it. A spout of bright white fire fizzed into the air, lighting up *Aviva*'s foredeck against the dimming light of a filthy May evening. The wind whipped away the smoke and all around us breaking waves rushed on up-Channel, but the flare kept blazing brightly and I held it up like an Olympic torch. It was done. After 29,227 of the loneliest miles in the world, *Aviva* and I were coming home.

EPILOGUE

Every time I tried to tack *Aviva* a huge wave shoved us aside and the bow fell back again. The Southern Ocean seas were so huge that we could not get across. So I furled the headsails and bore away. As we charged downwind we lost distance to weather at an alarming speed but suddenly the apparent wind speed dropped and it was quiet. The difference between battling upwind and running downwind was incredible. Then I wore round on to the new gybe and rounded up and we resumed our crashing journey against the wind.

It was on one of these occasions that I started to think I would like to experience what it was like to work with the elements and ride them as fast as I could. By the time I reached the Cape of Good Hope I was sure of it: I wanted to sail round the world again, next time the right way round.

As I was sailing homewards through the South Atlantic I confided in Harry and we discussed how we could make it happen. There are quite a few round the world races and various ways of sailing with the prevailing winds and currents but the toughest of all, the absolute pinnacle for a solo sailor, is the Vendée Globe race. This takes place every four years and begins and ends in France. There are no stops. It is single-handed and contested by some of the best sailors in the world. I knew this would be a big step up for me but that is what I decided I wanted to do next.

When I stepped ashore in Southampton in May 2006 there were crowds of people lining the dock. I held two flares aloft in the triumphant pose I had seen so many other sailors strike. The first person to come onboard was Mum. Her eyes were filled with tears of pride and relief and she hugged me to her tightly. Then the Princess Royal came onboard to greet me. I was dazed by it all. All these faces, the TV cameras, the noise and the festival atmosphere after six months of solitude was overpowering, but most of all I was excited and overjoyed. I longed for the taste of everything I had been deprived of for six months and any thoughts I'd had of going back to sea again evaporated.

When the intense euphoria of my homecoming had subsided, however, I struggled to get my bearings. I loved seeing people and talking to them again but it took some getting used to. I had been in complete control of my life for six months and I did not like running to other people's schedules. I found I needed people to slow down and explain things to me. To my surprise I discovered the speed at which I processed information had actually slowed during the voyage. It underlined the breakneck pace at which we all function in the modern world. Within a few weeks, I had adjusted but I missed the opportunities for reflection I had enjoyed on *Aviva*.

I noticed things I had been completely unaware of before. When I travelled up to London I flinched at the pollution, the noise and the crowds of people. It felt claustrophobic and the idea of being crammed into an underground train actually frightened me.

The biggest adjustment I had to make was to my sleeping patterns. For four months after coming ashore my sleep was unsettled. I had trained my body to get used to an average of four hours' sleep in 24 hours and the longest nap I ever had was for an hour-and-a-half. This was always dependent on the weather; day and night were irrelevant. The idea of spending a night in my own bed at home was exciting but three hours after falling asleep I was wide awake and bored. This went on night after night, driving Harry to distraction. After a few months I was able to sleep for four hours, then five hours, but one thing has never changed: as soon as I hear the alarm I am up and ready for action.

Gradually I settled back into life ashore and as I did my ambition to sail round the world again grew back stronger than ever. In retrospect, my voyage in *Aviva* felt more like a new beginning than an end. All during the summer of 2006 I worked on these plans and did everything possible to persuade Aviva, which had been such supportive sponsors, to come along with me on an even bigger adventure. So I am excited to say that the dreams I had in the Southern Ocean will, I hope, become a reality in 2008 when I set off in the Vendée Globe.

The race is sailed in Open 60 yachts, cutting edge, high technology carbon fibre monohulls that are some of the fastest boats in the world. This is the Formula 1 of solo sailing and I have a lot to learn in the short time before it starts in November 2008. I am really excited that Aviva has agreed to sponsor me again and help me become the first woman in history to sail single-handed, non-stop round the world in both directions. The Aviva Ocean Racing Campaign will be an exciting project.

I am often asked why I want to do these things. Why would I want to go back into the Southern Ocean again? The answer is because it is a challenge that makes sense to me. Pain is temporary and you recover. Success lasts for ever.

I never thought of myself as a solo sailor before the Aviva Challenge but once you have experienced sailing alone I think you are always drawn to it. It is difficult to explain. The bad times feel twice as bad when you are dealing with troubles alone but the sense of satisfaction when you succeed is immense. My diary summarises it best:

'I went back on deck and we had sailed into the clear sky in perfect time to see a beautiful sunset. We had found some breeze and finally started sailing in the right direction. Aviva was cutting through the water easily at eight knots, bathed in a warm pink glow. I sat on deck and reflected on the week. I was exhausted but I had come through it all. I shed a tear as I sat there. All the effort was worth it.

'If I could freeze frame that moment, it would illustrate exactly why I took this project on. This is what it was all about to me, these 20 minutes, these rare moments of fantastic, relaxed sailing in an amazing and beautiful part of the world. We just have to endure lots of bad stuff to make the good bits really special.'

I admit my natural character is rather unusual for a solo sailor. I am not a loner. I do not crave solitude but I value my time alone now and I enjoy the challenge of being self-sufficient. I am proud of the things I manage to do and I get frustrated with my mistakes but every day on the water I learn something. The conditions are never the same. The sea makes unceasing demands but it pays its rewards.

The world's oceans are the most awesome and frightening environment on earth. The sea can be incredibly beautiful but it is fickle and sailors face it with a degree of apprehension. The Southern Ocean is the loneliest stretch of ocean in the world but it is much more than just wind and waves. I have seen two versions of this ocean, one that was benign and rich in life and another that hunted me with indifference and pushed me to the absolute limits of my endurance. I was hooked by both.

Lessons in life come from all directions and I learned a huge amount from facing the elements on my own. I learnt I possessed an inner strength that I am convinced we all have hidden inside ourselves. It takes determination and perseverance to make it through the hard times and achieve a goal. Life outside the comfort zone is all about taking small steps but you can do more than you think you can. You just have to dare to dream.

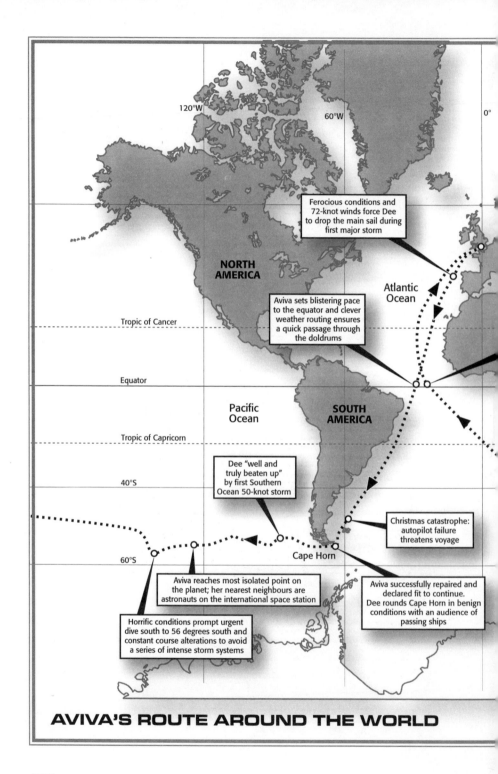

Ferocious conditions and 72-knot winds force Dee to drop the main sail during first major storm

Aviva sets blistering pace to the equator and clever weather routing ensures a quick passage through the doldrums

Dee "well and truly beaten up" by first Southern Ocean 50-knot storm

Christmas catastrophe: autopilot failure threatens voyage

Aviva reaches most isolated point on the planet; her nearest neighbours are astronauts on the international space station

Aviva successfully repaired and declared fit to continue. Dee rounds Cape Horn in benign conditions with an audience of passing ships

Horrific conditions prompt urgent dive south to 56 degrees south and constant course alterations to avoid a series of intense storm systems

120°W
60°W
0°

NORTH AMERICA

Atlantic Ocean

Tropic of Cancer

Equator

Pacific Ocean

SOUTH AMERICA

Tropic of Capricorn

40°S

60°S

Cape Horn

AVIVA'S ROUTE AROUND THE WORLD

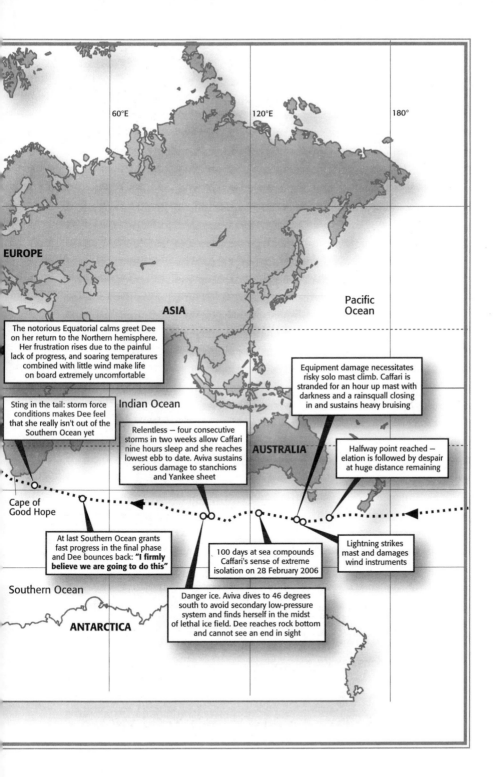

60°E   120°E   180°

EUROPE

ASIA

Pacific Ocean

The notorious Equatorial calms greet Dee on her return to the Northern hemisphere. Her frustration rises due to the painful lack of progress, and soaring temperatures combined with little wind make life on board extremely uncomfortable

Equipment damage necessitates risky solo mast climb. Caffari is stranded for an hour up mast with darkness and a rainsquall closing in and sustains heavy bruising

Sting in the tail: storm force conditions makes Dee feel that she really isn't out of the Southern Ocean yet

Indian Ocean

Relentless — four consecutive storms in two weeks allow Caffari nine hours sleep and she reaches lowest ebb to date. Aviva sustains serious damage to stanchions and Yankee sheet

AUSTRALIA

Halfway point reached — elation is followed by despair at huge distance remaining

Cape of Good Hope

At last Southern Ocean grants fast progress in the final phase and Dee bounces back: **"I firmly believe we are going to do this"**

100 days at sea compounds Caffari's sense of extreme isolation on 28 February 2006

Lightning strikes mast and damages wind instruments

Southern Ocean

ANTARCTICA

Danger ice. Aviva dives to 46 degrees south to avoid secondary low-pressure system and finds herself in the midst of lethal ice field. Dee reaches rock bottom and cannot see an end in sight

AVIVA
Challenge 72ft Class Yacht

APPARENT WIND RANGE	MAINSAIL	HEADSAILS	
0 – 22 Knots	Full Mainsail	No 1 Yankee	Staysail
22 – 25 Knots	Full Mainsail	No 2 Yankee	Staysail

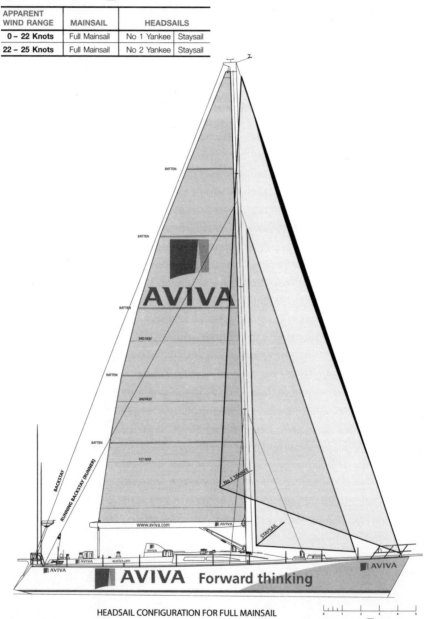

HEADSAIL CONFIGURATION FOR FULL MAINSAIL

APPARENT WIND RANGE	MAINSAIL	HEADSAILS	
32 – 45 Knots	Three reefs in Mainsail	No 3 Yankee	Storm Staysail

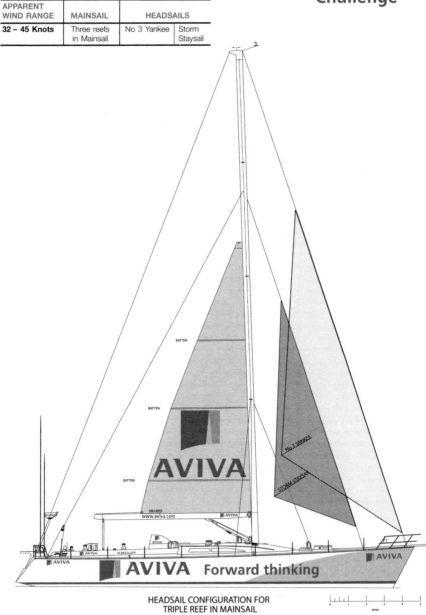

HEADSAIL CONFIGURATION FOR
TRIPLE REEF IN MAINSAIL

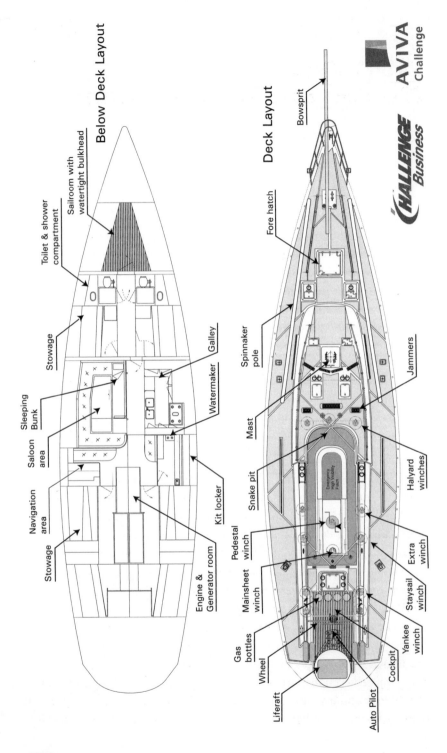

Below Deck Layout

Toilet & shower compartment

Sailroom with watertight bulkhead

Stowage

Sleeping Bunk

Saloon area

Galley

Watermaker

Navigation area

Kit locker

Stowage

Engine & Generator room

Deck Layout

Bowsprit

AVIVA Challenge

CHALLENGE Business

Fore hatch

Spinnaker pole

Jammers

Mast

Snake pit

Halyard winches

Pedestal winch

Extra winch

Mainsheet winch

Staysail winch

Gas bottles

Yankee winch

Wheel

Cockpit

Liferaft

Auto Pilot

APPENDIX 2

AVIVA'S
Design and Modifications

ANDREW ROBERTS
AVIVA CHALLENGE PROJECT DIRECTOR

Aviva is one of a fleet of 12 identical steel Challenge 72 one-design yachts designed by Rob Humphreys and a team from Challenge Business, and they were built specifically to race around the world against the prevailing winds and currents in the 2000/2001 BT Global Challenge Race, dubbed 'the World's Toughest Yacht Race'.

There are very few sailing boats strong enough to withstand beating to windward for over 10,000 miles across the hostile Southern Ocean, but we had built an earlier fleet of Challenge 67 yachts for previous round the world races that, between them, had battled their way west between the Great Capes 26 times, and it was the lessons learned from these yachts that helped create the Challenge 72.

Aviva, in common with nine of the identical Challenge 72s, was built by Devonport Yachts of Plymouth UK and two by Kim's Yacht Company in China.

Steel was chosen for the construction material because safety, strength and reliability were the overriding requirements in the design, build and fit-out. The design concept was for a heavy displacement boat to be sailed by a skipper and 17 crew, and there were no concessions for shorthanded sailing. By the time Dee was preparing for the Aviva Challenge, the design had already sailed a combined distance of over one million miles and we were confident that, with Dee's experience, she could sail *Aviva* alone given the right equipment.

The great strength of *Aviva*'s design was her exceptional seaworthiness and ability to keep sailing in any of the conditions Dee would encounter. The success of the voyage depended, however, on Dee not being injured even in extreme conditions, and here the design and detail of the deck and accommodation helped. Heavy displacement does not help performance in light conditions, but it does allow a kindly motion in a seaway and sturdy upwind performance in heavy conditions. The loads on the hull and structure of a yacht in the worst Southern Ocean gales are incalculable and beyond the ability of most boats.

A smaller or lighter boat would potentially have been faster, but there was no time to plan, build or trial a custom boat. In any case, to achieve the required strength (with its weight penalty) and carry the essential stores is difficult. At the planning stage it was predicted that *Aviva* could be at sea for between 160 and 180 days, and Dee had reserves to allow for up to 200 days. The fuel, stores, food and equipment required amounted to nearly 5.5 tonnes, which would have dramatically affected the performance of a lighter boat. All in all, we felt that *Aviva* was the right boat for the job.

The size and weight of the sails and the huge loads on each sheet and halyard, however, were the most daunting prospect. The deck layout was labour intensive, designed to be a safe working platform for a large crew, and there was no way we could change it in the available time, so we concentrated on trying to make sail handling easier. Furling gears were fitted to the jib and staysails (foresails) to enable them to be set and reefed from the safety of the centre cockpit, but they are still very large and heavy sails, so a powerful three-speed coffee grinder winch (a Harken pedestal drive winch) was installed in the centre cockpit to achieve this. It could be used to winch the headsail sheets as well as the mainsail sheet and helped Dee sheet the sails in faster, thus reducing flogging and damage to her sails. It also meant she could tack and trim from the centre cockpit, which was the safest position on deck and required the least possible movement round the deck.

To improve the boat's performance downwind, we fitted a carbon fibre bowsprit on which to set one of two incredibly powerful 350m^2 asymmetric spinnakers.

The success of the voyage was totally dependent on an effective autopilot system, and we mounted the electronic and hydraulic units aft of the wheel for easy access and fitted two completely separate systems for reliability. Touchpad autopilot controls were sited on the foredeck, in the centre and aft cockpits, and down below so that adjustment to the course could be made and the yacht tacked from anywhere Dee was working. In addition, she had a handheld wireless controller that worked from up the mast. The subsequent problems we had with the autopilots were very largely down to a lack of time for sea trials in rugged conditions.

Because the autopilots and communications systems consume large amounts of power the generator was run over 8 hours (as predicted) a day, so two additional fuel tanks each holding 500 litres of diesel oil were installed in the forward cabins. This increased the total tankage to 3,150 litres, of which 2,316 were used. The generator was run for 1,481 hours and was fully serviced three times at sea. The watermaker was run for only 44 hours, or less than two hours a week, to produce a total of around 2,700 litres. A lack of use was probably a factor in some of the problems with the watermaker.

On the whole, *Aviva* arrived back in good enough condition to go again. The sails and rigging showed little signs of the arduous and very long voyage, a testimony to Dee's great seamanship.

APPENDIX 3

THE AVIVA CHALLENGE
Technical Support

ALISTAIR HACKETT
AVIVA CHALLENGE LOGISTICS DIRECTOR

Before Dee left on her voyage, *Aviva* went through a ten-week intensive refit and, along with her, our support team had to decide what special equipment she needed and how she was going to sail the yacht alone. The most obvious thing to fit was a complete hydraulic autopilot system. We fitted two identical units that were able to switch over to give full redundancy. The specification had to be customised because there wasn't a system on the market that could do what we wanted. It was driven from Brookes & Gatehouse electronic instruments and these, in turn, directed the hydraulic pumps and rams to move the rudder to keep the yacht on course. No system had ever been asked to drive a heavy displacement yacht in such conditions over such a long period of time (Dee only helmed the yacht for about 5 per cent of the time she was away). Of all the equipment on board this was the most important and, as we found out, the one that gave us the most to worry about.

Sail handling was also vital, so we had to turn the yankee headsail and the staysail into furling sails in order to make it easier to reduce their size or stow them away completely. This was done with two Harken furling systems. The stowage of the mainsail was made easier by using 'hayracks' fitted to the side of the boom and lazyjacks to catch the mainsail as Dee reefed the sail. Hood Sailmakers provided slightly modified sails which withstood the trip without any major problems and required no special work when the yacht arrived back. This is a great testament to their quality but also to the wonderful seamanship that Dee demonstrated during the voyage.

Many other small things were changed to make life easier. These included a special bunk that was built in the saloon, though Dee only used it once; she preferred to sleep at the chart table most of the time; and two single burner gas hobs replaced the large cooking hob which was originally designed for a crew of 18. All this new equipment and its fitting had to be carried out in such a way that it would withstand the punishing environment we knew she would face.

Panasonic Toughbook computers were put onboard to allow Dee to run all the communications equipment, which consisted of an Inmarsat C satellite system, an SSB radio and an Iridium/Telaurus satellite telephone system on which Dee sent or received nearly 2,000 emails to and from the shore team during the trip, plus all her other emails. The Iridium/Telaurus system also allowed Dee to make phone calls just as if she was using a mobile phone. This became a real morale booster for Dee.

With Dee's help we also talked about and planned for as many different and life-threatening situations as we could think of. One of these was what action should be taken in a case of collision. It was this action plan that Dee put in place when she sailed into the ice field in the Southern Ocean. That included locking all the watertight doors, preparing an emergency grab bag and sleeping in an immersion survival suit. For our part, we could request extra position reporting from the yacht and track her position every few minutes.

Once Dee left, the support didn't stop. There is nothing in the rules governing a round the world sailing record that prevents a sailor obtaining advice about weather or technical equipment from outside, although it is not permitted to take anyone or anything onboard. This allowed us to send a constant stream of emails to and from the yacht and to answer questions from Dee, pass on advice and recommend different options and courses of action.

The support team knew *Aviva* intimately. We knew the inventory of spares that was on the yacht and how and when certain items were to be used. An example was making sure that Dee had service packs for essential equipment such as the generator which included all the filters, replacement injectors, and a video that illustrated exactly how to carry out a generator service and injector change.

For all the advice and help we were able to give Dee during the trip, she still had to do it all herself. When Dee crossed the finish line at The Lizard, *Aviva* looked immaculate. It was not until later that I was able to see in detail and appreciate how hard Dee had worked. The Aviva Challenge was a wonderful example of superb seamanship.

TECHNICAL SPECIFICATION OF *AVIVA*

Length overall:	72ft	22 metres
Length of waterline:	61ft	18.82 metres
Beam:	18ft 2ins	5.5 metres
Height of mast above waterline:	95ft	29 metres
Draft – full load:	10ft	3.05 metres
Displacement – half load:		38.5 tonnes
Ballast keel weight:		12 tonnes
Displacement at start of Aviva Challenge:		43 tonnes
Ballast keel weight:		12 tonnes
Sail area – max windward:	2825 sq ft	262.5 sq m
Sail area – max downwind:	5247 sq ft	487.5 sq m

TANK CAPACITIES

Water:	390 gals	1,775 litres
Weight of water		1.8 tonnes
Fuel tankage:	736 gals	3,310 litres
Additional fuel tankage:	244 gals	1,100 litres
Weight of fuel:		2.7 tonnes

DESIGN TEAM

Rob Humphreys	Rob Humphreys Yacht Design
Jim Moore	Jim Moore Designs
Roger Scammell	Key Designs
Andrew Roberts and Matthew Ratsey	Challenge Business
Devonport Yachts Ltd	Devonport Royal Dockyard

BUILDER

Devonport Yachts Ltd, Devonport Royal Dockyard

CONSTRUCTION

Hull – 50A mild steel
Keel – steel fin and lead bulb
Deck and coamings – 316 stainless steel
Coachroof – GRP balsa sandwich

SAFETY STANDARDS

The Challenge 72ft class yachts are designed and fitted out to comply with the MCA requirements for unlimited operations (worldwide in high latitudes)
Design approval – Bureau Veritas
Challenge Business Yacht Building Quality Assurance Programme
Certifying Authority – MECAL for MCA
Surveyor for annual and special surveys – John Fearnley

Safety Standards compliance for the Aviva Challenge – MCA Cat 0, ISAF and Royal Ocean Racing Club, ORC Cat 0 where appropriate, as well as specific requirements for the voyage.

Challenge Business policy for safety at sea.

EQUIPMENT SUPPLIERS

Autopilots
Brooks & Gatehouse Electronics
Hamilton Jet Hydraulics

Communications Equipment
RADIO COMMUNICATIONS EQUIPMENT

HF radio – 200 watt SSB	ICOM (UK) Ltd
VHF radio – 25 watt	Shipmate
GMDSS	ICS Electronics Ltd
Handheld VHF radios	ICOM (UK) Ltd

SATELLITE COMMUNICATIONS EQUIPMENT

Imarsat Standard C	Thrane & Thrane/TMI 2000
Iridium	Iridium/TMI 2000

Cameras

Still cameras	Panasonic Lumix 8.4 Mega Pixel
Video cameras	Panasonic 3 Chip Mini DV

Computers

Computers X 2	Panasonic Toughbook CF29
Computers X 1	Panasonic Toughbook CF-W2
Computer monitors	Sony

Computer Software

Operating system	Windows NT/windows XP
General software	Microsoft Office
Electronic charting	MaxSea/ARCS Charts
Communications software	Telaurus/SeaCOM
Sat C communication	PC Sat C
Weather fax	M Scan Meteo
Data logging	Brooks & Gatehouse Deckman
Battery management software	BMVLink

Deck Equipment

Hatches and portholes	Lewmar Ltd and Nemo (Italy)
Steering gear	Edson USA
Winches and deck equipment	Harken USA

Pulpit, pushpit, stanchions, handrails etc | Hercules CSMD of Dartmouth
Custom Deck Equipment
Blocks, jammers etc | Designed by Roger Scammell, Manufactured by Hercules CSMD

Electrical
Power management systems | Energy Solutions Ltd
Batteries (gel) | Sonescheim

Mechanical
Main engine | Sabre Engines Ltd
Propeller | Bruntons Propellers Ltd
Generator | Northern Lights/Energy Solutions
Engine and generator exhaust system | Halyard Marine Ltd
Watermaker | Aquafresh Ltd
Accommodation heater | Mikuni

Navigational Equipment
Wind data, water speed, depth | Brookes & Gatehouse Ltd
GPS | C A Clause Ltd
Radar | Raymarine

Paint, Protective Coatings and Fairing Materials
International Paints Ltd and Awlgrip

Rig
Mast and spar maker | Atlantic Spars Ltd
Carbon fibre bowsprit | Multimarine
Rigging terminals | Norseman Gibb
Dyform standing rigging | Norseman Gibb
Running rigging | Liros, supplied by Seago Yachting
Spectra running rigging | Southern Ropes
Mainsail batten system | Bainbridge Aquabatten Ltd

Sailmaker
Hood Sailmakers Ltd

SAILS CARRIED
Mainsail, Trysail, No1 Yankee (furling), No2 Yankee (furling), Staysail (furling), Spare staysail, Code 0 (furling reacher), Asymmetric spinnaker, Flanker (2.3 oz spinnaker), 1.5 oz spinnaker, 0.75oz spinnaker.

Rudder and Keel
Rudder, skeg and keel fin fabrications | Hercules CSMD of Dartmouth
Lead bulb keel | Iron Brothers Ltd

Safety Equipment
Liferafts | Zodiac
Lifejackets/harnesses | Ocean Safety Ltd
EPIRBS | Ocean Safety Ltd
Watertight doors | Hercules CSMD of Dartmouth

ACKNOWLEDGEMENTS

Writing this book has been a journey in itself. I have had to remember and rediscover parts of my life that I had long forgotten. I have enjoyed the journey and also found it incredibly frustrating at times. I reached the end with assistance and encouragement from Jo Uffendell to ensure my time was protected to complete this commitment. The words would not have flowed without the guidance and conviction of Elaine Bunting, without whom I would never have written this book.

There are many people to thank for their contribution to my adventure. Sir Chay Blyth told me I could achieve the impossible voyage and helped me all the way to the finish line. His team at Challenge Business, led by Andrew Roberts, was dedicated and committed to the project and had my safety and success as the imperative throughout.

Special thanks also to Mike Broughton, who navigated me along the safest passage for the whole voyage. I arrived feeling and looking so well thanks to Allie Smith, who organised my food. Ultimately the voyage made me realise how lucky I was to have such an understanding and patient boyfriend in Harry Spedding.

I thank Aviva for their support and for welcoming me into their family. Sarah Loughran, Stephen Pain and Sue Winston worked with me on a day to day basis to make it all happen. Many thanks, too, to Patrick Snowball, Andrew Moss, Philip Scott and Richard Harvey for their belief and vision.

The team at Karen Earl Sponsorship kept everyone informed of my progress and also passed on the fantastic messages of support that gave me the strength to keep going. I also thank the young Swallows and Amazons sailors with their fearless leader Richard Baker-Jones, who gave me Sizzles the bear to keep me company around the world.

The Aviva Challenge also had some friends involved that it was great to have in support. OnEdition and APP captured the adventure.

My medical support was provided by Dr Spike Briggs. The guys who cast off my lines at the start and took them at the end have been through this and more in my sailing career: Loz Marriott, Paul Kelly, Andy Forbes, James Allen and Tom Snowball.

I would also like to express my thanks to Dave Greenberg and the helicopter team for the rendezvous off New Zealand, and the crew in South Africa. I got a huge morale boost from the Royal Navy crew aboard *HMS Chatham* and *HMS Cumberland*. *Aviva* and I became partners in our adventure together, and I would like to thank Amelia Hackett for naming her and giving us a lucky omen.

The steps in my life that led me to the Aviva Challenge have had many influences. Mike Golding and Graham Tourell gave me my break into the marine industry. Paul Bennett offered sound advice and great contacts that have served me well. Professor Carlton Cooke at Leeds University took me on my first offshore sailing trip off the West Coast of Scotland in the early nineties.

My friends Rachel Ansell and Claire Edis have always been there as we were growing up and we remain best friends to this day. I thank them for their patience and commitment.

Above all, my life would not have been anything without a loving family. Jane, Nick and my nephews Alex and Matthew are friends as well as family and I love making them proud. Uncle Michael, Aunty Anne, Sarah, Rae and Stephen may have drifted away in the past but I am thankful my adventure brought us closer as a family once more.

Most importantly, I want to say thank you to my Mum, Barbara Caffari. Water is not her natural habitat but she has always listened, supported and loved me unquestioningly.

PHOTO CREDITS

All photos by Dee Caffari unless otherwise credited

Page 7 (bottom): Harry Spedding
Page 9 (top): onEdition
Page 10 (bottom): Dave Greenberg
Page 11 (top): onEdition
Page 11 (bottom): Getty images for Aviva
Page 15 (both): onEdition
Page 16: onEdition